SILENCE UNHEARD

SUNY series in Hindu Studies
Wendy Doniger, editor

SILENCE UNHEARD

DEATHLY OTHERNESS IN PĀTAÑJALA-YOGA

YOHANAN GRINSHPON

State University of New York Press

Published by
State University of New York Press, Albany

Printed in the United States of America

For information, address State University of New York Press,
90 State Street, Suite 700, Albany, NY 12207

Production by Diane Ganeles
Marketing by Fran Keneston

Library of Congress Cataloging-in-Publication Data

Grinshpon, Yohanan, 1948–
Silence unheard : deathly otherness in Patañjala-yoga / Yohanan Grinshpon.
p. cm.
ISBN 0-7914-5101-1 (alk. paper)—ISBN 0-7914-5102-X (pb : alk. paper)
1. Patañjali. Yogasūtra. 2. Yoga. I. Title.
B132.Y6 G68 2001
181'.452—dc21 00-054791

10 9 8 7 6 5 4 3 2 1

To Rivka, My Wife
With Love

Contents

Foreword by David Shulman ix

Acknowledgments xi

Introduction: Challenges of an Oxymoronic Genre 1

1. Eight Characters in Search of the *Yogasūtra*: The Lively Banalization of Yogic Deathly Silence 13

2. Daily Life in *Samādhi*: The Dying Yogin's Real Life and a Plea for Holistic Presentation of the *Yogasūtra* 37

3. The *Yogasūtra* and the Dying Yogin's "Lively Interior" 53

4. Causality, False Linearity, and the Silent Yogin's Presence in the *Yogasūtra* 65

5. Untying the Knot of Existence: Liberation, Deathly Silence, and Their Interpretation in Pātañjala-Yoga 79

6. The Dying Yogin's Challenge; Homelessness and Truth 91

The Essential *Yogasūtra*; An Exercise in Rereading as Rewriting 95

Notes 123

Bibliography 147

Index 153

Foreword

Familiar perspectives die hard. We mostly think the world as it has been thought before. This habit, one of the hallmarks of our humanity, afflicts scholars and scientists no less than others, as Thomas Kuhn elegantly showed. On the other hand, another feature of being human is an ability to see and understand things differently. When we are finally convinced, paradigms of perception change, collapse, expand under the pressure of something truly new.

The problem is perhaps even more severe for those of us who read ancient texts. Patañjali, the "author" of the *Yogasūtra*, if he lived at all as an empirical individual, has been dead for over two millennia, at a conservative guess. It is extremely difficult to have a conversation with him. Rather little of the textural features that determine the experience of living dialogue—the very subtle but crucial components of tone, movement, shadow, depth of looking—comes through in the sutras that we have. In any case, the sutra genre allows little more than traces, tiny, energized, almost invisible flashes of the once living fire. Sutras are compact devices for fixing memory, hence mostly enigmatic and in need of commentary. Like the medieval Sanskrit commentators, we interpret them in the light of whatever system seems most likely to make sense of them. And like these medieval scholastics, with their strong rationalizing tendencies, we too are in constant danger of imposing on the parent text some prefabricated structure we have inherited and to which, perhaps out of anxiety or lethargy, we continue to cling.

Still, occasionally rarely, someone appears who is able to listen to the texts in a fresh way—a listening rooted in a certain recalcitrant originality of spirit, and also in humility. Yohanan Grinshpon's book is in this category. This essay should change the way classical yoga is treated in our histories of Indian thought. At a time when yoga has become a worldwide industry, and when the conventional wisdom is repeated monotonously in book after book, even by skilled practitioners and teachers, this short, densely argued study, philosophically informed and philologically sound, opens up the *Yogasūtra* and its commentaries as if revealing a striking and unfamiliar landscape.

In doing so, the author has had to clear away the veils that were previously in place—for example, the prevalent Eliadean notion of yoga as "integration," or the conventional, apologetic understanding of the *siddhi* powers that accrue to the advanced yogi as distractions or temptations, negative in force. A radically altered yogic anthropology emerges, and with it a yoga-informed metaphysics of language that repositions the experience of meditation in relation to the sutras' (rather unsuccessful) attempts to speak of it.

The profound otherness of the classical meditative transformation of awareness now stands at the center of the proposed reading of the ancient foundational text and of the Sāṅkhya system that frames it. The vision that Yohanan Grinshpon offers—though stated in minimalist arguments—has very welcome features of boldness, novel insight, and philosophic rigor. He is not afraid to experiment, to the point of tentatively and rather playfully rearranging the sutras in terms of their competing "voices." He speaks of a range of experience that can, I think, be known and studied critically. Mediated in different forms by many of the classical Sanskrit authors, it is one of the great contributions of Indian civilization.

Not everyone, inside and outside our disciplines, will be able to see this new landscape. That is hardly surprising. Familiar perceptions die hard. In this case, as so often, it is largely a matter of how we look or listen.

—DAVID SHULMAN

Acknowledgments

Sometimes I consider Pātañjala-Yoga the epitome of cool sobriety. Its envisaged end-of-ends, the ultimate default of life, postdisintegration silence, seems to me profoundly reasonable, an only, inevitable, necessary end. At other times, yoga philosophy ("darkness covered by darkness") is beyond the range of my mind.

Aside from my own openness to philosophies of a somewhat morbid nature and my interest in "possible transformations," I owe this book to four presences. The first is Professor David Shulman, my first mentor in Indian studies. In the beginning (twenty years ago), he seemed to me incredibly scholarly, poetic yet strangely personal, beyond the ken of my life experience and reading. But, in his presence and under his guidance, I have gradually discovered the connection between reading and writing, and one's own being (self). It is this connection—as it has revealed itself to me in what David does and says—that makes intellectual life meaningful. For me, at least, this is what has inspired and informed my entire effort in the study and interpretation of ancient India. That is a teacher's and friend's most precious power; there is no higher gift.

The second presence is that of Professor Wilhelm Halbfass, my mentor at the University of Pennsylvania. I cannot accept his premature death; indeed, I still address him often in my mind. Feeling inferior and lacking true scholarship, I once complained about a chapter I had given him: It is mere interpretation, I said. And he responded emphatically: "Interpretation, this is what we want!"

Dr. Nita Schechet is the editor and producer of this book. I still suspect that she resents the underlying message of the *Yogasūtra*—the urgent plea for disintegration and end. She is, I am afraid, too much into life. Her intense interest in "textual realities" initiated and intensified my curiosity about others' thoughts and verbal expressions of yogic reality. The focus in this book on the tension between the practitioner's yogic silence and the various—inherently deficient—verbalizations thereof is largely due to her commitment to the value of speech and talent in penetrating texts. In the course of our relationship she has become a real co-author of *Silence Unheard*.

On many occasions I joke with my wife, Rivka, telling her that she was "born from the truth." I, for my part, would often prefer to stay with a more softened, less poignant sense of truth. However, Rivka, with her disturbing truthfulness and power of discernment, is a source of dear inspiration. She is present behind any touch of truth available in this book.

Two of Hebrew University's promising graduate students also helped in the long journey from idea to book. Anna Kventsel provided many helpful suggestions concerning meaning and translation of sutras and commentaries thereupon. Spartack Arbatov bridged classical India and contemporary computer science at crucial moments in this production. I thank them and the others who have accompanied me on my way.

Introduction: Challenges of an Oxymoronic Genre

The interior is not easily revealed and understood; Who really knows what is in there? Compared with the lucidity of the congealed, objective, and well-bound external, the inner—though close and familiar—is dubious and dark. Normal vision and ordinary experiences may not be enough as data and grounds for healthy conceptualization of innerness and selfhood. Freud's fascinating conjectures about the human interior originated in fertile circumstances of abysmal anxiety, dreaming, hypnosis, symptoms of pathology, and other unusual phenomena such as hysteria. Commonplace, seemingly simple and well-adjusted perceptions of reality may be too narrow, insufficient expressions of human nature and reality.

The more remote and surprising reaches of the interior—and the "spiritual potential of man"—may yet be digested. More extreme "symptoms" and "aberrant" behavior have yet to be explored and understood. Patañjali's *Yogasūtra* is one of the more viable, systematic conceptualizations of such symptoms and behavior, and an impressive articulation of the human end—disintegration. Even people less receptive to Patañjali's allegedly healing—transformative—intentions may be interested in the system of Pātañjala-Yoga, for in its courageous explication and openness to distant areas of human experience and modes of being it is admittedly singular. Yoga is an instructive example of the rich modes of otherness apparently available in ancient India.

However, the emaciated, frightfully disciplined, as if free and happy (alleviated of sorrow) figure of the yogin portrayed in the *Yogasūtra* threatens us in his singularly critical attitude towards normal life. Yoga insists on its harsh diagnosis of the human condition; victim of innate predispositions and ignorance, humans are conditioned and afflicted by the accumulated impact of past lives and behaviors, by the vicissitudes of life from moment to moment, by the antagonistic powers of nature.[1] Moreover, the remedy is as harsh as the diagnosis. Yoga requires that the person disintegrate; it seeks separation of subject and object, and consequent dissolution. It is the absolute, unfathomable end, the end of ends. While death is at most an incomplete completion, the end according to yoga is a complete completion, infinitely deeper and more final than death. The color, taste, sound, and flavor of this end of ends can hardly be imagined. It is a most indigestible, inaccessible kernel of otherness embedded in the universe of yoga pointed at by the *Yogasūtra.*

Commentators on and scholars of Pātañjala-Yoga do not share in the yogin's universe and experience, and cannot touch—among other things—the depth of diagnosis and prognosis of "life" expressed in the *Yogasūtra.* While Patañjali himself heard about it, was closely familiar with and deeply moved by the spectacle of the yogin immersed in meditation, he may not have substantially shared it. However, in his thought he conceived the images of disintegration and separation underlying and pervading Sāṅkhya metaphysics, and combined them with the vision of the silent yogin, visibly dissociated from the world, as if fallen apart, disintegrated. Though terribly impervious and dark, the silent yogin stimulates and moves the philosopher committed to dualism. The yogin's deepest silence had its enduring verbalized echo in the imageries of disintegration correlated with the unabridgeable gap between the light of consciousness and objective reality. Patañjali has thus found his spiritual hero, the embodiment of his Sāṅkhya theory of liberation.

Indeed, the most compelling of the voices vibrating in the *Yogasūtra* is a Sāṅkhya interpretation of the yogin's silence. The yogin unties the knots of existence, dismantling combinations, resisting "integrations," breaking entities apart, living in the spirit of analysis and separation (the spirit of Sāṅkhya) until he decombines his very own being into the densest possible silence. Patañjali's statement in YS 3.35 seems the epitome of the integration of Sāṅkhya metaphysics with yogic immersion in meditation. Meditation (*saṁyama*) on the infinite difference between the *sattva* component of the mind and the seer (purusha) brings about the knowledge of the pure subject. We may thus visualize Patañjali's visualization of the yogin absorbed in meditation. What does the latter meditate on? The ultimate principle of Sāṅkhya metaphysics, the dualism of purusha and prakriti. The dead-to-world yogin is an extension of Patañjali himself, a philosopher in action (however beyond discursive verbalization). Thus, Patañjali imagines the silent yogin as he disentangles the three constituents of objective reality; as he distinguishes—and separates—pure subjectivity (purusha) and objectivity (prakriti), the human being and the world fall apart.

Thus, the crux of Patañjali's intuition is the association of dualism and disintegration with the yogin's silence and behavior. Immersion in meditation, dissociation from the world, indifference to violence and pain, disregard for hunger and thirst, reported experiences of invisibility and levitation, unusual powers of memory, apparently close contacts with animals, and so forth, have all been associated with the vision of disintegration and Sāṅkhya metaphysics. In the history of philosophy and ideas of classical India, Patañjali's interpretation of yogic silence has come to be the most authoritative and viable. And yet, though integrative and particularly stimulating in its approach to the quality and meaning of ("postdisintegration") silence, his *Yogasūtra* is another scholarly attempt to overcome stark otherness in the figure of the lonely, inaccessible yogin.

This book joins a distinguished library of scholars attempting two elusive challenges, aural and verbal. Beginning with Patañjali, I trace and join writers who attempt both to hear and to articulate the depths of the silence reached in yogic pursuit. The ineffable quality of this condition has challenged all those who have attempted to approach it textually. To facilitate my attempt, doomed by this same ineluctably shared mismatch of tenor to vehicle, I have created seven archetypal characters, imaginary composites of centuries of textual yogic pursuit. The Complacent Outsider, the Ultimate Insider, the Romantic Seeker, the Universal Philosopher, the Bodily Practitioner, the Mere Philologist, and the Classical Scholar appear throughout this book. Theirs are the shoulders on which I stand. Recalling Hamlet, I have called myself the Observers' Observer. This book tracks these eight characters in search of the *Yogasūtra*, a trail of words which aims at bringing readers closer to that ineffable experience while recognizing itself as an oxymoronic genre.

Serious commentators and scholars have been sympathetic in their primary evaluation of Pātañjala-Yoga. But organically, so to speak, they are committed to the value of "life." In the face of the uncompromising, active yogic negation of the very combinations that constitute human life, one must say that scholars of yoga are also in favor of life in *saṁsāra*. This impossibly positive evaluation of both *saṁsāra* and yoga leads to an inner contradiction, and the essence of yogic otherness (the uncompromising experience of life as disease and the consequent need for disintegration) reflected on in the *Yogasūtra* is violated. Like a neurotic approaching therapy in the hope of improving upon neurosis (preserving rather than eradicating the disease), the more engaged commentators on yoga perceive its value for life *in saṁsāra*. Yoga, they maintain, is for integration, health, life. They are often fond of referring to the meaning of the name "yoga" (yoking, harnessing; but there are other possibilities).[2] The dominance of unification, merger, integration, and connectedness as images associated with fulfillment and satisfaction obstruct contact with the most compelling imagery of yoga (falling apart).

I.K. Taimni concedes that if the separation of the pure subject (purusha) and pure objectivity (prakriti) were indeed to take place (as is Patañjali's unequivocal assertion), it would be "horror and not the consummation of bliss."[3] He thus offers "complete unification" of one with the One Reality as the ultimate import of Yoga. R. Mehta refers to Pātañjala-Yoga as the "art of integration," the highest degree of fulfillment in life. M. Eliade does not commit himself to Patañjali's harsh, primary evaluation of life, and yet he is excited by "absolute freedom," "perfect spontaneity," "inexpressible freedom,"[4] as the yogin's assets and virtues regardless of the original frightful diagnosis and "end of ends" envisaged in Pātañjala-Yoga. And Eliade, too, is in favor of integration: "all these exercises pursue the same goal, which is to abolish multiplicity and fragmentation, to reintegrate, to unify, to make whole."[5] Another distinguished scholar, Barbara Stoler Miller, is also for "reintegration" and thus reluctant to accept the obvious—denied by no one—prescription of yoga for "separation" (*viveka*) and disintegration. She insists on the yogin's possibly considerable contribution to our world and time "with its bewildering complexity and seductive material culture."[6] In accordance with the role of yoga "to eliminate the control that material nature exerts over the human spirit,"[7] Miller objects to the dissociation of the yogin from the world: "The antiworldly isolation prescribed for certain stages of yoga is not the ultimate yogic state."[8] But the ultimate state of yoga is complete "aloneness" (*kaivalya*), deathly silence following the cessation of any activity of the three forces of nature (*guṇa*). This, indeed, is not only "antiworldly isolation" but absolute isolation, as the light of subjectivity becomes black, *turning upon itself* (rather than on objects).

Thus Pātañjala-Yoga cannot satisfy the integrative mood underlying the spirit of our time. The silence following disintegration is untouchable by the integrated and those thirsty for more integration. Integration is accompanied by the sound and aura of growth, fullness, continuity, expansion. The stuff of disintegration is real nothing and icy silence.

The ideal of separation and disintegration is the hallmark of Patañjali's Sāṅkhya yoga; it is a unique and fascinating expression of otherness (unattractive as it is for the integration-bound). However, Sāṅkhya yoga protagonists are also philosophers claiming truth, and as such they share our universe of philosophy and rational discourse. However, truth regarding human nature is unlike other truths. Paradox and tension accompany the search (and research) into innerness and selfhood. Research into the interior is in itself transformative, partially constituting its object. This is an exciting drama, where the narratives developed in the course of thinking about oneself are fateful.

The most well known Hindu philosopher, Śaṅkarācārya, was excited in the course of heated debates with imagined opponents about the nature of the self. The main source of excitement was the utter relevance of knowledge of self to human fate and destiny. Thus, for example, in a fight with an (imagined) Sāṅkhya opponent: if the *śāstra*, considered as a means of right knowledge, should point out to someone desirous of release but ignorant of the way to it, a nonintelligent self as the real self, such a person would—comparable to the blind person who had caught hold of the ox's tail—cling to the view of that being the self, and thus never be able to reach the real self different from the false self pointed out. Hence such a one would be debarred from what constitutes human good, and would incur evil.[9] Thus, under this description, research into innerness (or selfhood) offers the highest benefits as well as terrible risks.

However, the scope of research into human nature is necessarily limited if confined within the boundaries of our normal lifestyle and powers of observation and thought. We may have many advantages in our balanced condition of eating and drinking, reading, traveling, having families. But harsher, more "extreme" modes of living and experience have value too. Experimenting with the interior is groping not only for what the human person "is" but also for what it could be. What is possible may even carry more weight than what has actually been visible so far. The essence (nature) of the seed of corn lies in its potential to become corn, not in the seed manifested in its pregermination condition. In this context, extreme, latent, and foreign circumstances—such as those created by yogins—may be invaluable for human self-understanding.

The remote—almost inaccessible—yogic universe is potentially instructive by virtue of its remarkable otherness. On the other hand, this universe is not found outside the ken of humanity, beyond the range of human experience. Heeding the viability of traditions associated with Pātañjala-Yoga, and the obscure attraction exerted by yogins through the ages, one must concede that yoga represents a real possibility in the womb of potentiality we call human nature. The late Wilhelm Halbfass—particularly acute in reviewing culture in its various expressions, East and West—once said to me: "Thinking about it, if yoga did not exist, something vital would indeed be missing in our civilization." And W.B. Yeats simply said: "I want to hear the talk of these naked men."

Indeed, the ideal of disintegration—the goal of yoga—does provoke resistance; connectedness and inner unity are more appealing to the heart of one active in life and wishing for progress and amelioration. In this sense, Advaita Vedānta seems more satisfying and natural to people in *saṁsāra*. Merging in the One evokes images of expanded ego-boundaries and is thus closer to the human heart. Thus, for example, like many others, Pandit Usharbudh Arya defines Pātañjala-Yoga in the Advaitin's eyes: "Yoga is the union of the individual soul with the Absolute One,"[10] ignoring that essential way in which yoga is different from Advaita, prescribing disintegration rather than merging and "integration." It is thus opposed to powerful innate drives inherent in the human condition. From the vantage point of yoga, dominant spiritual motivations that seek modes of merging and "combination" (with the absolute, a deity)—as expressed by *bhakti*-movements or in Advaita Vedānta—may well be variations of the basic disease of "integration."

In the "therapeutic paradigm"[11] unfolded by Vyāsa in his commentary on YS 2.15, it is the combination (*saṁyoga*) of purusha and prakriti that is the cause of disease (*roga-hetu*). Philosophically, the existential drive of yoga is for analysis rather than synthesis, close to the spirit of Buddhism and opposed in this respect to Vedānta. Thus the essential principle of yoga psychology involves an enquiry into the nature of "combination." Undoing the ideal of combination ("decombination") and seeking an enlightened falling apart has its subdued, deep enchantment; and thus the incredibly harsh yoga survives.

The motifs and propositions offered in this essay are grounded in the recognition of the special challenge to understanding posed by the *Yogasūtra*. Three such motifs are particularly emphasized:

> a) Yoga is essential otherness. Along with the disturbing ideal of discombination, the yoga conceived by Patañjali implies the creation of a yogic universe[12] based on difficult and prolonged observances and practices culminating in actual sensory renunciation (dissociating the senses from their objects—*pratyāhāra*).
>
> b) This otherness of yoga is expressed also in the numerous supranormal experiences (*siddhi*) particularly emphasized and described in the third section of the *Yogasūtra* (the *Vibhūtipāda*).
>
> c) The scholarly tradition underestimates the significance of yogic otherness. Even the classical scholars (Vyāsa, Vācaspati, Vijñānabhikṣu, King Bhoja) exemplify this gap between the commentator and yogic silence. Patañjali himself—with his powerful connective and integrative drives—testifies as if unaware of his own separation from the reality of yoga.

The reality of yoga is the silent, dying yogin's lot, and Patañjali's *Yogasūtra* is (a most intelligible) conceptualization of this reality. Thus, the *Yogasūtra* attests to the coherence of the yogic universe and its reality. In most cases, the classical commentators fall short of this integrative, reality-affirming spirit of Patañjali. The commentators' typical strategy is the selection and glossing of one component of the sutra. Thus, for example, in referring to YS 3.29 where Patañjali connects meditation on a certain point (*nābhi-cakra*) with awareness of bodily structure (*kāya-vyūha*), commentators focus on the various components of the body while ignoring the connection of meditation to the knowledge thereby obtained. Or, for example, Patañjali connects *samādhi* with the destruction of "karmic impressions" (*saṁskāra*).

In YS 1.50 he connects highly charged consciousness which "carries ultimate truth" (*ṛtam-bharā*)[13] with the creation of new karmic impressions. Such an assertion—among numerous others—highlights the basic causal pattern of explanation embedded in the *Yogasūtra*. Above all, Patañjali is an intellectual who *explains*. His explanations connect various dimensions of the universe of yoga and the yogin's life. Through his powerful connections he forcefully points to the reality—inherently connected, integrated as any reality is—of the yogin and the yogin's world. None of the commentators on the *Yogasūtra* has ever reached the degree of coherence and connective spirit vibrating in the *Yogasūtra* itself.

Patañjali, according to our myth, is no practicing yogin but a Sāṅkhya philosopher deeply moved by the spectacle of the silent yogin, making this lonely figure the embodiment of liberation, *kaivalya*, or pre-*kaivalya* condition. This dramatic description of the *Yogasūtra* as generated by an encounter between an as-it-were dumb yogin and a curious, verbal Sāṅkhya philosopher differs from others, but it does not contradict them. We know nothing of the "historical Patañjali" (if he existed). It may well be that the author of the *Yogasūtra* collected information available in various sources. He was thus a "mere compiler" whose contact was with texts (rather than with, say, the reality of yogins immersed in meditation). However, our myth of "the philosopher and the dying yogin" reflects on the existential nature of the very speech-act, which is the *Yogasūtra*. In his very first sutra (YS 1.1; *atha yogānuśāsanam*), Patañjali defines himself as a *speaker* on yoga, outside the ken of "beyond-speech" yogins. References to speech and verbalization in the *Yogasūtra* clarify the meaning of speech as possible demarcation and boundary between yogin and nonyogin. The author of the *Yogasūtra* gives full and self-reflexive expression to such boundaries.

Thus, the tension between speech and postspeech silence is present in Patañjali's own reflections on verbalization in the *Yogasūtra*. There is a prescription for withdrawal from speech—and particularly referential speech—for the yogin immersed in a "post-samsaric" condition, while this condition (of immersion in silence) is addressed by intense—though technical, cool, unexcited—verbalization in the form of the *Yogasūtra*.

Among other phenomena of harmful combination (or "integration")—such as the very person (the human as being a combination of subject and object)—the *Yogasūtra* mentions speech itself. YS 3.17 refers to superimposition (*adhyāsa*) of word (*śabda*), object (*artha*) and "idea" (*pratyaya*) as something worthy of reflection. The sutra consists of two propositions; the first asserts that (referential) speech implies ignorance and lack of discernment: "the mutual imposition of word, object, and idea thereof is an unlawful combination (*saṅkara*)" (*śabdārtha-pratyayānām itaretarādhyāsāt saṅkaras*). The second proposition suggests that a cure for speech—the cessation of referential speech—is possible by meditation (*saṁyama*) on the difference between the aforementioned components of speech whereby (apparent) silence and mysterious knowledge of the sounds of all the creatures are obtained (*tat-pravibhāga-saṁyamāt sarva-bhūta-ruta-jñānam*). (Paradoxically, postspeech silence is productive of [supranormal] knowledge of speech.) Indeed, the dying yogin seems to block referential speech similarly to the way he controls light waves emanating from his body. Control of the latter produces invisibility (see YS 3.21), while the former means control of referential speech and results in silence.

Other attempts made in the *Yogasūtra* to define the role of speech and verbalization in the (silent) yogin's life point in the same direction. The purification of meditation from overt verbal traces is clearly seen in Patañjali's fourfold classification of *samāpatti* (YS 1.42–46). In these programmatic statements, Patañjali considers verbalization as a hindrance, a veil covering truth and reality. Thus, he recommends progressive purification (*pariśuddhi*) of the mind in the form of eradication of speech (YS 1.43). In this context, Vyāsa mentions the conventional (*saṅketa*) mode of speech as a contamination of mind to be removed. In addition, the list of mind-fluctuations (*vṛtti*) to be extinguished[14] strongly suggests Patañjali's interest in the yogin's postspeech silence.[15] Altogether, there are quite a few statements in the *Yogasūtra* addressing speech and postspeech silence. At the center there stands the richly empty and silent *Vivekin*.

There are thus at least four levels of auditory existence traced in this book: the yogin's primordial silence, Patañjali's verbal reflection on this silence, the commentators' and scholars' reflections on Patañjali's reflection and, finally, our reflections on the various distortions in hearing the yogin's inaccessible silence.

Speech acts addressed to the nature of otherness such as the yogin's materialize an obvious risk, the presumption of understanding. With respect to extreme modes of otherness, no one is exempt from the price for saying "I understand." Yogic otherness—foreign, inaccessible—invites particular, infinite caution. Who can claim satisfying, warm, enlightening understanding of the emaciated, intelligent yogin? Suppose there is reality pointed at by the *Yogasūtra* and that the *Vivekin*, the spiritual hero portrayed by Patañjali, embodies a true possibility of human nature. Who is qualified to understand the lonely *Vivekin*? Who can share experiences such as levitation and invisibility, the flavors of his scorching meditation (which burns previous conditioning, karma)?[16] It is virtually impossible to verbally address the yogic universe with true understanding; each statement of the yogin is engulfed by an aura of falsehood. Let us illustrate this by a historian's sober and useful falsification about a lesser figure in this tapestry, which demonstrates the potential for violation, projection, objectification, and banalization inherent in the scholar's gaze:

> The Maharajas are now fast disappearing and the rope-trick was at best a hallucination. Only the snake-charmer remains: generally an ill-fed man who risks his life to catch a snake, remove its poisonous fangs, and make it sway to the movement of the gourd-pipe; and all this in the hope of the occasional coin to feed him, his family, and the snake.[17]

While sobriety and truth prevail, we do sense an aura, the flavor of the objectifying subject (author), the ironic, even joking mode of approach, its reductive insistence on economy (the food, coin, the survival of the family). It may well be, of course, that the snake charmer is fully known, no other at all; he seeks food. However, a measure of presumptuous understanding is—no harm done in the case of the snake charmer—also there.

The case of addressing the yogin who creates a new life, dissociating himself from the world and *from us*, is obviously more complicated. Since understanding yoga is our goal in approaching the *Yogasūtra*, and since presumptuous understanding is no understanding, the hazards of gross presumptuous understanding are great.

However, we do not address the yoga universe alone. Rather, we walk on Patañjali's verbal bridge. Most probably, he violated the yogin's silence and otherness for our sake. But even thus, flavors of the other are preserved, adhering to the *Yogasūtra*. In addition to the Sāṅkhya principle of disintegration of the person into pure subjectivity (purusha) and pure, potential, invisible objectivity (prakriti), one meets with remembrance of lives past,[18] creation of other minds,[19] alleviation of relentless, subtle pain (*duḥkha*),[20] invisibility,[21] refusal of gifts and property,[22] yogic (invasive) cleanliness,[23] controlled breathing,[24] experiencing celestial tastes, overcoming hunger and thirst.[25] This is but a tiny sample of attitudes, practices and experiences in the alternative world of yoga. This world, mediated, violated, partially preserved, is still present in the *Yogasūtra*.

A major assumption of this chapter is that heeding the impervious otherness of the yogin's world of experience, discipline, attitudes, and philosophy, heightened contact with and awareness of presumptuous understanding—including our own—invites better—less presumptuous—understanding. Any attempt to approach Pātañjala-Yoga demands an awareness of the text and its "author." Many scholars address Patañjali's person, intellectual profile, and even "mode of existence." Indeed, there is much room for speculation. Except for tales of his obscure origin, nothing is known of him. Some scholars think he is the same as Patañjali the grammarian (author of the *Mahābhāṣya*). J. Varenne wonders whether he existed at all. G. Feuerstein thinks he "was clearly an adept of Yoga with a penchant for philosophy."[26] Barbara Stoler Miller sees Patañjali as a real philosopher, not just a technical compiler: "An attempt to teach the *Yoga Sūtra* through extant translations convinced me of the need to rescue the text from the overly technical language and scholastic debates that obscure Patañjali's brilliant analysis of how the workings of thought trap us in misconceptions about ourselves and the world" (p. xii).

I have stated an obvious fact: Patañjali is a verbalizer, a philosopher. His ideas include Buddhist sensibility and attitudes concerning *duḥkha*, *ahiṁsā*, and therapeutic imagery, Sāṅkhya metaphysics. His mode of being is that of a scholar who explains, as succinctly expressed in Patañjali's self-understanding in the very first sutra: *atha yogānuśāsanam*. Most of the sutras are vehicles for explanation (rather than description); the descriptive component is embedded in a structure of explanation. Pressing my reading further, I end this book offering an "essential *Yogasūtra*" which attempts to separate the descriptive from the explanatory in the sutras and to "rewrite" them in translations ranging from literal to loose, a kind of palimpsest translation meant to be read as a complementary, interactive entity.

Focusing on the otherness of the yoga universe, I have placed the yogin's "supranormal attainments" (*siddhis*) as a focal point of reference. For indeed, viewing these *siddhis* or *vibhūtis* as *experiences* (akin to those reported as the "near-death" condition) embraces *both* the otherness of the yogic universe and its inclusion within the range of humanity. Among the various dimensions of Pātañjala-Yoga, "supranormal attainments" have been consensually denigrated and rejected by the majority of commentators and scholars. Not incidentally, in the context of his presentation of the *siddhis,* M. Müller raises the hypothesis of a second Patañjali, one who inserted the *vibhūtis* into yoga, a Patañjali different from the sublime philosopher.

Reference to "supranormal powers" as experiences is a decisive invitation and challenge to understanding. The semantics of "miracles," "powers," and "attainments" has been, in the long and mostly repetitive tradition of commentaries on the *Yogasūtra*, suggestive of idiosyncrasy — irrelevant if not abnormal (the declaration that "[this] book does not deal with any of these mystical practices nor does it lay any stress on the performance of any of those miracles described by Patañjali"[27]). Relegation of these "powers" to the domain of "experience" is a move towards understanding their relevance and significance.

Similarly, Pātañjala metaphysics and psychology, evidently more respectable than unusual yogic experiences, have not been addressed with due courage and honesty. Latent fears have hampered or obstructed descriptions of yoga metaphysics and correlate psychology. The outlook of yoga incorporates a frightfully negative evaluation of what we consider normal life, provoking resistance in people attached to the cluster of values and motivations associated with "integration." The light of consciousness turns upon itself, becoming dark, as it were. Harsh and relentless indeed is Patañjali's vision of reality, incompatible with the spirit of our time. Our desire for experience meets with absence.

We have created the myth of the dying yogin as a narrative strategy for incorporating the *siddhis*; thus Patañjali the philosopher and the conceptualization of the *Yogasūtra* emerge from an encounter between a Sāṅkhya philosopher and a virtuous practitioner. Earlier traditions of thought and practice refer to yogic experiences affiliated with conceptualizations of *mokṣa*. Thus, for example, there are references to free motion (*kāma-cāra*) and playful bodilessness (*aśarīratva*) in the Upanishads. Thus, consequently, Patañjali embeds yogic experience within his primarily Sāṅkhya receptivity. Near-death condition is featured as potent ground for yogic experience. The narrative (myth) concerning Patañjali's encounter with the dying yogin facilitates a reading of the coherent reality of yoga.

However, although I cannot resist the urge to describe the yogic universe in this book, I also intimate the inaccessibility of this universe to outsiders and nonpractitioners of many kinds. I have described the hermeneutic situation prevailing in the field of Pātañjala-Yoga as a particularly challenging one. The yogin portrayed in the *Yogasūtra* is really an other; yogic otherness is real. It remains only to join eight characters in search of the *Yogasūtra*, listening to and for silence unheard.

1

Eight Characters in Search of the *Yogasūtra*: The Lively Banalization of Yogic Deathly Silence

Sages and scholars, no less than others, desire to live on and on. Not only continuity of living is desired, but also the indefinite extension of a certain essence of life and identity. Scholars are people; they are what they are. They seek to live on and remain the same. Sometimes they come forward to grope for the unfamiliar and foreign, projecting themselves onto the dark of the unknown. The encounter with the overwhelming otherness of yoga, a tradition particularly inimical to "normal life," has the mirror potency of stark otherness. Such otherness reflects and refracts the scholar's identity—nature, concepts, affiliation, education, fears, hopes, incompetence—in the light of day. How does one fill the gap between strikingly unfamiliar otherness and oneself?

Many indeed are the voices speaking for and instead of Patañjali, desperately closing and reclosing the gap between normal consciousness and the dying yogin's terribly dense innerness. But can it be done? If so, under what conditions? Perhaps Patañjali knows; most probably he too does not. He himself tried to close the gap between his normal consciousness (that of a highly verbal Sāṅkhya philosopher) and the dying yogin's testimony of the interior.

Here they are, then, approaching the *Yogasūtra*: the Complacent Outsider, the Ultimate Insider, the Romantic Seeker, the Universal Philosopher, the Bodily Practitioner, the Mere Philologist, the Classical Scholar, the Observers' Observer. These, of course, are archetypes, not found in reality. None of the Spiritual and Romantic Seekers would readily relinquish the scholarly voice and tacit access to objective truth. Though himself a Romantic Seeker, W. B. Yeats advances a general theory on the impact of Buddhism on Indian history.[1] M. Eliade is a great scholar, but also—essentially—a Romantic Seeker. He seeks deconditioning, freedom, and immortality. B. K. S. Iyengar is primarily a Bodily Practitioner, but is also a Spiritual Seeker who moves from the body to the innermost core of the soul. G. Feuerstein is a Seeker offering scholarly speculations on the history of yoga, the structure of consciousness, and many other scholarly subjects. R. Mehta, a sage and seeker affiliated with Krishnamurti, interprets the *Yogasūtra* as an Existential Seeker, though with much attention to detail such as correct Sanskrit wordings and diacritical signs. He thus understands his mission not only as an expression of his own personal and spiritual values and experience, but also as an exegesis of the *Yogasūtra*.[2]

S. Radhakrishnan—a Universal Philosopher—thinks highly of merging in the Absolute, but he also seems to have a special esteem for family life and brotherly cooperation, which—he admits—are not found in yoga. Thus he is concomitantly a Universal Philosopher and a Hostile Outsider. M. Müller is also a great scholar partially hostile to yoga, which he claims contains—among other things—"all these postures and tortures" as well as materials which are solely "of interest for the pathologist." Swami Vivekanada is definitely a Seeker, but also precise about diacritics and translation. Paramahansa Yogananda and J. H. Woods are an Ultimate Insider and a Mere Philologist, respectively.

The above is a kind of a commentary on one of Patañjali's sutras, YS 2.9. Patañjali asserts here that sages as well as fools are activated by a common and forceful current underlying normal life, the desire to preserve one's essence on and on.[3] This is one of the *kleśas*, omnipresent roots of misery.[4] Vyāsa conceives of *abhiniveśa* as "fear of death" (*maraṇa-trāsa*). Such a fear, he observes, is perceived even in worms which have just been born (*kṛmer api jāta-mātrasya*). Vyāsa seems to wonder whence this fear, for—he suggests—such a desire (to live on) could not possibly have arisen if the quality of death had not been experienced before (*na cānanubhūta-maraṇa-dharmakasyaiṣā bhavaty ātmāśīḥ*). Vyāsa concludes that the pain of death experienced in previous lives (*pūrva-janmānubhūtaṁ maraṇa-duḥkham*) has been inscribed into each creature's being, and is activated and remembered anew time and again in each life cycle. Thence the consciousness of all creatures: "May I never cease to live; may we live on and on."

Patañjali's *Yogasūtra* is a collection of 195 short sentences (sutras), composed or compiled around 200 A.D. Several centuries after the life of the Buddha, Pātañjala-Yoga addresses humanity with the diagnosis of life as misery, and seeks remedy in the creation of an alternative yoga universe. Patañjali puts forth the ideal of "yogic death" (*samādhi*) as one such remedial alternative to normal consciousness. *Samādhi* is indeed a "drive from humanity" and a "transcendence of the human condition" in terms of reality and value. Vivekananda puts this blatantly in his introduction to Patañjali's aphorisms: "Every soul must disintegrate to become God. So, it follows that the sooner we get out of this state we call 'man,' the better for us."[5] The creation of the yoga-reality involves shunning contact with other human beings,[6] a harshly disciplined lifestyle (celibacy, nonviolence, nonpossessiveness), postures, breathing control, meditation, and absorption. The end result is complete sensory deprivation and darkening of the world, at which point the yoga universe comes into being.

Most probably, none of the commentators mentioned above has shared fully in the yoga universe. The abysmal gap between yoga reality and its interpreters calls for bridges, and these are provided by commentators and scholars in the tradition of Pātañjala-Yoga. Inevitably, they extend or project their needs, fears, preferences, and aspirations onto the yoga universe; thus otherness becomes, in effect, a mirror.

Insufficient contact with the dying yogin's world as well as with its most immediate conceptualization—Patañjali's *Yogasūtra*—is visible in all the attempts to approach Pātañjala-Yoga. The Complacent Outsider preserves his or her "empiricist" identity, remaining aloof and suspicious; the Ultimate Insider exemplifies harmony and lack of discord, taking Patañjali's assertions for granted, making yogic phenomena commonplace, and thus resisting in his or her own way the yogin's otherness. The Universal Philosopher pays attention solely to metaphysical and religious dimensions, and becomes hostile once other components—incommensurable with the scholarly mode of seeking truth—are concerned. The Seekers vary in their mode of rejection of the yogin's mental culture and experience. Many talk of their very own "freedom"—conspicuously different from Patañjali's.[7]

Thus scholars and others act out their wish to live on and on. It is somewhat paradoxical—but true—that the more strikingly unfamiliar (or "other") the other, the more enhanced its mirror potency becomes. The remarkable variance among contemporary commentaries on the *Yogasūtra* attests to the stark otherness of this tradition.

In his intention to expose the reality behind all sorts of occult phenomena, D. H. Rawcliffe includes yoga.[8] In his exposition of the nature of *samādhi*, he says:

> The Yoga trance, like the trances of many mystics, is undoubtedly a source of great happiness and inspiration. Its psychiatric interpretation, however, sheds a ray of disillusion over the whole subject. The trance is almost certainly in most instances the product of autohypnosis. In a few cases a technique of very rapid breathing may result in a cataleptic trance through the exhaustion of the CO_2 content in the blood (as sometimes occurs in hysteria). Otherwise no particular importance can be attached to the acrobatic postures and special breathing techniques in the induction of the trance; they teach the yogi control of the will and the body and no more.[9]

Rawcliffe further elaborates on the yogin's "delusions of significance":

> It is through a process of autohypnotisation and autosuggestion that the yogi attains his euphoric trance.[10] The euphoria and delusions of significance which it brings are remembered by the yogi as a blissful experience which makes him long to repeat it.[11]

Rawcliffe is indeed a Complacent Outsider. He is somewhat aloof and superior to the tradition he examines, and his dealing with miraculous phenomena is a paradigm for his interpretation of yoga in general. In the context of his dealing with the "Indian rope trick," he mocks the "gullible and suggestible audiences of the Orient."[12]

The Complacent Outsider does not encourage serious study of the yoga-universe. He pays little attention to what the yogin says, and does not bother with the particular connections made by Patañjali.[13] Although seemingly sober and sincere in his reductionist program as well as in his attempts to expose frauds of yogins and fakirs, he does not make room for pondering the possible value of the other's remote experience. He is not truly challenged by Patañjali's *Yogasūtra*. Exploration into the yogin's domain of experience as a meaningful organic whole amounts—in Rawcliffe's exposition—to research into the dynamics of hallucination.[14]

At the other edge of the continuum is the Ultimate Insider, a devotee who speaks as an actual yogin and who sees into the truths of yoga from within. W. B. Yeats' guru, Shree Purohit Swami, is an Ultimate Insider who often interprets and corroborates Patañjali's statements by reference to his own experience. Thus, for example, he supports YS 3.16 by testimony from his own life:

> The sage Bhrigu worked out sometime in the past, the horoscopes of thousands of men, some alive today, some yet to be born. I saw my own horoscope, carved on palm leaves, written in Saṁskṛt, giving an account of my past as well as present life. There are various copies of this collection of horoscopes; I know of one which is at Benares, I saw another which belonged to a pundit from Malabar. It is called Bhrigu-Samhita. Generally three lives are described, or rather one life in relation to the past and the future life.[15]

For ordinary Westerners—largely Complacent Outsiders—such accounts by an Ultimate Insider sound naive and untrustworthy. However, Purohit's translation and commentary on the *Yogasūtra* is straightforward and unpretentious. His testimony about a transformative Kundalini experience is sincere, interesting, and has a ring of truth:[16]

> It is a terrifying experience when the kundalinee is awakened. The first day the fire was kindled in me, I thought I was dying, the whole body was, as it were, on fire, mind was being broken to pieces, the bones were being hammered, I did not understand what was happening. In three months, I drank gallons of milk and clarified butter, ate leaves of two nimba trees till they were left without a single leaf, searched everywhere for mudra leaves and devoured those insipid things.[17]

Purohit often refers to his personal experiences when interpreting Patañjali's sutras.[18] However, while Purohit's commentary is often fascinating by virtue of his personal testimony, his contact with the dying yogin's reality—as conceptualized by Patañjali—does not seem adequate. In particular, he seems to maintain a certain monistic type of metaphysics, incompatible with Patañjali's dualism. His statements are sometimes ambiguous. Thus, for example, his assertions that yoga "joins the personal Self and the impersonal Self," and that "when the three qualities of mind, purity, passion, ignorance, are controlled, the two Selves are yoked,"[19] are characteristically eclectic and inaccurate.

Another Ultimate Insider, Paramahansa Yogananda, considers yoga phenomena to be extensions of nature, and makes use of science to corroborate and support the truths manifested in his own life as a yogin. Although Paramahansa Yogananda does not refer extensively to the *Yogasūtra*, his *Autobiography of a Yogi* is a rumination on the viability and meaning of yogic experiences. Yogananda is an Ultimate Insider, in that he sees the world exclusively through a believer's eyes, relating—for example—with total belief his control over children's kites[20] and his tacit denial of real suffering in the world, a denial made possible by the theory of the relativity of consciousness.[21] Yogananda seems to deny any discontinuity between the normal world and the yoga universe. He looks upon yogic experiences as extensions of ordinary ones where, for the enlightened yogin, suffering disappears.

In this regard, Yogananda tells in detail a personal episode from the time of the First World War:

> In 1915, shortly after I had entered the Swami Order, I witnessed a strange vision. Through it I came to understand the relativity of human consciousness, and clearly perceived the unity of the Eternal Light behind the painful dualities of *māyā*. The vision descended on me as I sat one morning in my little attic room in Father's Garpar Road home. For months the First World War had been raging in Europe; I had been reflecting sadly on the vast toll of death (p. 317).

Yogananda continues and tells his story of the dead captain into whose body his consciousness had entered.[22] Then, back in his room, apparently alive and totally confused, he asks the Lord: "Am I dead or alive?" And the answer is given:

> A dazzling play of light filled the whole horizon. A soft rumbling vibration formed itself into words: "What has life or death to do with light? In the image of My light I have made you. The relativities of life and death belong to the cosmic dream. Behold your dreamless being! Awake, My child, awake!" (p. 317)

Yogananda integrates this paranormal occurrence with Western science through the notion of light: "With a few equational strokes of his pen, Einstein banished from the universe every fixed reality except that of light" (p. 316). The identification of light as the sole reality provides the yogin's opportunity: "A master is able to employ his divine knowledge of light phenomena to project instantly into perceptible manifestation the ubiquitous light atoms. The actual form of the projection (whatever it be: a tree, a medicine, a human body) is determined by the yogi's wish and by his power of will and of visualisation" (p. 316). " [A] yogi rearranges the light atoms of the universe to satisfy any sincere prayer of a devotee" (p. 317). Sympathy for science is associated by Yogananda with the ideal of mastery over nature: "For this purpose were man and creation made: that he should rise up as master of *māyā*, knowing his dominion over the cosmos" (p. 317). Science is viewed as fully compatible with Hinduism: "Twentieth-century science is thus sounding like a page from the hoary Vedas."[23]

A disturbing question comes to mind at this point: Why don't the masters of yoga rearrange light atoms in a more satisfactory way?

I. K. Taimni, one of the leading commentators on Pātañjala-Yoga in our age, is also an Ultimate Insider, though much different from Purohit and Yogananda in style and character. Taimni does not speak of personal experiences as they do, but is fully committed to the scientific viability of the *Yogasūtra* as well as to its spiritual value. In his book *The Science of Yoga* he refers to yoga as "the Science of sciences."[24] He explains the value of integrating yoga with science:

> The philosophy of *Yoga* deals with some of the greatest mysteries of life and the Universe and so it must inevitably be associated with an atmosphere of profound mystery. But much of the obscurity of *Yogic* literature is due, not to the intrinsic profundity of the subject, but to the lack of correlation between its teachings and the facts with which an ordinary educated man is expected to be familiar. If the

> doctrines of *Yoga* are studied in the light of both ancient and modern thought it is much easier for the student to understand and appreciate them. The discoveries made in the field of Science are especially helpful in enabling the student to understand certain facts of *Yogic* life, for there is a certain analogous relationship between the laws of higher life and life as it exists on the physical plane, a relationship which is hinted at in the well-known Occult maxim, "As above, so below."[25]

Trying to explain yoga—like Yogananda and Taimni—as extension of the laws of nature, S. Radhakrishnan is an exemplary Universal Philosopher. Yet he is no devotee or Ultimate Insider, and he is conspicuously open to Western culture and values. Radhakrishnan is very learned, and in addition to the commentators of classical yoga—such as Vyāsa, Vācaspati, Bhoja—he discusses Plato, Lao Tse, Tennyson, Plotinus, Schelling, and others. Abstract philosophy is, to him, the "inmost being" of yoga. Other elements—practice, *siddhi* experiences—are irrelevant.[26] In general, Radhakrishnan is not very interested in the yogin's reality. His interests are primarily textual; in his series of four lectures (*East and West*) he does not mention yoga at all.

As an illustration of the central concept of the *Yogasūtra* tradition—*samādhi*—Radhakrishnan offers Tennyson's beautiful account of his experience:

> A kind of waking trance I have often had, quite from boyhood, when I have been all alone. This has generally come upon me through repeating my own name two or three times to myself silently, till all at once, out of the intensity of the consciousness of individuality, the individual itself seemed to dissolve and fade away into boundless being; and this not a confused state, but the clearest of the clearest and the surest of the surest, the weirdest of weirdest, utterly beyond words, where death was an almost laughable impossibility, the loss of personality (if so it were) seeming not extinction, but the only true life.[27]

But such remarkable reports of mystical experiences are insufficient to endear yoga to Radhakrishnan. He seems to suspect yoga with respect to family values and morality:

> The goal of *jīva* is detachment and independence. It is not compatible with the human relationships of family life, society, etc., and accordingly the Yoga is said to be an unethical system. Ethical considerations cannot have any place in a system that aims at the breaking of all bonds connecting the individual to the world.[28]

According to Radhakrishnan, Pātañjala-Yoga is inherently incoherent. There is in yoga "low naturalism" as well as "high idealism,"[29] and consequently yoga is confused:

> The system did not feel prepared to cut off all connection with its surroundings and so incorporated elements which did not belong to its inmost being.[30]

Here the "inmost being" is the philosophy, while attendant elements are deemed lowly, unworthy, and are dismissed: "The habit of drug intoxication prevalent in primitive tribes was mixed up with the higher mysticism of the Yoga."[31] The Universal Philosopher is thus fortunate in knowing the difference between genuine and specious spirituality:

> There is such a thing as unconscious suggestion from the environment, and so the Yoga exhibits features determined by the conditions of the age in which it arose. But it is easy for us to separate these secondary accidental characteristics from the primary and the integral. The *Yogasūtra* does not take any further notice of drugs and spells, thus suggesting its considered conviction that the signs and wonders which the uncultured seek after, even if well authenticated, possess no spiritual value.[32]

While "less universal" than Radhakrishnan, S. N. Dasgupta is also a philosopher who considers the abstract contents of the *Yogasūtra* his main interest.

> The philosophical, psychological, cosmological, ethical and religious doctrines, as well as its doctrines regarding matter and change, are extremely interesting in themselves, and have a definitely assured place in the history of the progress of human thought; and, for a right understanding of the essential features of the higher thoughts of India, their knowledge is indispensable.[33]

Many are the Seekers inspired by the *Yogasūtra*. They want radical, existential, metaphysical change. The *Yogasūtra* is indeed a description of a yoga universe drastically different from the normal one. However, it is virtually inaccessible. None of the commentators—Seekers, Mere Philologists, Ultimate Insiders—has ever reached the yoga universe and lived there. Even a person such as Rajneesh, who pours so many compliments on Patañjali—particularly in terms of his *realistic and effective* teaching—cannot be said to have reached yogic death (*samādhi*) and the yoga universe. This is the sunless world of the emaciated yogin's innerness, which—most probably—even

Patañjali did not actually visit. For Patañjali only met with dying yogins, and was not—as this Observers' Observer notes—one of them.[34]

Actually being one of them is ostensibly the goal of the Romantic Seeker, who diagnoses life as unsatisfactory, conditioned, repetitive, or disenchanting. Heinrich Zimmer seems tired of the "virtuous fulfillment of the tasks of the decent, normal, human career (*dharma*)." Once such normal life becomes "stale routine," "there remains, still, the lure of the spiritual adventure."[35]

It is likely that Zimmer speaks from his heart when he suggests that our life (in *saṁsāra*, apparently) is "an intolerable bore," and hence the "possibility of discovering the secret of the workings of the cosmic theater itself . . . remains as the final fascination, challenge and adventure of the human mind" (p. 284). The romantic air is enhanced as Zimmer refers to the inner person revealed by yoga. "Yoga, however, stills the mind. And the moment this quieting is accomplished, the inner man, the life-monad, stands revealed—like a jewel at the bottom of a quieted pond" (p. 285).[36]

But who is this "inner man," the jewel at the bottom of the pond? He is apparently the purusha, the infinitely passive, motionless, unseen and pure subject, dissociated from any trace of objectivity, not even thinking or feeling. Is this state the desired release from intolerably boring life?

Missing in Zimmer's narrative of yoga is a more sober, less romantic, account of Patañjali's metaphysics as well as a realistic appraisal of the yogin's terrible choice. This is not an escape from the "intolerable bore" of the "cosmic theater." It is the creation of awful inner density, gained by the harshest of disciplines.

Though less personal and somewhat more scholarly than Zimmer, M. Eliade is also a Romantic Seeker. While sounding scientific, there are strong notes of romantic search in his writing. In his introduction to *Yoga: Immortality and Freedom*, Eliade contemplates the particular compatibility of our time with the core of Indian spirituality:

> The problem of the human condition—that is, the temporality and historicity of the human being—is at the very center of Western thought, and the same problem has preoccupied Indian philosophy from its beginnings. . . . What modern Western philosophy terms "being situated," "being constituted by temporality and historicity," has its counterpart, in Indian philosophy, in 'existence in *māyā*.'[37]

Thus Eliade describes the development of different disciplines, sciences, and moods in the West, which he wisely correlates with certain approaches to India. He then articulates the particular correspondence of Western interest in the "conditioning of man" with Indian spirituality: "From the Upanishads onward, India has been seriously preoccupied with but one great problem—

the structure of the human condition" (p. xvi). Obviously, Eliade's main interest is in the "human condition" (for the sake of its transcendence). He is keenly interested in "deconditioning" and "freedom," interests which he allegedly shares with fellow Westerners as well as with spiritual India. According to Eliade's description of the East-West hermeneutic situation, he himself exemplifies the very situation he describes. However, for a happy correspondence between Western mood (or receptivity) and Indian message, the description of spiritual India must be independent of Western interests. This is seemingly the scholarly ideal. But is this possible? A certain sense of circularity, mirroring and cultural colonialism becomes more perceptible as one heeds these generalizations about India's "one great problem." It is likely that India also had other interests and problems "from the Upanishads on." The gap between Eliade and Patañjali is closed at a price—the elision of the yogin's otherness. The encounter with yogic death (*samādhi*)—a starkly dark and unfamiliar condition—becomes a somewhat familiar, promising, and even comfortable condition, compatible with the seeker's needs and fulfillment. For Eliade is a resolute Romantic Seeker in quest of "indescribable freedom," "absolute freedom," "immortality," and so forth.

In addition to conditioning and deconditioning, Eliade seems to have other interests and motives which affect his exposition of yoga. Eliade starts his *Patañjali and Yoga* with the story of an unworthy Indian fakir by the name of Haridas.

> At about the middle of the nineteenth century Dr. J. M. Honigberger astonished the scholarly world with the story of a yogi called Haridas. In the presence of Maharajah Ranjit Singh and his court in Lahore, Haridas put himself into a state of catalepsy and was buried in a garden. For forty days a strict watch was kept over the tomb. When the yogi was exhumed, he was unconscious, cold and rigid. Hot compresses were placed on his head, he was rubbed, air was forced into his lungs in a kind of artificial respiration, and finally Haridas came back to life. (p. 3)

Why does Eliade tell this story? What is its relevance to his focus, and why does he give it primacy of place? Indeed, Eliade troubles to denigrate Haridas, expressing interest in this lowly man:

> But the story of Haridas is significant for another reason too: His mastery of yoga in no way implied a spiritual superiority. Haridas was known, rather, as a man of loose morals. He finally fled with his wife and took refuge in the mountains. There he died and was duly buried according to the custom of the country. (p. 5)

Eliade then reveals his own conviction: "But obviously true yoga should not be confused with the possession of a fakir's powers" (p. 5). There is evidently a puristic note in this statement; unusual experiences and "powers" are denounced so that pure, legitimate, worthy, absolute, indescribable freedom be possible. Indeed, Haridas's story might subserve both ends; the purification and reality of absolute freedom.[38]

The most suggestive transition in Eliade's narrative is that between Haridas's story and the definition of yoga as a potent means for deconditioning and attaining absolute freedom. In *Patañjali and Yoga*, Eliade does not explicitly connect these two components. Does he tacitly suggest that absolute freedom does not entail freedom from conventional morality? Why begin with the curiosity of the buried fakir? The underlying theme of the fakir's story is the reality of yogic phenomena. Indeed, in the course of his introduction to *Patañjali and Yoga*, Eliade reaches the point of subscribing to the reality of yoga. Eliade is fascinated by Haridas's achievement, and he considers it the essence of liberation and yoga. Haridas is, seemingly, the *Jivan Mukta* who embodies in Eliade's view the yogin par excellence.[39] But such a yogin does not *really* die but lives indefinitely in the body; thus his death is merely "anticipatory death," "initiatory death," followed—necessarily—by rebirth.

The Romantic Seeker is thus close to viewing yoga as actual abolition of the profane and effective constitution of the sacred. "For Yoga, the initiatory rebirth becomes the acquisition of immortality and freedom."[40] However, Haridas's disappointing end reflects a tension in the scholarly, Romantic Seeker's mind. Eliade seems undecided about the precise modality of yogic death, immortality, and freedom; towards the end of his—most valuable and informative—book, he sees yoga as essentially and paradoxically involved with "magic" and "mysticism."[41] Is yoga then a real promise of redeeming transformation (from the impure, profane plane onto the sacred) or a road to unfulfilled aspiration for immortality and freedom? Eliade ends the main body of his most important book with a clearly undecided note of doubt: "Everything depends upon what is meant by freedom."[42] Unable to resolve ambivalence and ambiguity, Eliade remains with empty freedom and ambiguous immortality.

W. B. Yeats is more aware than Eliade of his own position as a Romantic Seeker: "I come in my turn, no grammarian, but a man engaged in that endless research into life, death, God, that is every man's reverie."[43] Yeats identifies himself as different from philologists and other scholars; "I want to hear the talk of those naked men, and I am certain they never said 'The subliminal impression produced this (super repetitive balanced state)' nor talked of 'predicate relations'" (pp. 11–12). Yeats sees in Patañjali a man who "unlike Buddha turned from ordinary men; he sought truth not by the logic or the moral precepts that draw the crowd, but by methods of meditation and contemplation that purify the soul. The truth cannot be found by argument, the soul itself is truth, it is that Self praised by Yadhnyawalkya which is all Selves" (p. 15). Though an avowedly nonscholarly ("romantic") seeker, Yeats advances his own scholarly ideas about the development and history of Indian spirituality: "The school of Yadhnyawalkya and its historical preparation replaced the trance of the soma drinkers (I think of the mescal of certain Mexican tribes), or that induced by beaten drums, or by ceremonial dancing before the image of a god, by a science that seems to me as reasonable as it must have seemed to its first discoverer" (p. 15).

Yeats shares the diagnosis of yogic trance with the Complacent Outsider, but he has his own evaluation of the facts: "Through states analogous to self-induced hypnotic sleep the devotee attains a final state of complete wakefulness called, now conscious *samadhi*, now *Tureeya*, where the soul, purified of all that is not itself, comes into the possession of its own timelessness" (p. 15).

Similarly, R. Mehta and Bhagavan Rajneesh are Stimulated Seekers; they express in their own way the dissolution of the yogin's otherness and thus the banalization of yogic death and Patañjali's enterprise. The *Yogasūtra* is a stimulus which enables Seekers such as Mehta and Rajneesh to elaborate on ideas and themes already present and well-established in their intellectual and spiritual lives. R. Mehta is an original thinker. His interpretations of many of Patañjali's sutras are notably different from more traditional or conventional commentaries. Although he seems to pay homage to tradition, with impeccable punctuation of the sutras, Mehta does not consult in his book (*Yoga; the Art of Integration*) any of the Classical Scholars such as Vyāsa or Vācaspati. His commentary is always original and independent of the overt meanings of Patañjali and tradition. Thus, for example, commenting on YS 2.45,[44] Mehta interprets *Īśvara-praṇidhāna* ("surrender unto *Īśvara*") as "right orientation", *Īśvara* being "Reality." "To contemplate is to view with a totality of attention. *Īśvara-praṇidhāna* or right orientation enables a spiritual aspirant to look at everything with total attention" (p. 182). Thus, *tapas* is "simplification," the removal of unnecessary adornments. Mehta often recognizes his deviation from the conventional meaning of words; "*brahmacārya* is commonly translated as celibacy, but this is not its real meaning. It really means the cessation of the frittering away of one's energies. One's energy is frittered away through resistance and indulgence" (p. 167). "Non-possessiveness indicates the rendering of the mind completely homeless" (p. 170). "*Saṅtoṣa* is usually translated as contentment, but its real meaning is self-containment" (p. 177). "The word *antardhāna* appearing in this sutra is translated generally as being physically invisible. To regard this sutra as indicating a state of physical invisibility would be to interpret it in a very superficial sense" (p. 321).

Mehta's constant deviation from traditional and conventional interpretation of Patañjali's sutras signifies originality and independence of thought as well as lack of openness to the other's import. Indeed, Mehta seems to exclude the other's existence from that very reality whose heightened contact he so relentlessly advocates.

Similarly to R. Mehta, Bhagavan Rajneesh desires (and educates for) intense openness to reality. Unlike Mehta, he emphasizes Patañjali's character as a great scientist:

> Yoga is pure science, and Patañjali is the greatest name as far as the world of yoga is concerned. This man is rare. There is no other name comparable to Patañjali. For the first time in the history of humanity, this man brought religion to the state of science: he made religion a science, bare laws; no belief is needed.[45]

Rajneesh himself is an Existential Seeker rather than a scientist. His voice is religious, seeking transformation, the abolition of mind and normal existence:

> A total frustration is needed—the revelation that this mind which projects is futile, the mind that hopes is nonsense, it leads nowhere. It simply closes your eyes; it intoxicates you; it never allows reality to be revealed to you. It projects you against reality. The mind is a drug. (p. 5)

The Seekers' identity, ideology, and interests often becloud certain aspects of importance in the *Yogasūtra*. Thus many Seekers disregard Patañjali's status as a Sāṅkhya philosopher. Swami Prabhavananda and Christopher Isherwood are modern Vedāntins who collaborated in the translation of and commentary on the *Yogasūtra*, disregarding the actual metaphysics contained therein. In their book *How to Know God*, they address the difference between Patañjali's convictions and their own. They justify their values and mode of commentary by asserting the reader's welfare as well as the insignificance of metaphysical differences:

> Since yoga, prior to Patañjali, was originally grounded in Vedanta philosophy, we have interpreted the aphorisms, throughout, from a Vedantist viewpoint. In this we differ from Patañjali himself, who was a follower of Sāṅkhya philosophy. But these are merely technical

differences, and it is best not to insist on them too strongly, lest the reader become confused.[46]

Thus, for Seekers like Isherwood and Prabhavananda, Patañjali's otherness as a Sāṅkhya philosopher is explicitly avoided; they superimpose on the *Yogasūtra* their own (Vedāntist) position: "but Prakriti is not the ultimate Reality. Behind Prakriti is Brahman."[47] They seem to accord primacy to their educational goal, claiming that "the majority of Western psychotherapists do not, as yet, recognize the existence of the Atman, the Godhead within man; and do not, therefore, attempt to help their patients achieve the union of perfect yoga."[48]

At the other extreme of temperament and orientation is the Mere Philologist. James Hauthon Woods's *The Yoga-System of Patañjali* has received much attention as the epitome of scholarship on the *Yogasūtra*.[49] Woods's interests are patently textual and scholarly, and he avoids any reference to the reality of yoga. Woods refers to the "historical importance" of the yoga texts as "forming a bridge between the philosophy of ancient India and the fully developed Indian Buddhism and the religious thought of today in eastern Asia."[50] Scholarly interest—this historical importance—"emboldens one to the attempt" at exegesis (p. ix). Woods further expounds on the nature of Pātañjala-Yoga as "a bridge": "For this system, together with the Nyāya and Vaiśeṣika systems, when grafted upon the simple practical exhortations of primitive Buddhism, serves as an introduction to the logical and metaphysical masterpieces of the Mahāyāna" (p. ix). Woods is the ultimate Mere Philologist. After a brief reference to his "reasons for taking up the work," his preface addresses "difficulties of comprehending the work," "difficulties of style," "translation of technical terms," "punctuation," and "texts and manuscripts."

The narrative of Woods's introduction focuses on the authorship of the *Yogasūtra*, the "tradition of identity of two Patañjalis," the date of the *Yogasūtra* and the main commentaries. This narrative does not contain a single statement about the *contents* of the *Yogasūtra*. The Mere Philologist's most intimate reference to the reality of the yogin's experience is expressed in his "translation of technical terms," when he confesses to a difficulty in translating the concept of *prasaṅkhyāna*: "I have weakly consented to use 'Elevation' as equivalent to *prasaṅkhyāna*; the original word denotes the culmination of a series of concentrations; the result is the merging of the Self in the object of contemplation."[51] This last statement—quite standard in descriptions of yoga—is the boldest gesture of the Mere Philologist towards the bodily yogins who dimly provide a certain manifestation of *prasaṅkhyāna* and "merging of the Self."

Woods sees Pātañjala-Yoga as a "system" rather than a way of life or reality, not a drama of the human spirit but a mode which resists translation and acculturation. In his view, "a system whose subtleties are not those of Western philosophers suffers disastrously when its characteristic concepts are compelled to masquerade under assumed names, fit enough for our linguistic habits, but threadbare even for us by reason of frequent transpositions" (p. x).

Totally different from the Mere Philologist—in his interests, language, and mode of disregarding the other's otherness—is the Bodily Practitioner. B. K. S. Iyengar is one of the leading contemporary teachers of Haṭha yoga. He is well-known as a tough and exacting teacher of *āsana* (posture) as well as a commentator on the *Yogasūtra.* Iyengar's absorption in the performance of *āsanas* provides him with an intellectual opportunity in the interpretation of life and Patañjali's *Yogasūtra.* "By studying in depth the performance of *āsana*, I have shown how, even by performing one *āsana*, the entire human system can be integrated."[52] Iyengar is thus a holistic Bodily Practitioner, and accordingly he criticizes current trends in the dismembering of yoga: "Yet we unnecessarily disintegrate yoga, which, by definition, is an integral subject, when we call it physical yoga, mental yoga, spiritual yoga, *jñāna*-yoga, *bhakti*-yoga, *kuṇḍalini*-yoga, *siddha*-yoga, and so on. It is very unfortunate. Why do we demarcate and divide that which unites each individual from the body to the soul?" (p. 68). Describing the road from *āsana* to *samādhi*, Iyengar sometimes sounds like an Upanishadic sage: "And yet we say that the end of yoga is to forget the body and to forget the mind. As the essence of the tree is hidden in the seed, so the essence of the tree of man is hidden in the seed of the soul. You cannot see the tree in the seed, and you cannot see the self in the innermost seat of the soul" (p. 69).[53] Iyengar the Bodily Practitioner is also an Existential Seeker. "I don't want yesterday's experience. I want to see what new understanding may come in addition to what I had felt up to now. In this quest, my body is my bow, my intelligence is my arrow, and my target is my self" (p. 69).[54]

Among the various commentators, interpreters, and seekers of yoga, Iyengar is the only one who is "a yogin." The others—Romantic and Existential Seekers, Universal Philosophers, Mere Philologists, Ultimate Insiders, and Complacent Outsiders, are all beyond the ken of actual yoga. Yoga has been Iyengar's preoccupation for his entire life. Practice and teaching for over sixty years have resulted in a well-established perspective on life and yoga, a perspective centered on the value and potency of yogic postures. These postures—to which Patañjali refers as the third limb of *aṣṭāṅga* yoga—are for Iyengar the roots of the tree of yoga. "All the eight limbs of yoga have their place within the practice of *āsana*."[55]

Sometimes Iyengar interprets his experience with *āsana* in a genuinely interesting way, making new connections among the various practices and insights of yoga:

> Suppose that in performing an *āsana* you are stretching more on the right side and less on the left. An unethical state is setting into your body. There is violence on the right side where you are stretching more, and the left side, where the stretch is less, appears to be non-violent. On the right side you are being violent because you are saying, "Do as much as you can! Stretch as much as you can!" It is a deliberate violence because you are overstretching. On the left side, where you are not stretching so much, maybe you have the idea that you are not being violent. But an intelligent practitioner of yoga observes that at the same time as he is consciously doing violence on one side, he is also doing violence on the other. . . . One side thus manifests deliberate violence, and the other side non-deliberate violence (p. 48).

Iyengar elaborates and connects other *yamas* with the "root of the tree of yoga"—the *āsana*:

> When the right and the left are integrated, there is truth, which is the second principle of *yama*. You need not observe truth—you are already in truth, but you are not escaping by failing to perform on the weaker side. And where there is total stretch in the *āsana*, there is a tremendous understanding and communication between the five sheaths of the body from the physical and from the spiritual and from the spiritual towards the physical. (p. 49)

However, to this Observers' Observer the practice and experience of *āsana* do not seem sufficiently powerful as an integrating principle of the yoga universe as a whole. Iyengar's definitions of the various "limbs of yoga" reveal obvious deviations from meanings accepted by Patañjali. Let us take as an example Iyengar's definition of *samādhi*. In accordance with his experience with *āsana*, Iyengar reaches an original definition of *samādhi*: "Diffusing the soul into each and every part of the body is *samādhi* " (p. 69). This statement seems to be an expression of an experience of "wholeness," most probably an important and real experience of Iyengar. It is, however, remarkably different from Patañjali's conceptualization of *samādhi*;[56] according to the *Yogasūtra*, *samādhi* is essentially a condition in which the distinction between consciousness and object disappears. It is not impossible that certain of the Bodily Practitioner's experiences correspond with loss of boundaries between "subject" and "object." However, Iyengar's definition of *samādhi* seems particularly compatible with *āsana*-practice, and somewhat removed from yogic death and utter innerness as these are expressed in the *Yogasūtra*.

Thus Iyengar disposes of the other's otherness in his own way. His creative acquaintance with the culture and concomitant experiences of yogic postures makes him see certain meanings and connections. These are often interesting and important; yet, the Bodily Practitioner's perspective reflects his own being, similarly to the other characters who approach the *Yogasūtra*.

Indeed, silence, when approached, is alarming, makes extraordinary attending demands and is easily distorted. The Seekers, Philosophers, Outsiders, Insiders, and Mere Philologists preserve their identity and essence of their life experience. Approaching the silent yogin, they are thus unable to hear and attend to the nature and meaning of his or her silence.

This auditory deficiency is shared by the Classical Scholars. The Classical Scholars—Vyāsa, Vācaspati, King Bhoja, the author of the *Vivarana*, Vijñānabhikṣu—are essentially Mere Philologists. Crucially, they never address the truth value of statements in the *Yogasūtra*. They do not consider observation and experience as major sources of interpretation and they avoid discussion among themselves when strictly practical or experiential topics are the issue.[57]

While eluding our perception, the yogin's life is harsh and wonderful. He knows the pain of separation from "satisfaction," human warmth, and "pleasure."[58] He is also familiar with exceptional experiences, power, control, and unusual insights. The yogin's loneliness, the excruciating discipline of yoga—the yogin's engagement with potent postures, control of breathing, meditation, altered states of consciousness and, in general, the near-death condition—create yoga experience. This is inaccessible and incredible for most people and hence to most scholars.

We Scientists, Seekers, Bodily Practitioners, Outsiders, Philosophers, Observers' Observers, and Mere Philologists are doomed, of course, to a shadowy reflection of essentially foreign territory. Most likely, we will never breathe the crisp air of pleasure-free contact with "objects." We shall not experience total sense deprivation, and our minds will always be hopelessly beclouded by the "veils," conditioned by and consisting of primordial tendencies such as the *gunas* of passion and sloth. We shall probably not even sit stably and comfortably in an *āsana* position, clean-minded, endowed with readiness (*yogyatā*) for meditation. Above all, yogic unconsciousness, yogic death (*samādhi*) and disembodiment, along with its accompanying experiences (the *siddhis*), are beyond our reach. We will not savor this dense and soothing darkness, the yogin's promising, liberating death. And—consequently—we will not reach the miraculous, substantial dreaming available to one who has crossed the frontier into innerness. Thus our contact with yoga is substantially impaired, insufficient even with respect to the more overt, explicit dimensions of the tradition of yoga.

We—Seekers, Practitioners, Scientists, Observers—do feel, however, the reality behind some of the traditional classifications made by scholars of yoga. We have some glimpses into the hierarchy of levels (*bhūmi*) of concentration, awareness, and being. We too have our better and worse moments. We share with the yogin a certain yearning for freedom, transparency, and vision. Thus it is possible to sense some "reality," "an occasion for meaning," a distant echo of "experience." But lacking the excruciating yogic discipline and practice, it is unlikely that we can ever transcend the human condition and have more than a marginal share in the outstanding existence in yoga. Yoga experience is and has been necessarily remote, shared by very few.

By virtue of his observation of these colleagues, the Observers' Observer is aware of the difficulty involved in interpreting the *Yogasūtra*. He or she perceives the insurmountable gap between the dying yogin's ultimate silence and the philosopher's (Patañjali's) eloquent speech. While Patañjali's is an immensely significant attempt at closing the abysmal difference of being which lies between himself and the silent yogin, the Seekers, Philosophers, Classical Scholars, Outsiders, and Insiders do not attain the connective and integrative quality of the *Yogasūtra*. In fact, the characters approaching the *Yogasūtra* reenact Patañjali's primary—though instructive—failure (to close the gap of otherness with the silent yogin). For Patañjali—a Sāṅkhya philosopher—also wanted to live on and on.

Unlike his colleagues, the Observers' Observer greatly values experience. Yoga experience is the least accessible dimension of the yoga universe, the least intelligible dimension of the dying yogin's life. The other dimensions—attitude, metaphysics, practice—are more available for thought and understanding. Among the various characters pursuing the *Yogasūtra*, the Philosopher is interested in metaphysics and attitude; the Bodily Practitioner finds meaning in moving from practice to metaphysics; the Seeker looks for means of transcendence through metaphysics and attitude; the Classical Scholar emphasizes the coherence of metaphysics; they all consider the *siddhis* embarassing.

Unable to have any existence in yoga ourselves, we depend heavily upon Patanjali's verbal expression of the yogin's experience and mental culture. Thus we reach out for some understanding of the *Yogasūtra*. Patañjali's *Yogasūtra* is an integrative reflection on yogic life, experience, and practice, on the yoga universe as a whole. The *Yogasūtra* is a unity, not only in its coherence, but also in its expression of an organically whole reality. It is a philosophical work, wondering at the yogin's dense and unbearable silence and the remarkable, extraordinary experiences of yogins who crossed the boundary between life and "after life." Accounting for the yogin's experiences makes sense of the relationship of practice, attitude, experience, and (metaphysical) interpretation. Thus the *Yogasūtra* is an attempt to make sense of "life-in-yoga" as a whole. Underlying Patañjali's project is the conviction that the yoga universe, steeped in silence, is valuable as a genuine alternative mode of being, a way to knowledge and liberation; its study, then, is not a world of vicarious fantasy.

The *Yogasūtra* teaches a way of transcendence, culminating in dissociation from externality, and thus crossing the boundary between normal consciousness into dark silence and otherness. It is, indeed, a crisis. In total darkness, practically disembodied, the person experiences an unfamiliar, different "reality." At this point the reality of yoga experience becomes apparent. Many unusual experiences occur; levitation, extraordinary feats of memory, entering into others' bodies, unnaturally powerful perceptions of remote and subtle objects, invisibility, telepathy, precognition, understanding animal sounds. These are the *siddhis*, the unusual experiences carefully listed and detailed—and explained, one by one—by Patañjali. These experiences are an integral aspect of the organic whole of yoga. The *Yogasūtra* is a unity, both coherent and referring to an organic whole of some reality, and yoga-experiences are necessary symptoms and unifications of the universe of yoga. Without these unusual experiences the description of yogic practice, attitude, and Sāṅkhya interpretation would lack an essential aspect.

The *Yogasūtra* contains implied metaphysical principles, such as in the following statements: pure subjectivity becomes colored by mind activities;[59] when mind activities cease, subjectivity rests on its own.[60] *Īśvara* is a particular subject, unaffected by karma and *kleśa*;[61] and so on. Such propositions must have emerged after a long process of reflection. They do not have the biting immediacy of proximity to the yogin's experience. At the other pole of the continuum of expression there are propositions such as: immeasurable happiness comes from the practice of yogic contentment;[62] meditation on the boundaries of body and space produces an experience of unusual lightness and movement in the air;[63] yogic meditation on the bottom of the throat brings about the cessation of hunger and thirst;[64] meditation on the shape of the body brings about the experience of invisibility;[65] meditating on karma as faster or slower to ripen brings about knowledge of the time of death and exit (from the body);[66] there is an experience of the mind entering another's body,[67] of divine hearing (*divyaṁ śrotram*),[68] and so on. If we consider the class of sutras which are closest to the immediacy of yogic experience, we observe that yoga experience is communicated most directly through the doctrine of the "unusual experiences," the *siddhis*; and these constitute the essence of the yogin's otherness, the most foreign dimension of the yoga universe.

Though essential to the structure of the *Yogasūtra*, within the elite culture of commentators and scholars, Seekers, Practitioners, Philologists, and Philosophers, this inaccessible progeny of yoga and thus yogic experience itself has been denigrated as unworthy, spiritually inferior, dissociated from Vedic culture, even foreign to the essence of yoga. Classical commentators tended to view the *siddhis* as marginal epiphenomena on the yogin's road to liberation. Vyāsa suggests that yogic meditation (*saṁyama*) is practiced for the sake of the "desired objects."[69] Yogins whose minds are open to the world (*vyutthita-citta*)—and pursue the *siddhis*—are inferior to the more superior, "recollected ones" (*samāhita-citta*).[70] The *siddhis*, if useful at all, are "signs" (*sūcaka*) of the yogin's progress.[71] Vācaspati elaborates on this point and says that as the yogin produces certain *siddhis*, he knows what he has already accomplished and what remains to be done.[72] Vijñānabhikṣu distinguishes between the yogin who desires powers (*vibhūti-kāma*) and the one who desires liberation (*mumukṣu*).[73]

Most modern commentators and scholars succumb to this "language of power and desire" in their interpretation of the *siddhis*.[74] Their denigration and rejection of the *siddhis* is much harsher and more pronounced than that of their classical predecessors. Even scholars who are closer to understanding the *siddhis* in terms of "experience" consider them totally insignificant. The great Indologist M. Müller suggests that these supranormal attainments are "superstitions which have little claim on the attention of the philosopher, however interesting they may appear to the pathologist."[75] Müller is pained by the inclusion of the *siddhis* within Patañjali's outlook. He laments his own dealing with these unusual experiences, saying apologetically: "These matters (the *siddhis*), though trivial, could not be passed over, whether we accept them as mere hallucinations, to which, as we know, our senses and our thinking organ are liable, or whether we try to account for them in any other way. They form an essential part of the yoga philosophy."[76] He also says that the inclusion of the teaching of the *siddhis* in the elevated system of yoga, a system which establishes the sublime distinction between the pure subject (purusha) and the object (prakriti), suggests the possiblity that the Patañjali who wrote the wonder-full section of the *Yogasūtra* and the Patañjali who composed the more serene parts of this text are not the same person.[77] In the same vein, though more emphatically, the 19th-century mystic Ramakrishna declared that "*siddhis* or miraculous powers are to be avoided like filth."[78] Al-Bīrūnī, the eleventh-century Muslim philosopher and traveler, warns against the appeal of the *siddhis* as an obstacle to liberation. The *siddhis* involve "a sort of self-aggrandizement and pride."[79] Ramana Maharshi suggests that "one should not accept thaumaturgic powers etc. even when directly offered to one, for they are like ropes to tether a beast and will sooner or later drag one down."[80] P.V. Kane also sounds apologetic about dealing with the *siddhis*, explaining his attention to them as a textual constraint: "From the fact that with most yogins the *siddhis* are an important part of the yoga doctrines and the fact that, out of 195 *sūtras* of the *Yogasūtra*, thirty-five (3.16-50) are devoted to the description of the *siddhis*,[81] the present author is constrained to say that the *siddhis* are an integral part of yoga."[82] Another great Indologist, S. Radhakrishnan, suggests that power yoga infiltrated the yoga tradition by a "popular cult of magic."[83] He offers his own explanation of the inclusion of yoga experiences in the *Yogasūtra* tradition, an explanation which represents Patañjali as a cunning manipulator: "The attractions of unlimited physical and intellectual power were perhaps employed to induce the worldly to take to the higher life. The foolish always seek after signs."[84] S. Dasgupta, the great historian of Indian philosophy, sums up his treatment of the *siddhis* by saying that, apart from the contribution of the *siddhis* to the yogin's faith, they "have no value."[85]

Similarly, many scholars associate the *siddhis* with temptation and danger. Thus, for example, M. Eliade: "On the one hand, the 'powers' are inevitably acquired in the course of initiation, and, for that very reason, constitute valuable indications of the monk's spiritual progress; on the other hand, they are doubly dangerous, since they tempt the monk with a vain 'magical mastery of the world' and, in addition, are likely to cause confusion in the minds of unbelievers."[86]

P. T. Raju also uses the concept of temptation in his understanding of the *siddhis*. "Patañjali advises the yogi, if he is intent on final liberation, not to be tempted by those powers. To be tempted by them is to be attached to them; and to be attached to them is to be lost in them without rising higher."[87] A. Danielou perceives greater danger here, viewing the 'temptation' that Eliade sees in the *siddhis* as a grave impediment. He includes a description of 38 *siddhis* in his book on yoga. "These attainments are the greatest obstacles of the adept in his journey towards reintegration. Nature herself, in a final effort to keep the adept within her bonds yields him magic powers; if he uses them for any worldly end, he is apt to fall back into the arms of worldly enjoyments. All true seekers, therefore, are careful not to perform miracles except in very special circumstances."[88]

J.Varenne also warns of the dangerous potential of the utter significance of the *siddhis* in yoga. "Needless to say, there can be no question of the true yogi's indulging indiscriminately in the use of such superhuman powers. If he did, he would simply be proving that he has not succeeded in annihilating desire within himself, showing that he is still a long way from attaining liberation."[89] K. Kloistermaier's reference to the reality of the *siddhis* along with his conception of the nature of *samādhi* are typical of the attitude of power yoga negation:

> More than anything else those *vibhūtis* have been described and dreamed about in literature about Indian yogis. Biographies and autobiographies of yogis are full of reports about achievements following

> the line of the *Yogasūtras*. In actual Indian life one hardly ever encounters any miracles of this sort. Living for two years in a place where thousands of holy men and women dwelled and where countless rumors of such things circulated, I never witnessed a single incidence corresponding to this idea of the miraculous.[90]

J. Ghosh seems somewhat embarassed by the *siddhis*, expressing his own linear view of human progress by apologizing for them: "If, however, we bear in mind that science was in its infancy when this system was developed, and that the yogi never set much store by these results, but regarded them as so many obstacles to spiritual progress, we would not let the weakness of the illustrations affect our judgement on the soundness of his main contention."[91] While conceding that supranormal powers "may be possible," S. Chatterjee and D. Datta caution that "the yoga system warns all religious aspirants not to practise yoga with these ends in view. Yoga is for the attainment of liberation. The yogin must not be entangled in the quagmire of supernormal powers. He must overcome the lure of yogic powers and move onward till he comes to the end of journey, viz. liberation."[92]

As we have seen, this view of the *siddhis* as an obstacle is shared by many. J. Filliozat is one of the most sympathetic interpreters of yoga and yoga experiences. He strives to confirm the reality of the *siddhis* while at the same time negating their value. "The powers of action are the least important. Their pursuit is considered rather as a hindrance to an integral realisation of yoga. That is why they are presented as potential: the yogin feels their presence in him without feeling a need to exercise them. What is indisputable is that the yogin must not be attached to them, otherwise he would be unfaithful to his initial intention of keeping out all feeling of appropriation."[93]

Along with the yogic silence of *samādhi*—conceptualized by Patañjali as the ground from which unusual experiences sprout—the *siddhis* are the epitome of the otherness of yoga. They are also the most intimate unifications of the yoga universe, reflecting the autonomy and essence of the dying yogin's world; as the immediate and concrete manifestations of *samādhi*, the *siddhis* are extremely unfamiliar, the essence of otherness for the many who attempt interpretation of the *Yogasūtra*. However, Patañjali conceived of them as ultimately real.[94] The yogin's intense, "absolute" silence, together with the unusual experiences available therein, constitute the hard core of his otherness. Patañjali's description of yoga as an organic whole is interpreted here as an account of the yogin's near-death silence and its products. However, Patañjali the Sāṅkhya philosopher is but another character approaching the yogin's otherness, seeing in him a mirror of his own Sāṅkhya identity.

The Outsider, Insider, Philologist, Philosopher, Bodily Practitioner, and Seeker—a range of humanity—are represented above as failing in their approach to the *Yogasūtra*, as they succeed in their wish to live on and on. Patañjali's success in the representation of the yogin's silence and experience is partial at best, since he succeeds in preserving his mode of life as a philosopher, a Sāṅkhya thinker. The question that may be asked, then, is why the quest for the yogin's otherness if the end result is mirroring? Would the best and most courageous minds—often experimental in their nature—pursue stark otherness for narcissistic reflection, refraction, and satisfaction? This is unlikely.

A more likely hypothesis would be the essential identity of the yogin's otherness with one's innermost being. Such identity—if true—would powerfully attract all creatures capable of consciousness. *Tapas* and renunciation do provide a certain opportunity for freedom; perhaps such yogic freedom and death are connected with "being oneself." In this case, Patañjali's failure in the primary encounter with the dying yogin, as well as his numerous followers' secondary vicarious reenactments of meeting with the other, are not necessarily uninstructive.

2

Daily Life in *Samādhi*: The Dying Yogin's Real Life and a Plea for Holistic Presentation of the *Yogasūtra*

The yogin chooses certain death over life in this world; this death is good insofar as it is necessary for awakening. The Pātañjala yogin—the *Vivekin*—is a courageous philosopher, if indeed he is terribly bound for truth. According to Patañjali, the dying yogin creates and lives within an organic whole which is totally different from ours; only in this yoga universe do knowledge and truth allegedly arise. Indeed, as a risky quest for truth, this is daring *philosophy*.

The yoga universe is mysteriously coherent, complex, and paradoxical. It is harsh as well as genuinely playful, infused with a sense of freedom as well as with the harshest discipline and effort. Old patterns of conditioning are drastically loosened, thus exempting the yogin from the laws of karma. His world becomes a different universe.

In YS 4.7 Patañjali explicitly addresses the unique "flavor" (or color) of the yoga universe. The yogin's karma is neither white nor black. Other people's lives are colored in three ways.[1] Like God—Īśvara—the yogin forsakes desire and—disembodied and free—floats in his own world.[2] Within this strikingly unfamiliar oceanic liberty, the yogin *moves* in time, space, and identity. He or she reexperiences the remote past, leaves the body behind, and enters "with the mind" into others' bodies and becomes aware of the naked truth about one's own identity; they are an entity composed "by mistake." Decomposition of this personal identity is the only escape from pain and illusion, while liberating insights and experiences emerge solely in the yoga universe, as expressions of the yogin's entire life of euphoric starvation, solitude, concentration, training in metaphysics. Patañjali's *Yogasūtra* is a reflection on the yoga universe as an organic system.

The bottom line of Pātañjala-Yoga is a demand for respect for yoga as an organic whole. The yogin lives in a unique mental space, one's own world, a life of a certain flavor, hardly relished by ordinary humans. It is "multidimensional" and yet whole, a "form of life," a "yoga universe." Thus the *Yogasūtra* describes and prescribes a variety of practices, attitudes, principles of metaphysics, and experiences such as celibacy, solitude, physical exercises, breathing control, meditation, levitation, and invisibility, the struggle to distinguish "subject" from "object," the conception of life in *saṁsāra* as misery. All these betoken the coming into being of an "organic whole," distinct from its various dimensions and manifestations; the *Yogasūtra* is the conceptualization of this "wholeness." Numerous indeed are Patañjali's statements connecting "practice," "metaphysics," and "experience." The *Yogasūtra* is characteristically a connective, integrative work.

Pātañjala-Yoga stresses the unity of the yoga universe; it is a tradition which bases its self-definition on this very interdependence, integration, or connection of the various dimensions of life on the road to liberation. The spiritual hero of yoga is the *Vivekin*, the yogin philosopher, a practitioner of yoga as well as a sage on the road to realization of the ultimate truth about the distinction between purusha and prakriti.[3] He also undergoes unusual experiences such as levitation,[4] invisibility,[5] and incredible expansions of knowledge,[6] thus embodying the essence of yoga as an organic, interdependent system of practice, attitude, experience, and metaphysics.

The yoga universe emerges into existence, correspondingly less real to others as it becomes more real to the seeker. As the various attitudes, metaphysical convictions, yogic practice and experiences come together to form the yoga universe, the yogin's reality looks more fantastic and unreal. The more dense and well-integrated the *Vivekin*'s life, the more incredible it becomes to the rest of humanity. Thus the *Vivekin* in his unreal reality is apparently hopelessly lonely and misunderstood.

Let us review—as illustrations—a few expressions of the "wholeness" of the yoga universe. The most immediate ones concern the import of individual statements, Patañjali's sutras. These are invariably integrative, connecting practice to attitudes, experience and metaphysics, experience to attitude and metaphysics. At the root of particular connections of various levels and dimensions of the yogin's life, there is the perception of yoga as an organic whole.

In YS 2.40 Patañjali connects practices of "cleanliness" (*śauca*) with a positive evaluation of solitude and a certain attitude (and experience) of aversion to one's body. From the practice of cleanliness arises disgust towards one's own body and avoidance of the company of others (*śaucāt svāṅga-jugupsā parair asaṁsargaḥ*).

Practices of "cleanliness" are not further described in the *Yogasūtra*, though such practices are referred to in detail in other treatises of yoga such as the *Hathayogapradīpika*, the *Gheranda-Saṁhitā*, the *Śiva-Saṁhitā*. Thus, for example, the *Hathayogapradīpika* describes the practice called *karma-*

basti: "squatting in navel-deep water, and introducing a six inches long, smooth piece of 0.5 inch diameter pipe, open at both ends, half inside the anus; it (anus) should be drawn up (contracted) and then expelled. This washing is called the *basti-karma*."[7] Other similarly aggressive practices of cleanliness are the *hṛd-dhauti*, the *daṇḍa*, *vamana*, and *vāsa-dhauti*.[8] Patañjali might have such practices in mind under the label of *śauca*.

Vyāsa, the most authoritative commentator in the tradition of Pātañjala-Yoga,[9] combines the two results of cleanliness—distaste towards one's body and non-association with others—into one process. According to Vyāsa, efforts to clean the body are never fully successful and, as one realizes the impossibility of bodily purity (*kāya-śuddhi*), one becomes all the more reluctant to engage with others.[10] Vyāsa is probably familiar here with the consequences of the practice of cleanliness. In this addition to his perceptive observation concerning the yogin's despair of complete—or even satisfactory—cleansing of his body, Vyāsa creatively meets the challenge of expressing Patañjali's connective mind. In the case of YS 2.40, he is successful in following the integrative mood of the sutra.

YS 3.38 asserts that entrance into others' bodies is obtained by weakening the "causes of bondage" and by knowing the movements of the mind,[11] apparently a reference to the yogin's experience of entrance into others' bodies. In addition there is an interpretation of what makes this experience possible. In this case, the entire teaching of yoga concerning karma and bondage is involved. Vyāsa suggests that the very connection of the (naturally unstable) mind to the body is due to the power of karma (*lolī-bhutasya manaso 'pratiṣṭhasya śarīre karmāśaya-vaśād bandhaḥ pratiṣṭhety arthaḥ*), and asserts that by the power of *samādhi* bondage to karma is loosened (*tasya karmaṇo bandha-kāraṇasya śauthilyaṁ samādhi-balād bhavati*). Movements of mind become known, particularly in the condition of *samādhi* (*pracāra-saṁvedanaṁ ca cittasya samādhi-jam eva*). Such an observation about creative disembodiment and the value of awareness touches upon many themes of significance in the teaching of Pātañjala-Yoga.

Thus the Sāṅkhya theory of the evolution of the body and ego from abstract primordial nature (prakriti) into the manifest world is present in YS 3.38. In addition, the negation of *saṁsāra*—perhaps the most common theme and attitude underlying the sutra-statements—is also implied, as the loosening of one's connection with the body and this world is recommended. The power of *samādhi* and yogic practice to affect deeply buried layers of karma[12] is also implied in Patañjali's YS 3.38, thereby reflecting an entire gestalt of Sāṅkhya interpretation. Classical commentators as well as scholars of neo yoga do not fail to capture and express this spirit of integration.

In YS 2.39 Patañjali connects "nonpossessiveness" (*aparigraha*) with knowledge of the past. Practice—or observance—of *aparigraha* brings about the experiential reality of awareness of one's birth (*aparigraha-sthairye janma-kathaṅtā-saṁbodhaḥ*). As in other sutras, there does not seem to be any obvious thematic or causal relationship between nonpossessiveness and knowledge of (previous or future) births (*janma*). Indeed, Vyāsa is at a loss; he cannot connect *aparigraha* with its result. He focuses his attention on the contents of the knowledge consequent upon observance of *aparigraha*; the yogin apparently raises questions such as: "Who was I?" "How was I?" "How will we be?" Yet Vyāsa does not mention *aparigraha*. Thus in the case of YS 2.39 Vyāsa does not maintain the connective mood of Patañjali's sutra.

Vācaspati seems similarly helpless. Like Vyāsa, he does not comment on the connection of *aparigraha* to knowledge of the type and nature of previous (and possibly future) births. Neither does Vācaspati offer any explanation of the nature of *aparigraha* and its impact. He refers to the yogin's *desire* to know the future (*anāgataṁ jijñāsate*) and at the end of his commentary, to the rule concerning the general efficacy of desire: "whoever desires something, gets it (or does something about it)" (*yo hi yad icchati sa tat karotīti nyāyāt*).[13]

Vijñānabhikṣu follows Vācaspati in his emphasis on the yogin's desire to know the past and the future. At the end of his commentary on YSBh 2.39 he refers to the surrender unto Īśvara (*Īśvara praṇidhāna*) as connected with *aparigraha*. By observing *aparigraha* it is possible to attain all these (cognitions of past and future) at once, through mere surrender unto Īśvara (*ato 'parigraha-sthairyāt tāḥ kṣaṇaṁ praṇidhāna-mātreṇaiva gṛhyante*). However, Bhikṣu fails (like Vyāsa and Vācaspati) to account for the nature and particular impact of *aparigraha* in this context. The author of the *Vivarana*—allegedly Śaṅkara[14]—suggests that the "consciousness of the occurrences of birth" (*janma-kathaṅtā-saṁbodhaḥ*) is "a perception of one's *ātman*." He says that once external possessiveness is overcome, view of the *ātman* is easily achieved (*bāhya-parigrahāsaṅgābhāvāt svātma-viṣayālocanam ayatnena pravartate*). For others tormented by the desire for possessions, this is not possible even with much effort (*nānyeṣāṁ parigraha-santāpa-vitāni tatṛṣāṁ yatnenāpi jāyate*).[15]

The neo yoga commentators are conscious of the basic explanatory pattern of the sutras and in general try to recover Patañjali's corresponding connective mood. The vast majority of modern commentators on the *Yogasūtra* are often closer to Patañjali's spirit of integration than the classical interpreters (Vyāsa, Vācaspati, the author of the *Vivarana*, Bhoja, Vijñānabhikṣu, and others). Vivekananda explains the impact of *aparigraha* as follows: "When a man does not receive presents, he does not become beholden to others, but remains independent and free. His mind becomes pure. With every gift, he is likely to receive the evils of the giver. If he does not receive, the mind is purified, and the first power it gets is memory of past life."[16] I. K. Taimni considers the remembrance of things past a "natural result" of the practice of nonpossessiveness. He assumes that apart from the personality of this particular life, there is a subtle and more permanent foundation to the myriads of transmigrating bodies:

> The development of non-possessiveness frees us to a very great extent from this habit of identifying ourselves with our bodies and the things with which they are surrounded and thus *loosens the bonds of the personality*. The natural result of this loosening is that the centre of consciousness gradually shifts into the higher vehicles of the *Jīvātmā* and the knowledge present in those vehicles is reflected more and more into the lower vehicles.[17]

R. Mehta resists the usual bind to Vyāsa's *bhāṣya* and interprets cognition or awareness (*saṁbodha*) of the "whereabouts of birth" (*janma-kathaṅtā*) as the "meaning of existence." "While nonpossession may imply the giving up of the home, nonpossessiveness indicates the rendering of the mind completely homeless."[18] Mehta correlates nonpossessiveness with giving up projections onto reality and concludes: "It is only when all projections, even the most idealistic, cease that the intrinsic significance of life can be understood."[19]

In YS 3.26[20] Patañjali connects meditation on the "sun"[21] with knowledge of the universe. Vyāsa produces a very long *bhāṣya*. He describes in much detail the various subunits of the universe, along with their inhabitants and the different flavors of the oceans. But Vyāsa fails to connect meditation on the sun with its result. Why and how does meditation (*saṁyama*) on the "sun" produce "knowledge of the universe"? Vyāsa concedes failure in this regard when he says that the result (knowledge of the universe) can also be derived from the application of *saṁyama* on points *other* than the sun (*anyatrāpi*). But this, of course, contradicts the essential principle in the *Vivekin*'s life, namely that the particular object of meditation is connected to the nature of the *siddhi* experience.

Classical commentators follow Vyāsa in his failure to recapitulate Patañjali's connective statement of YS 3.26.

In YS 3.17 Patañjali connects meditation (*saṁyama*) on the difference of "word" (*śabda*), "object" (*artha*) and "idea" (*pratyaya*) with the unusual power or attainment of "knowing the sounds of all creatures." YS 3.17, like all of the *siddhi* sutras, is difficult to understand. Testimony of experiences such as the "mental transparency" of other creatures makes the otherness of the yoga universe strikingly painful. Classical commentators focus exclusively on the nature of the object of meditation (the difference between word, object, and idea), and add nothing to our understanding of the nature of the *siddhi* experience (knowledge of the sounds of all creatures), or to the connection of practice and experience in this instance.

Neo yoga commentators feel the urge to recapitulate the spirit of connection typical of Patañjali's work. YS 3.17 is a particularly difficult case. G. Feuerstein considers the ordinary confusion of word, object, and idea as an occasion for a yogic exercise: "The yogin makes a virtue out of our natural inclination to fuse and confuse these three distinct components by using it as a starting-point for an exercise in concentration and meditative-absorption and, finally, enstasy."[22] Yet, the challenging otherness embedded in Patañjali's connection of meditation with the unusual transparency of all creatures remains unmet. Feuerstein indirectly addresses this challenge as follows:

> Whether or not it is literally true that the yogin can have knowledge of the language of all beings, only yogic practice can verify—or falsify. So long as we have no means of settling this question either way, it would seem advisable to suspend our judgement on the matter. This, of course, applies to all other claims made by the protagonists of Yoga.[23]

It is difficult to see how "yogic practice" could simply verify or falsify the yogin's claims. Yoga is an organic whole of attitudes, metaphysical consciousness, practice, and experience tightly linked together by the *Yogasūtra*. The yoga universe is presented as a unified piece of life. However, G. Feuerstein's caution with respect to the unusual experience of understanding the sounds of all creatures is a good expression of the otherness of yoga.

No such caution is seen in I. K. Taimni's exposition of YS 3.17. He conceives of Patañjali's statement as almost trivially true:

> If we are to understand how the yogi can comprehend the meaning of the sounds uttered by any living being, we have to consider the composite mental process which produces the sounds. Take, for example, a nightingale calling to its mate. We hear only the external sound, but that sound is the final expression of a complex process in which two other elements are involved. One is the image of its mate present in the mind of the nightingale and the other is the desire or purpose (*Artha*), namely, to see the mate. Without both these elements the sounds could not be produced. If anyone could enter the mind of the nightingale he would become aware of both these factors and gain immediately a comprehension of the meaning of the external sounds. Now, it has been shown already in explaining YS I.42 that when several factors of this nature are present together in

> a complex mental process they can be resolved and separated from each other by performing *samyama* on the factor which is outermost. The three factors together constitute a "seed" which can be split open and the meaning separated out as explained already. This will immediately enable the Yogi to comprehend the meaning of the sound uttered by the nightingale. Since the sounds uttered by all living beings are produced by the same kind of mental process referred to above, the Yogi can always come to know their meaning through *Samyama*.[24]

W. Halbfass considers the paucity of references to the theory of karma and rebirth in the more ancient scriptures of India "one of the familiar paradoxes of the Indian religious and philosophical tradition."[25] Pātañjala-Yoga embodies one of the more systematic conceptualizations of the idea of karma, and the integrative nature of Patañjali's speech act is clearly reflected in his dealings with this subtle and difficult theory.[26] Quite a few of Patañjali's sutras deal with the theory of karma.[27] The yogin is capable of approaching the reality of karma in his own experience and direct perception (*sākṣāt-karaṇa*). In YS 3.22 the *Vivekin* is described as one who is capable of knowing the "time of death." This is obviously an unusual, and possibly a profound, experience. Ordinary people live in darkness in this regard, the unknowability of the precise time of death constituting an essential aspect, so it seems, of the "denial of death." By meditation on karma—which is fast or slow to bear fruit—or by means of omens, the yogin knows the time of his death.[28] Vivekananda says that "when a Yogi makes a *Saṁyama* on his own *karma*, upon those impressions in his mind which are now working, and those which are just waiting to work, he knows exactly by those that are waiting when his body will fall. He knows when he will die, at what hour, even at what minute."[29]

Vyāsa beautifully illustrates the difference between the two types of karma. Karma is like a wet cloth. If left to dry up when spread out, it would dry in (a short) time. If left to dry up when "squeezed" (as a ball) (*saṁpiṇḍita*), it would dry up slowly. Or, as fire burning freely on dry grass spreads fast in the wind, such is the karma that immediately ripens and bears fruit. Vācaspati considers karma to be *dharma* or *adharma*. He says something interesting about the dynamics and benefit of knowing the time of one's death. Yogins can create for themselves as many bodies as they like. Once they know their fast-to-bear-fruit karma, they create many bodies for themselves, and then experience simultaneously—or instantly (*sahasā*)—the fruits of their karma. Thus, he can die at will.[30]

Foreign indeed is this world which emerges in the condition of yogic death, *samādhi*. We face the yoga universe as total strangers. The connective nature of Patañjali's statements makes interpretation of the *Yogasūtra* particularly difficult. Defining the yoga-universe as an organic whole, no single statement may be interpreted without access to metaphysics, practice, attitude, and experience. Thus there is built-in incompetence in the interpretation of the *Yogasūtra*. In Vyāsa's commentary on the *Yogasūtra* the essential split of the entire tradition of Pātañjala-Yoga emerges.

The organic wholeness of yoga is reflected not only in the connective character of individual sutras, but also in the formation of subsystems of interrelated components of practice, attitude, metaphysics and experience. A good example of such an organic unit concerns the meaning and nature of "suffering" (*duḥkha*) and its cure in the *Vivekin*'s universe. In my exposition of this instance, emphasis will be placed on the role and relevance of experience to the evaluation of life in *saṁsāra*. The somewhat paradoxical outcome will be that within an organic unit there is the temporal coexistence or even reversal of prognosis and diagnosis.

Patañjali's assertion that "all is suffering for the one who really understands (*Vivekin*)"[31] is well known. Thus Patañjali shares with the Buddha the "therapeutic paradigm"[32] within which life in *saṁsāra* is diagnosed as disease. The first two truths of the Buddha's Four Noble ones can be said to be the diagnosis, while the two latter ones constitute the prognosis. Vyāsa explicitly likens the teaching of yoga to the science of medicine (*cikitsā-śāstra*). In his *bhāṣya* on YS 2.15 he says that the teaching of yoga is fourfold (*caturvyūha*), precisely like the teaching of medicine.

According to Vyāsa, the science of medicine is based on the following parts; definition of the disease (*roga*); definition of the cause of the disease (*roga-hetu*); availability of a condition without disease (*ārogya*); the procedure (or medicine) bringing about the transition to health (*bhaiṣajya*). The teaching of yoga, Vyāsa says, is similarly fourfold. The disease is *saṁsāra* (and abundance of misery); there is the cause of *saṁsāra* [the connection (*saṁyoga*) of objectivity (prakriti, *pradhāna*) and the subject (purusha)]. There is liberation (*mokṣa*); and there is the means of reaching liberation (*mokṣopāya*). It is reasonable to describe medical procedure in a linear way; indeed, diagnosis often precedes prognosis. The patient complains and describes symptoms. The doctor observes some of these symptoms, and makes use of his knowledge to identify the cause of the disease. Proceeding to envision a condition without the disease, he then prescribes the medicine to be used in order to restore health. Indeed, as symptoms of the illness are considered first, causes second, and remedy (which implies the recognition of a condition of health) given last, the doctor's procedure seems to be essentially *linear*.

But can diagnosis and prognosis in the yoga universe be understood on the same pattern of linearity? Not necessarily; the nature of the yoga universe as an organic whole suggests other possibilities. For example, diagnosis may coexist with prognosis, or prognosis may even precede diagnosis. The connections of practice, attitude, experience, and theory in Pātañjala-Yoga point in this direction. The advanced yogin's experiences—available only at a relatively late stage of his training and transformation—might be vital for a realization of certain metaphysical principles. Or—in the present illustration—to the diagnosis of *saṁsāra* as "suffering." Let us explore this structure of "wholeness" in greater detail.

A major aspect of the definition of *saṁsāra* and suffering—in Pātañjala-Yoga as well as in other Indian traditions—is the "nauseating repetition" of samsaric life cycles and experiences. The Indian tradition seems to capture a certain neurotic dimension in the phenomenon of repetition. The repetitious quality of *saṁsāra* is expressed in the imagery of the "wheel of *saṁsāra*" (*saṁsāra-cakra*) as well as in expressions such as rebirth (*punar-janma*) and its antecedent version—redeath (*punar-mṛtyu*),[33] rereturn (*punar-āvṛtti*). The human is born again and again and again. There is a nightmarish quality to this cycle of rebirths. This intercycle repetition is reflected in the essence of life within a given birth; conditioned life in *saṁsāra* is disgusting. Vyāsa says that a yogin who goes back to the ordinary way of the world is like a dog who licks his own vomit.[34] The cessation of the cycle of rebirths is "release," liberation. The relief over the end of rebirth must have been tangible for Bādarāyaṇa, the author of the most important work of Indian philosophy. He asserts—in a somewhat repetitious way—at the very end of his *Brahmasūtra*: "According to scripture there is no return, according to scripture there is no return."[35]

A modern Hindu yogin, Paramahansa Yogananda reflects on the nauseating quality of repetitive *saṁsāra*. He is disillusioned about the merits of *saṁsāra* and rebirth: "This cyclic pattern assumes a certain anguishing monotony after man has gone through a few thousand human births; he begins then to cast a hopeful eye beyond the compulsions of *maya*."[36]

As suggested above, the neurotic flavor of repetition is an important aspect of samsaric cycles and recycles. But—the question may be asked—how does one avail oneself of this diagnosis? How does one perceive the neurotic quality of transmigratory repetition? The endlessly recurring transmigration and rebirth might shed light on the essence or quality of samsaric life. The thought of repetition and recycling of experience and "life" may detract from a sense of the uniqueness and value of a single human life. However, suppose one cannot rely on any evidence in this regard (transmigration). In fact, people often question the cogency of the Buddha's or Patañjali's diagnosis of life as misery. There is something appealing in the vision of life as separation from what is dear and association with what is hateful (old age and death). And yet we often hear other voices, life-affirming, accepting pain and even death as aspects of the overall positive value of "life."

While there is much to commend Patañjali's assertion that "all is misery for the one who really understands," there is also room for doubt. Although the diagnosis of life as disease is one of the most accessible dimensions of the Indian culture of consciousness therapy, there is room for caution even with respect to this dimension. Thus, S. Collins notes that "interpreters of Buddhism have often been puzzled by the idea of *duḥkha*—it is clearly wrong to suggest that life is experienced as continuous suffering, and Buddhism has been thought a little overpessimistic and peevish to suggest that what suffering there is overshadows any pleasure."[37]

The Indian sage has another means of evaluating *saṁsāra*. The *Vivekin* seems capable of approaching the reality of repetitive birth by "experience." In YS 3.18, Patañjali tells us that the yogin who meditates on "residual impressions" (*saṁskāra*) obtains knowledge of one's previous lives. King Bhoja remarks that the yogin remembers everything which happened in the past (*sarvam atītaṁ smarati*), and sees (or reexperiences) previous lives by "actual perception" (*pratyakṣeṇa paśyati*), saying: "this object was experienced by me in this way, this action was performed by me in this way" (*evaṁ mayā so 'rtho 'nubhūtaḥ, evaṁ mayā sā kriyā niṣpāditeti*).[38]

Thus, in the tradition of Pātañjala-Yoga the experience of seeing one's previous lives is conducive to a firsthand evaluation of *saṁsāra* along with its wheellike, endless recurrences. Indeed, in his *bhāṣya* on YS 3.18, Vyāsa focuses on this feature of the evaluation of *saṁsāra* made possible by the *siddhi* experience of seeing one's previous lives.[39] He tells the story of the two sages, Jaigīṣavya and Avatya. By meditating on the *saṁskāras*, Jaigīṣavya—a most advanced yogin—is capable of remembering previous lives during ten great cycles of creation. Answering Avatya's questions, Jaigīṣavya diagnoses desire and *saṁsāra* as pain. As one who can retrieve past life experiences—having been an animal, a god, and the like—he is in a position to evaluate *saṁsāra* and rebirth; and he does. Having been cooked in *saṁsāra* for such a long time, he finds out that even the ultimate virtue in *saṁsāra*—"calm self-sufficiency" (*saṅtoṣa*)[40]—is nothing compared to transcending *saṁsāra* altogether.

Vyāsa's rejection of *saṅtoṣa* as an alternative to *mokṣa* sheds more light on the *incurability* of *saṁsāra*. Apparently, Jaigīṣavya's reexperience of his thousands of previous births makes the incurability of *saṁsāra* accessible to him, and hence also to the adept yogin. This access to one of the most essential features of *saṁsāra* is the yogin's prerogative.

Thus the *siddhi* of reexperiencing previous lives is presented by Vyāsa as most helpful in diagnosing *saṁsāra*. This means that only at a relatively advanced stage of his training and development, the yogin—such as

Jaigīṣavya—reaches the diagnosis of *saṁsāra* as incurable pain. Indeed, it seems reasonable to assume that this harsh diagnosis of transmigratory existence is a necessary condition for seeking the excruciating medicine of yoga. This is indeed typical of the physician/patient field. Obviously, medicine is not given unless there are perceivable symptoms. It is both the presentation and practice of the science of medicine which require the precedence of diagnosis over prognosis. But, as suggested here, the nature of the yoga universe as a tightly interdependent system of many dimensions (such as practice, metaphysics, attitude, experience) implies that the diagnosis of *saṁsāra* as an incurable illness is an exclusive aspect of the advanced yogin's world, not found in the beginner's.

Patañjali himself seems aware of the role of the advanced yogin's experience in the formulation and corroboration of the dianosis of life as pain. Patañjali's diagnosis of life—in YS 2.15—is given along with a causal argument, "by the pain involved in change, the tormenting heat and the (impact of) the *saṁskāras*, and also because of the contradictory action of the primordial tendencies (*guṇa*), everything is pain for the one who really understands" (*pariṇāma-tāpa-saṁskāra-duḥkhair guṇa-vṛtti-virodhāc ca duḥkham eva sarvaṁ vivekinaḥ*). As seen above, one of the causes of misery, residual impressions—*saṁskāras*—are the object of meditation (according to YS 3.18). Indeed, another cause of misery—according to YS 2.15—is "change" (*pariṇāma*). This becomes a focus of meditation according to YS 3.16; "meditation on the three modes of change brings about knowledge of the past and future" (*pariṇāma-traya-saṁyamād atītānāgata-jñānam*). The expansion of awareness, which is the "knowledge of the past and future," seems to subserve the diagnosis of life as pain similarly to the *siddhi* experience of reviewing previous lives. Knowledge of the future is essential to the medical paradigm of yoga, for it gives content and substance to the assertion that "future suffering should be avoided."[41]

The identity of the "one who really understands," one who is really discriminating (*Vivekin*), becomes clearer. The *Vivekin* is the one who meditates on the *saṁskāras* and consequently reviews his previous lives, as do people who undergo a near-death experience. The *Vivekin* also knows the future and makes use of this knowledge in order to integrate experience with practice and metaphysics. Thus the entire therapeutic paradigm—an essential feature, no doubt, of the Pātañjala-Yoga—is a tight combination of practice, experience, and metaphysics. Two of the pain-productive components mentioned in YS 2.15 are recognized and assimilated in unusual experiences obtained by the *Vivekin*—or dying yogin—already immersed in the yoga universe (*samādhi*). The prognosis is also supported by unusual experiences such as knowledge of the future. The interrelation of experience and metaphysics is characteristic of the organic whole. Thus within the yogic way of life different aspects are closely related and prognosis may precede diagnosis, as in the case of the diagnosis of suffering.

The wholeness of the yoga universe is difficult to interpret and understand. A linear reading of the *Yogasūtra*—divided into four *pādas* of allegedly distinct contents—is misleading.[42] In addition, individual sutras are often ambiguous. And above all, of course, looms the inaccessibility of the yoga universe itself. However, the requirement that underlies the composition of the *Yogasūtra*— to recognize the coherence and unity of the yoga universe as an organic whole—is emphasized by Patañjali. This requirement has not been recognized and respected in the scholarly expositions of Pātañjala-Yoga.

J. Varenne, a warm and reliable interpreter of yoga, is emphatic about the nature of yoga as an organic whole:

> And this seems a good place to repeat for the last time that attempting to reduce yoga to any one of its multiple aspects (metaphysics, physical exercises, breath control, etc.) is seriously to mutilate it. When a Westerner unilaterally decides that the metaphysics of yoga does not interest him, that the physiology of the "vital breath" is just plain silly, but that "there is an element of validity in the breathing exercises and the postures," he is guilty of ideological imperialism—an error I intend to avoid in these pages.[43]

However, it is difficult to maintain and preserve the vision of yoga as an organic whole. J.Varenne indirectly confesses to this difficulty:

> Yoga is presented here with sympathy . . . but also with a hint of Western skepticism, especially when it comes to describing the "miraculous powers" acquired by the yoga practitioner.[44]

Varenne is not only a "Western skeptic" regarding these "powers." He harshly denounces their role in the yoga universe:

> Needless to say, there can be no question of the true yogi's indulging indiscriminately in the use of such superhuman powers. If he did, he would simply be proving that he has not succeeded in annihilating desire within himself, showing that he is still a long way from attaining liberation.[45]

Essentially, Varenne reveals his priorities:

> The first systematic exposition of yoga is attributed to a certain Patañjali, about whom we know virtually nothing. His work (if it

> was in fact his) consists of a chain of aphorisms (*sūtra*) providing instruction in yoga in a concise, abrupt form that lays all its emphasis upon the doctrinal, metaphysical aspect rather than upon the practical exercises employed to assist the attainment of salvation.[46]

Even scholars who tend to recognize the unusual nature of yoga experience along with its essential significance for the yogin's journey and purpose share the perception of such experience as "fallen" and not worthwhile. Take, for example, M. Eliade's attitude. He divides human experience into three categories. The third one is yogic experience. On page 36 of *Yoga: Immortality and Freedom* he refers to the third category as "the parapsychological experiences brought on by the yogic technique . . . accessible only to adepts." On the following page he says: "The purpose of Patañjali's Yoga, then, is to abolish the first two categories of experiences (respectively produced by logical and metaphysical error) and to replace them by an 'experience' that is enstatic, suprasensory, and extrarational." By page 177 he expresses a much more reserved opinion of unusual yogic experiences:

> On the one hand, the "powers" are inevitably acquired in the course of initiation, and, for that very reason, constitute valuable indications for the monk's spiritual progress; on the other hand, they are doubly dangerous, since they tempt the monk with a vain "magical mastery of the world" and, in addition, are likely to cause confusion in the minds of unbelievers.[47]

Indeed, yogic experience seems to provoke resistance and suspicion.[48] And yet, experience is a powerful integration and expression of reality, in all the forms of life as well as in yoga. The paradigmatic yoga experience—the *siddhi* experience—is a most emphatic expression of Patañjali's connective mind. It must be assimilated and understood as an integral part of the yoga universe.

The yoga universe is thus an organic whole, a particular, unique life. It has its distinct atmosphere and flavors. Its quality is a fusion of disembodiment, absorption, or trance, play, transparency, infinite lightness, and contentment (the latter probably very mild). This is life in *samādhi*. Underneath lies the forceful attraction of ultimate balance (*nir-bīja-samādhi* or *kaivalya*).

Life in *samādhi* is heated, fluid, transparent, free, light, not unpleasant. Essentially, the yogin lives by "identification" or "absorption." This is, indeed, the essence of *samādhi*.[49] It embodies heightened paradoxality; for this peak condition—*samādhi*—is concomitantly utmost innerness and loss of consciousness (loss of self). It also gives rise to the paradoxical concept of "unconscious experience." The yogin loses himself in otherness, in "objects."

This requires, perhaps, the *Vivekin*'s great confidence. Life in *samādhi* is the yogin's playful perdition.

The yogin is bodiless. There are numerous tokens of this primary feature of life in *samādhi*; disconnection of the senses from their respective objects,[50] levitation,[51] invisibility, moving into others' bodies, overcoming the resistance of solids,[52] becoming infinitely minute or large,[53] disappearance of hunger and thirst[54] are but some of the more overt expressions of the yogin's disembodiment. Indeed, in Indian intellectual culture, bodilessness (*aśarīratva*) is a major issue. The last sutras of Bādarāyaṇa's *Brahmasūtra* reflect on controversies concerning *mokṣa* and disembodiment.

Given the dissociation of self from desire, karma and bondage, there remain mere shifts of absorption "from object to object," a series of identifications, embraces of "otherness." Thus everyday life in *samādhi* consists primarily of the yogin's absorption in objects. The yogin can identify with points in his "body,"[55] with the bodies and minds of others,[56] with the "sun"[57] or the "moon,"[58] with the (more abstract) differences between word, object and idea,[59] with the most abstract difference between subject and object.[60]

This vision of the yogin's bodilessness and the universe of identifications should be associated with the transparency of the world of yoga. The yogin sees through others' minds; he reads the thoughts of people and understands the sounds of animals. He sees the structure of his own body[61] and the most hidden and secret things in the world.[62] He can retrieve deeply buried experiences accumulated through thousands (!) of lives,[63] and he knows the time of the "death event."[64] Thus time, space, objects, and creatures all become transparent to him.

As a result of the dazzling transparency of the yoga universe, the yogin is *sensitive*. He can see through phenomena in worlds like ours. Life in the other world—in the reality of *saṁsāra*—is suffering and bondage. However distinct the *Vivekin*'s universe from ours, it is related to ours in its negation of *saṁsāra*.

It takes time for the yogin to develop. Starting his journey in this world of ours, he or she practices and observes nonviolence, *brahmacarya*, nonpossessiveness, truthfulness, cleanliness, yogic postures, and breath control. He or she changes, wrapped in ever-thickening layers of yoga reality.

The yogin's behavior and practices are invariably accompanied by specific experiences. He or she observes *ahiṁsā* and the environment changes accordingly.[65] He or she is busy cleaning the body, and the attitude to others changes.[66] He or she does not approach and does not think of women or men. If masculine, he does not spill his semen, becoming strong and energized.[67] He or she overcomes difficulties of temptation.[68] He or she gains in awareness as they relinquish possessive impulse.[69] Corporeal—or material—needs are satisfied.[70] He or she becomes more content, and—briefly—very happy.[71] He or she observes yogic truthfulness and thus becomes almost omnipotent.[72] He or she meets with well-fulfilled beings (*siddha*).[73] Life, of course, changes drastically as these practices and experiences accumulate.

Above all, the *Vivekin* establishes and re-establishes his world by meditation. He creates and re-creates his life through constant immersion in *samādhi*, especially by the use of the preliminary types of concentration and immersion in "objects" (*dhāraṇā*[74] and *dhyāna*[75]). Thus the yoga-universe flickers into existence. Paradoxically, the more real it becomes, the less real it seems. As these various attitudes, metaphysical convictions, practice and experiences come together to form the yoga-universe, the yogin's reality looks increasingly fantastic and unreal.

There are levels of commitment to, and immersion in, the yoga universe. Sometimes there are interventions and exchanges with the other world. Thus the yogin reestablishes his universe, overcoming various types of temptations by thoughts-to-the-contrary (*pratipakṣa-bhāvana*),[76] as well as by recurring efforts at yogic practices and meditation. There are fluctuations and levels of fulfilment in the yogin's life, as illustrated by the classifications of types of *samādhi* in YS 1.41–46. Meditation keeps the yogin in the yoga universe; if he quits meditation, he surfaces into externality. Thus he anchors himself in meditation.

The *Vivekin*'s life is very much a negation of our own. Bodiless, the yogin does not eat or drink. His senses are inactive. He does not touch sensory reality, he moves everywhere quickly.[77] He is light, content[78] and happy. He experiences neither hate[79] nor attachment.[80] He never feels "guilt." Exempt from the laws of karma, he is immensely free, not bound by the past. The defilements or sources of affliction (*kleśa*) do not affect him. He is not objectified in the eyes of others.[81]

Finally, he stops. Identifications are loosened, experiences fade away. He does not, of course, fear dying, nor is he eager to die. He already knows the moment of his death.[82] He "waits for the right time as a servant waits for orders."[83] Thus a subtle urge—somewhat subversive—underlies life in (*sa-bīja*) *samādhi*: the attraction of ultimate balance.[84] By this overwhelming, abysmal silence and balance (*nir-bīja-samādhi*, or *kaivalya*), the *Vivekin* is at last embraced.

3

The *Yogasūtra* and the Dying Yogin's "Lively Interior"

The teaching of yoga is a lesson in innerness. The emaciated, dying yogin seems to have had a glimpse into a new interior domain. The lonely figure of the yogin, isolated, immersed in a predeath (or deathlike) condition,[1] seems to attempt communication. He emerges from a condition of unconsciousness[2] and whispers his message. He tells of a transparent, marvelous, fluid interior, an amazing expansion of awareness and capabilities expressed in experiences such as unusual feats of memory,[3] exit from the body,[4] becoming invisible,[5] unusually powerful perceptions, visions of subtle, obstructed, and remote phenomena,[6] of encounters with superior beings,[7] of dreamlike motions through solids and air. Such experiences must have been immensely important, unforgettable, worth recounting repeatedly. For the yogin emerged, leaving behind that state of apparent bliss wherein the "self reverberates softly within itself through breathing/nonbreathing, moving in liquid rhythm to its own unconscious existence."[8] The one who listened, "Patañjali,"[9] tried to understand. The yogin's recurring reports prompted the composition of the *Yogasūtra.*

This is the core of the myth of the dying yogin, a narrative of a hypothetical encounter between a silent, dying yogin and an open-minded, often skeptical (or ambivalent) philosopher. This narrative places the unusual yoga experiences, the *siddhis*, at the center of the *Yogasūtra* as the primary datum around which this text is woven.

But was not the dying yogin Patañjali "himself"? Why assume that two were necessary for the transmission of the teaching of the interior? An inner dialogue on Patañjali's part, offering coherence, integration, and self-understanding, is perhaps a worthwhile narrative to be told and reworked.[10] It is not, of course, impossible that Patañjali was a "yogin" who conceptualized his own experiences in the *Yogasūtra*. However, this possibility (or narrative) is also somewhat unlikely. The dying yogin is an essentially silent person, beyond verbalization, deeply sunk into himself, oblivious to any external presence, resisting as it were reemergence into objectivity. True, at a certain point he (miraculously) addresses the other. But, we assume, he can only "minimally whisper." The philosopher's work is patently in a different voice. The *Yogasūtra* is conspicuously bereft of the vibrant, excited poetic quality available in the direct, creative expression of the interior.[11] The choice of the sutra-style is in itself an expression of a tendency to sum up, generalize, and conceptualize.

Thus the text of the *Yogasūtra* is apparently not a "primary verbalization" of yoga experience. It is not the dying yogin's whisper which is encoded in this organized speech act. The *Yogasūtra* is rather a reflective, intellectual project, removed from the terribly fresh touch of the reality of yoga. It is an effort at conceptualization in which Sāṅkhya metaphysics, current theories of meditation, epistemology, and Buddhist sensibilities have their share.[12] However, at the core of the *Yogasūtra* there is a certain openness to the yoga experience, to the *siddhis*. This openness—expressed in the very inclusion of a large body of *siddhi*-sutras as well as in the entire framework of its explanation by means of *samādhi* and the complementary negation of normal consciousness—is not only an abstract, benign attitude to eerie seers. The philosopher listens with a measure of approval to the challenging reports of the interior, of the phenomena which occur when one undergoes a certain training and transformation, and is finally cut off from any externality. Patañjali is open—at his own risk as it were—to the yogin's tale, and he accepts the dying yogin's testimony as worthy of understanding. The philosopher deems this testimony significant, true, and also—of course—in need of explication.

Thus Patañjali creates a philosophical use for the most important concept of classical yoga, *samādhi*, the condition of yogic death, silence, and creative disembodiment. However, endorsing the transforming power of yogic death is only one essential move towards an explanation of yoga experience. In addition, the philosopher launches an attack on normal consciousness. He senses that total intentionality and creative disembodiment are incompatible with the body, mind, and senses, and that these means of affirming the external should therefore be abolished.

Thence openness to tales of the interior is not easy. The dying yogin's testimony harshly challenges the philosopher's universe of thought and reality. Listening to the dying yogin might in itself be a transforming experience. Such listening (openness) involves a complex process of accommodation and adjustment. The end result—the *Yogasūtra*—represents a composite spiritual identity consisting of "mystical visions" contained in a net of explicit, scholarly voices of explanation and conceptual clarity. The philosopher's ambivalence might find expression in corresponding ambiguities within the text. Indeed, tokens of the philosopher's ambivalence and difficulty of assimilation are abundant in the *Yogasūtra* itself.[13]

What made the dying yogin so attractive to the philosopher? What made his reports so worth assimilating? Why attribute a measure of reality to the yogin's experiences in a deathlike condition? To what extent is Sāṅkhya metaphysics commensurable with the dying yogin's tales? Little has been said about this. Scholars have not paid attention to such questions beyond references to "superimposition" of Sāṅkhya metaphysics on yoga experience or "trance." And yet these are important questions, for they involve larger issues of different possible interpretations of that deathlike condition, probably a basic source of reflection in ancient India. But above all, as a committed endorsement of yoga experience, the *Yogasūtra* raises essential questions concerning the very value of yogic transformation and mode of being. What is the meaning of the yogin's deathly silence? Are yoga experiences of value to us? Is there any relevant insight in Sāṅkhya philosophy?

Patañjali's *Yogasūtra* is a Sāṅkhya work, and Patañjali is an active, creative Sāṅkhya philosopher. The main features of classical Sāṅkhya, as seen in Iśvarakrisna's *Sāṅkhyakārikā*, are also visible in the *Yogasūtra*.[14] Metaphysical dualism, the irreducible difference between the inactive, consciousness-made "subjectivity" (purusha) and the "creative," evolving, unconscious "objectivity" (prakriti);[15] the insistence of Sāṅkhya on ubiquitous and unavoidable suffering; its grounding in ignorance (*avidyā*); the possibility of overcoming suffering through liberating insight (into this difference of purusha and prakriti); the nature of the various levels of conditioning and bondage; prakriti as consisting of the three *guṇas:* all are Sāṅkhya principles active in Patañjali's thinking.

Above all, the quest for liberation must have been one of his major preoccupations. The excruciatingly harsh method of liberation prescribed in the *Yogasūtra* has its justification and source of attraction in the perspicacious diagnosis of human bondage and suffering.[16] Indeed, the human condition looks almost hopeless in the descriptions of the various levels of bondage detailed in the *Yogasūtra*. The natural human endowment consists of certain powerful dispositions to misery. These sources of misery (*kleśa*) constitute much of what we would call "human nature." The predisposition to mistake what is impermanent for what is permanent, displeasure for pleasure,[17] along with other "predispositions" such as egoism (*asmitā*), attraction (*rāga*), aversion (*dveṣa*) and the instinctive drive to survive (*abhiniveśa*) are characteristic of "human nature." In addition, the contradictory operation of the *guṇas*, the binding impact of karma and the *saṁskāras* are other dimensions of bondage and misery.[18] Under these circumstances, the desirability of liberation is perhaps obvious, but not so its feasibility. What can be done over and against the circumstances of human existence? A therapeutic motivation pervades the yoga school of thought and practice, as it is well known to constitute a major dimension of Indian mysticism and philosophy.[19]

Questions concerning the feasibility of liberation were not foreign to liberation-bound classical India. The feasibility of liberation is connected with "examples," observations with respect to "liberated persons." In the *Bhagavadgītā*, Arjuna becomes curious about the visibility of liberation (or liberating transformation), and he asks about the person who has reached *samādhi*: "How does a person immersed in *samādhi* talk, Krishna? How does he sit? How does he walk?"[20] The quest for signs of liberating transformation has apparently been common among the elite of seekers and interpreters of liberation. The compiler of the *Yogasūtra* most probably shared a keen interest in issues related to the feasibility question and the reality of the dying yogin's experience.

Some features of the yogin's lifestyle, appearance, and story perhaps account for liberation in Patañjali's own, Sāṅkhya version of *kaivalya*. In particular, phenomena of disembodiment, strikingly present in the emaciated, oblivious-to-bodily-existence yogin, might have been reminiscent of the possibility of *kaivalya*, or a momentous attainment on the road to the ultimate dissociation of purusha and prakriti, *viveka-khyāti*.[21] The yogin, disinterested in food, immersed in meditation, cut off from the world, responding exclusively as it were to inner occurrences, might have stimulated the philosopher, who probably discerned in the yogin's deathly silence a state of postdecomposition in accordance with the basic imagery of Sāṅkhya metaphysics and theory of liberation.[22] Patañjali apparently perceived the dying yogin as a person who knows the truths of Sāṅkhya "from within." Dying yogins were observed to be "immersed in *samādhi*."[23] Meditation has become a major characteristic of those desiring liberation (*mumukṣu*). The condition of deep meditation has been interpreted by Patañjali as the definitive attribute of the process of liberation. The condition of *samādhi* has been associated with *kaivalya*.

The primary assertion of the *Yogasūtra* is thus the identification of *samādhi* with *kaivalya*. The association of ultimate liberation (and insight) with meditation is central to the *Yogasūtra* and is suggested in numerous places. Quite a few statements in the third chapter of the *Yogasūtra*, the Vibhūtipāda, manifest the association of the meditating yogin with the attainment of *kaivalya*. The yogin reaches *kaivalya* by the application of meditation to the difference between *sattva* and purusha, according to YS 3.35. This meditation produces "knowledge of purusha" (*puruṣa-jñāna*). The ultimate Sāṅkhya insight, born of discernment (*viveka-jaṁ jñānaṁ*), comes about as a result of meditation (*saṁyama*) focused on moments and sequents.[24] The same Sāṅkhya knowledge (*viveka-jaṁ jñānaṁ*) is obtained by the yogin, according to YS 3.54. And *kaivalya*, again, is the condition of the yogin whose purity of *sattva* is equal to the purity of purusha.[25] Such statements possibly reflect, according to the myth of "the dying yogin and the philosopher," the initial perception of the yogin as a person who embodies certain spiritual possibilities particularly commensurate with the philosopher's own Sāṅkhya metaphysics. In the present exposition of Pātañjala Yoga, the narrative of the dying yogin is not—of course—construed as "history." This myth rather serves the interpretation of the connection of Sāṅkhya metaphysics and the yogin's silence and *siddhi* experiences, a connection totally inexplicable and even denied in the tradition of yoga commentary and scholarship.

The dying yogin's experience, grounded in silence and disembodiment, was most probably not an unfamiliar one in ancient India. The relationship of disembodiment and the deathlike condition (*samādhi*)[26] with "life in the interior" is an important theme in many myths and philosophical stories. Naciketas's journey into the world of Yama might well be an illustration of the cognitive value of reaching the condition of death (or predeath). Reaching the underworld of Yama makes Nāciketas' enlightenment possible. Entrance into the domain of virtual death contains an epistemic privilege impossible to obtain in a normal condition of openness to the world. In the language of the *Bhagavadgītā*, what is darkness and night for all normal creatures is (full) wakefulness for the (dying) yogin. What other creatures consider being awake, the sage who sees the truth considers darkness.[27]

The famous story in the *Chāndogyopaniṣad* 8.7–12 is also a good example of epistemic privileges inherent in the disembodied, deathlike condition. This is a tale of Indra's journey into the interior by means of explicit, progressive disembodiment. The *asura* Virocana accepts Prajāpati's misleading teaching of selfhood (*ātman*), and mistakes the body (or its reflection in a mirror or water) for the self. Thus by false understanding he ceases his quest. Indra, however, rejects this teaching and the two subsequent ones concerning identification of self with the subject in dreams and in deep sleep.[28] Finally, after 101 years of apprenticeship, Indra reaches his goal, the end of his journey to the interior. This end is a creative disembodiment where one is dissociated from one's body but also—and this is crucial—has certain experiences. The condition of disembodiment is the most conspicuous characteristic of the blissful interior, according to the *Chāndogya* story.[29] One who attains such a condition is a supreme person (*sa uttamaḥ puruṣaḥ*); he moves about laughing, playing, having pleasure with women, chariots and relatives.[30] Indeed, this is the Upanishadic version of the *siddhi* experience.[31] Most telling in this respect is the deep "forgetfulness of the body born of one's parents."[32] Creative disembodiment implies total dissociation from the body to the extent that even memory of bodily existence is wiped out. The passage ends with the saying that, under ordinary conditions, life is bound by the body as a horse is yoked to a chariot.[33]

This is also the essential paradigm of the *Yogasūtra*. Once the condition of total dissociation from the body (*pratyāhāra*)[34] is established, total intentionality and creative disembodiment (*samādhi*) become manifest in the *siddhi* experiences.[35]

For serious philosophers, fascinated by final, irreversible liberation, the climax of the *Chāndogya* story might be somewhat surprising or disenchanting. Playfulness with women, chariots, and relatives resembles life-in-the-world. What was all this journey for? Why is there no respite in the form of total, unchanging calm and quietude at the end of the road? Life in the disembodied interior is not a fulfilment of undifferentiated bliss by virtue of union with a Godhead or Absolute. Similarly, the condition of *samādhi*, the apex of the yogin's development, is connected by Patañjali primarily with the *siddhi* experiences.

We imagine that the dying yogin did not have concepts such as *samādhi*, *kaivalya*, *kleśa*, *saṁskāra*, karma, *vairāgya*, *viveka-khyāti*, purusha, prakriti, *guna* in his vocabulary. Distinctions between various mind fluctuations[36] and different types of meditation,[37] notions concerning differentiated impacts of *yamas* and *niyamas* such as *ahiṁsā*, *brahmacarya*, *śauca*, *aparigraha*, reflections on the nature of Īśvara,[38] surrender unto Īśvara,[39] the power of mantras and *prāṇāyāma* were likely those of the listener philosopher. The almost silent witness of the interior whispered about his most intimate and direct experiences. These experiences are listed, organized, conceptualized, and explained in the *Yogasūtra*.

The primary voice of the *Yogasūtra* is one of explanation, the business and mood of the entire text. The essential yoga experience is also embedded within the fundamental explanatory orientation. All the *siddhi* sutras contain an explanatory component. According to YS 3.30, the cessation of hunger and thirst has its cause in the application of meditation to the bottom of the throat (*kaṇṭha-kūpa*). The anatomical arrangement of the body is revealed by meditation on the navel wheel (*nābhi-cakra*).[40] Movement through air is possible through intense meditative contact with the boundary of body and space.[41]

Did the shaken yogin, probably pained, overwhelmed by rebirth—or reemergence into externality—bother to "explain"? According to our constructed story, the dying yogin did not "explain." He did not even say much about the structure of the interior, except for the "unconscious experiences" that he retrieves (remembers). Even the causal link of the *siddhi* experience with meditation and its particular objects—the major explanatory device of the *Yogasūtra*—is of a philosopher's making.[42]

This is then the myth concerning the composition of the *Yogasūtra*. It provides an occasion for thinking about the complex relationship between the primary verbalization (the yogin's story) and the secondary, reflective speech-act (the *Yogasūtra*). Patañjali, of course, could have misunderstood the yogin's story. Moreover, he might have resisted much of what he had heard or learned. His greatness lies in his openness to the silent, essentially non-verbal yogins, in being less defensive than others toward a particularly inaccessible segment of experience. Perhaps, unlike many of his colleagues (highly verbal thinkers of the Sāṅkhya and various Buddhist or Upaniṣadic schools), Patañjali is committed to the dying yogin's testimony, and he thinks the yogin's is a forcefully relevant experience, dimly compatible and somewhat incompatible with his existing interpretation of life. Thus he tries to incorporate the reports he heard and make them his own.

Indeed, Patañjali's *Yogasūtra* reflects an attempt at integration, expressive of an underlying conflict or controversy in the Hindu tradition of mysticism and philosophy. In the *Bhagavadgītā*, there are quite a few references to a controversy concerning the relationship of "Sāṅkhya" and "yoga."[43]

Committing himself thus to the cogency of the dying yogin's reports, what could the philosopher do? What would we—for we are more or less Patañjali-type verbalizers—do, facing the attraction of these tales of the interior? We would probably ask ourselves about the reality of the *siddhis*. Are these mere hallucinations which follow the extreme, deathlike condition of dissociation from all externality? Or are they real for this very reason (being a result of the deathlike condition)? Are they "real," consequent upon the "purification of consciousness" of contaminations or impurities?

The answer given in the *Yogasūtra* is that these unusual experiences are real. Indeed, according to the self-understanding of the *sūtra-kāra*, it is the very raison d'être of the *Yogasūtra* to account for these facts revealed in the yogin's story.[44]

The dying yogin's account of his experiences (the *siddhis*) significantly resembles accounts of "near-death experiences." One of the common themes in accounts of such experiences is a total commitment to their *reality*. The following is a typical example: "While I was out of my body, I was really amazed at what was happening to me. I couldn't understand it. But it was real. I saw my body so plainly, and from so far away. My mind wasn't at that point where I wanted to make things happen or make up anything. My mind wasn't manufacturing ideas. I just was not in that state of mind."[45]

C. G. Jung's account is also a good example. He tells of his visions and experiences from the beginning of 1944, when he had a severe heart attack and consequent unconsciousness: "In a state of unconsciousness I experienced deliriums and visions which must have begun when I hung on the edge of death and was being given oxygen and camphor injections." He tells of floating high in the air, a thousand miles above the surface of the earth. He then saw a huge dark stone with an opening which he entered, meeting with a Hindu who—apparently—was expecting him. Jung proceeds to reflect on the mode of reality involved in his near-death experience. "I would never have imagined that any such experience was possible. It was not a product of imagination. The visions and experiences were utterly real; there was nothing subjective about them; they all had a quality of absolute objectivity."[46]

Many other reports of near-death experiences focus on the distinction between "hallucination" and the reality of the unusual experience:

> It was nothing like an hallucination. I have had hallucinations once, when I was given codein in the hospital. But that happened long before the accident which really killed me. And this experience was nothing like hallucinations, nothing like them at all.[47]

For a sober philosopher such as Patañjali, the most significant move toward incorporation of the yogin's experience within his own universe would deal with the issue of "reality." Reality means positive, committed accommodation of thought and belief within one's universe. To be real is to be accounted for, to be part of a larger scheme of "the real." Patañjali's basic response to the dying yogin's testimony was the recognition that it referred to certain realities in need of understanding, explanation, and assimilation. The yogin's otherness (his tales of an unknown interior) challenged the philosopher. He created an air of intelligibility and reality for normally unknowable, inaccessible phenomena, thus introducing the concept of *samādhi* as the ultimate means of knowledge (*pramāṇa*). Ultimate reality is revealed in a state of "trance," a superior meditative condition, the apex of yoga training. *Samādhi*, as the primary cause of the *siddhi* experience, was made the foundation of the outlook of classical yoga. By introducing this fateful move, Patañjali anchored the dying yogin's tales of the interior to reality.[48]

In this way, two outstanding features of Pātañjala-Yoga become interrelated and intelligible; the definition of *samādhi* (YS 3.3) as a condition of object-intentionality and the invariable explanation of the *siddhis* by the nature of the objects meditated upon. The suggestion expressed in the myth of the dying yogin is that the *siddhis* are facts or data in relation to *samādhi*, which is a theoretical concept constructed for the sake of explaining the *siddhis*.

This myth of the dying yogin's reports is no different from other myths which address the role and place of the doctrine of the *siddhis* in the *Yogasūtra*. It is not different qua myth, from M. Müller's about "two Patañjalis,"[49] S. Radhakrishnan's concerning the "popular cult" which infiltrated the *Yogasūtra*, assimilated in order to persuade fools,[50] S. Dasgupta's suggestion about the need to motivate would-be yogins,[51] J. A. B. Van Buitenen's suggestion that a "primitive inducement of trance" is at the root of yoga,[52] M. Eliade's,[53] J. Varenne's,[54] A. Danielou's,[55] and P. T. Raju's rejection of the yoga experience as dangerous temptation,[56] Ghosh's apologetics concerning the infantile stage in the human intellectual development,[57] J. Masson's suggestion that the *siddhis* are fantasies rooted in the reality of child abuse in the guru's house.[58] These too are myths.

These "denigrating myths" of the "*siddhi* embarassment"[59] facilitate an evasion of the teaching of the *siddhis*, an understanding of their meaning and place in the *Yogasūtra*. For obviously, if there are two Patañjalis, one purely philosophical (who teaches the distinction between purusha and prakriti), and the other a kind of inferior magician (who talks about the *siddhis*), why bother with the latter's teaching? If the *siddhis* are meant to motivate fresh yogins, we—mere readers of the *Yogasūtra*—are certainly exempt from thinking too much about it. And if the *siddhis* are the dangerous temptations in Patañjali's view, is it not superfluous—a waste of time—to make a genuine effort to deal with them?[60]

However, most of the denigrating myths about the *siddhis* also have a scientific, "purely cognitive" aspect. They share a presupposition concerning the *siddhis* as epiphenomena of a generally high level of spirituality. "[We] now come to the celebrated 'miraculous powers' acquired by the yoga practitioner when he has reached the highest levels of spiritual experience."[61] The elevated human condition is usually said to be that of detachment, recall, egolessness, unworldliness, interiority. In this condition, the *siddhis* may appear. However, the condition seems independent of its possible outcomes; the "high level of spiritual experience" can exist *without* the *siddhis*. Indeed, questions concerning the reality of the *siddhis* become of little importance. Under these circumstances, one can go further and draw the conclusion—shared by all the denigrating myths of the *siddhis*—that the *siddhis* are even *incompatible* with the condition of high level spirituality (which produced them).

Thus, for example, the following statement suggests that *samādhi* is a prestigious condition, unfit to be the cause or ground of the unworthy *siddhis*. "The proper thrust of *samādhi*, however, is not backward into the world of objects, from which it is freeing the spirit, but forward into the discrimination of purusha from the *guṇas* that belong to prakriti."[62] The *siddhis* become negative epiphenomena of *samādhi*. Indeed, the *Yogasūtra* itself suggests a similar idea.[63]

It is indeed obvious that there can be descriptions of the human elevated or spiritual condition without reference to *siddhi* experiences. Thus the dissociation of the spiritual from *siddhi* experience is logically and empirically possible. However, the question remains whether this is the case in Pātañjala-Yoga. The teaching of the *siddhis* is extensive, spanning one-quarter of the text, and is evidently very important. It refers to the most obvious fruit of yoga training, consequent upon the consummation of yoga transformation. What is the point in embedding such a large body of references to the *siddhis* in a concise sutra-text such as the *Yogasūtra*? Viewing the *siddhis* as vicarious, marginal epiphenomena of the highly spiritual condition of *samādhi* may not accord with the overt structure of the *Yogasūtra*. Yet viewing the *siddhis* as the primary datum to be explained by Patañjali is conducive not only to a more balanced, coherent understanding of the *Yogasūtra*, but also to a more realistic approach concerning the "calling of the interior" according to classical yoga.

Pātañjala-Yoga represents a tradition and vision of life according to which the darkening of externality—the near-death condition—is an opening into a "lively interior," a marvelous, free, playful existence. This kind of spirituality might be somewhat exceptional or "alternative" to the central teaching of schools such as the Sāṅkhya or the Upanishads. Yet it is patently there, assertively expressed in the doctrine of the *siddhis*, mainly in the third section of the *Yogasūtra*. The myth of the dying yogin is the narrative which gives expression to the particular identity of Pātañjala-Yoga in this respect. This myth presents the *siddhis* not as vicarious epiphenomena of *samādhi*, but rather as the essence of yoga experience itself. And if the *siddhis* are recognized as the essence of yoga experience, and if it is admitted—as indeed it must be—that *siddhi* experience is emphatically connected in the *Yogasūtra* with the most elevated condition of yoga (*samādhi*), then the denigrating paradigm expressed in most of the myths mentioned above is noticeably lacking in explanatory power.

However simple the myth of the dying yogin, the picture of the *Yogasūtra* drawn or implied by this story is intricate. The encounter between the yogin and the philosopher is complex, prolonged, perhaps replete with tragic misunderstandings. In its course, much of the original receptivity to the dying yogin's whisper diminishes or disappears. And yet it is still there, constituting the most significant hallmark of Pātañjala-Yoga.[64]

As suggested above, Patañjali accounts for the reality of the yogic *siddhi* experiences by connecting them with the ultimate meditative condition (*samādhi*). *Samādhi* is the cause of the *siddhis*. In the *Yogasūtra*, the assessment of *samādhi* as the quintessential means of true knowledge and contact with reality implies that the *siddhi* experiences are strictly "real." This is indeed obvious, since the *siddhis* are the most conspicuous outcome or derivative of the condition of *samādhi*. If *samādhi* is a state of revelation and truth, so must be the *siddhi* experiences.

Yoga has often been conceived as the road to *samādhi*. Vyāsa says that "yoga is *samādhi*" (*yogaḥ samādhiḥ*).[65] According to the *Yogasūtra*, the condition of *samādhi* is the source of knowledge and true perception. In YS 1.48, Patañjali says that the cognition born of *samādhi* carries ultimate truth.[66] Mastery of *saṁyama* (yogic meditation, consisting primarily of *samādhi*) brings about the light of knowledge.[67]

All the commentators agree on this point, and feel comfortable extolling *samādhi*. "*Samādhi*, yogic 'enstasis,' is the final result and the crown of all the ascetic's efforts and exercises."[68] Indeed, the *Yogasūtra* makes *samādhi* a central concept of epistemological and philosophical importance. The references to different types of *samādhi*, to the truth value of cognitions arising out of *samādhi*, other consequences of *samādhi*, and so forth, are numerous. The first *Pāda* of the *Yogasūtra*—called the Samādhi-Pāda—consists of a classification of types of *samādhi*,[69] theses about the particular potency of *samādhi*.[70] The second section of the *Yogasūtra*—the Sādhana-Pāda—describes *samādhi* as the goal of *kriyā* yoga (along with the reduction of the *kleśas*),[71] as well as the final stage of the training in *aṣṭāṅga* yoga.[72] The third section—the Vibhūti-Pāda—contains a definition of *samādhi* as the pinnacle of the way of yoga[73] as well as dozens of experiences which result from the condition of *samādhi*. The last section of the *Yogasūtra*—the Kaivalya-Pāda—mentions *samādhi* as a condition from which yoga experiences profusely spring forth, as well as experiences such as the creation of other minds.[74]

In short, the meaning and significance of the condition of *samādhi* is a primary concern of the compiler of the *Yogasūtra*. The explanatory power of the concept of *samādhi* functions primarily with respect to the domain of yoga experience (the facts of yoga). Thus, the dying yogin provides the stimulus, the kernel around which the *Yogasūtra* is woven.

How then are the *siddhi* experiences understood (explained)? And how is (*sa-bīja*) *samādhi* described? *Samādhi* is defined as intense, distortion-free intentionality focused on objects.[75] YS 3.3 asserts that *samādhi* is a condition where the object only is in sight. "*Samādhi* is (a state of awareness) devoid as it were of its own nature, in which only the object of meditation shines forth" (*tad evārtha-mātra-nirbhāsaṁ svarūpa-śunyam iva samādhiḥ*).[76] The condition of *dhyāna* becomes devoid of its own "form" or "identity" (*svarūpa*). The *siddhis* are explained as the differentiated effects of intentionality according to its objects. Objects of meditation (*saṁyama*) are correlated with the resulting experiences. In some cases, the correlation of object and experience is obvious; in other cases a more indirect causality seems to be implied.

Thus the concept of *samādhi*—the fundamental (*pradhānya*) component in yogic meditation (*saṁyama*)—is intrinsically compatible with the explanation of the *siddhis* in the *Yogasūtra*. Its definition is of the philosopher's making, facilitating the explanation of the *siddhis*. The definition of *samādhi* as the final stage of *aṣṭāṅga* yoga is most relevant in assessing its explanatory function and power with respect to the *siddhi* sutras.[77]

As suggested above, *samādhi* is not an "experience" but a "condition." In YS 1.20 *samādhi* is grouped with faith (*śraddhā*), power (*vīrya*) and memory (*smṛti*). These components seem to be "conditions" rather than "experiences." YS 1.21 mentions the condition of *samādhi* as well as the results of *samādhi* (*samādhi-phala*), obtainable by the committed yogin. YS 4.1 also implies the condition modality of *samādhi* as the source of *siddhi* experiences. The *siddhi* experiences are, as Patañjali says in YS 4.1,[78] born of *samādhi* as they may be born of "birth," drugs, use of mantras and *tapas*. Types of birth, herbs, use of mantras and *tapas* are not "experiences" but rather sources, grounds, causes or conditions which generate the *siddhis*. Thus *samādhi* is a condition rather than an experience.[79] It is not of the same modality or ontic level as the *siddhis*. *Samādhi* is a kind of generative innerness, of which the most significant effect is the *siddhi* experience. Referring to a kind of (unseen) generative innerness, the concept of *samādhi* is essentially a theoretical concept, to be assessed and described by the measure of its explanatory efficacy.

Patañjali conceptualizes yogic deathly silence and experience by differentiating between two types of *samādhi*: silent innerness charged with objects (*sa-bīja-samādhi*) and ultimate silence, devoid of objects (*nir-bīja-samādhi*).[80] The peculiar meaning of *samādhi* as the essence of yoga derives from the two central goals of Patañjali's exposition; the explanation of yogic experience (*siddhi*) and the connection of Sāṅkhya metaphysics with yogic silence. The differentiation of *samādhi* into *sa-bīja* and *nir-bīja-samādhi* subserves these two goals of Patañjali. Silence charged with objects produces the *siddhis*; the other, totally dark, immobile silence, with no objective presence in sight, is *kaivalya-samādhi*—postdisintegration, post-*saṁsāra*.[81]

Yogic experience is the most salient expression of the yogin's otherness, suffused with silence on the verge of death. Like the family world or the living body, the wholeness of the yogin's life is irreducible to its parts. The impenetrable otherness of the yoga universe resides in the whole, in the complex flavor of celibacy, breathing-control, yogic postures, refusal of possessions, cleanliness, solitude, perception of life as suffering, meditation, Sāṅkhya metaphysical interpretation, and a host of unusual experiences and visions. Attitude, practice, metaphysics, and experience are combined in the creation of the yoga universe; the yogin's silence is its apex and completion.

4

Causality, False Linearity, and the Silent Yogin's Presence in the *Yogasūtra*

Beginnings are tense, paradoxical, pregnant. There is an outburst of meaning, but also—often—a strong sense of containment and self-reference. Certain desires find expression there, attesting to wishes to discharge, communicate, break a silence, and also to present oneself. Such are the energies which lie at the threshold. Thus an opening statement is not only a first encounter with an audience; it is often consciousness of oneself created and introduced. Sometimes, indeed, a prefatory text is a metastatement, almost paradoxical in its self-referential nature.

Thus too in the *Yogasūtra*. In YS 1.1 Patañjali identifies himself as a scholar who discusses yoga: "Now the exposition of yoga" (*atha yogānuśāsanam*). On the one hand, the author commits himself by the use of the word "exposition" (*anuśāsana*) to the role of an exponent who, essentially, repeats, reorganizes, reintegrates and reexplains a body of existing knowledge. On the other hand, Patañjali also pronounces a certain beginning: now, then (*atha*).

None of the commentators fails to note the importance of this opening sutra; many pay special attention to the word *atha*, which appears to break a previous state of silence, charged by a desire (intention) to speak. Thus, for example, Vācaspati Miśra refers to the "body of knowledge desired to be commenced" (*prāripsitasya śāstrasya*).[1] Pandit Usharbudh Arya devotes eight pages to discussing the meaning of this very first of Patañjali's words—*atha* ("now"). He quotes the commentators who say: "The words *oṁ* and *atha* came from the Creator's throat/in the beginning of the creation; hence both these words are auspicious."[2]

Tradition contemplates the tension between the sense of beginning or commencement (suggested by the word *atha*) and the sense of continuity (implied by the word *anuśāsana*). Thus the classical commentators emphasize two aspects of Patañjali's enterprise: Patañjali is authoritative, but the *Yogasūtra* is a treatise, a text. Moreover, most of the commentators share the basic presupposition that the *Yogasūtra* is a text *derived from texts*. In this context, Vyāsa introduces the notion of a well-established body of knowledge (*śāstra*): "The discourse on yoga here begun is a *śāstra* which should be known" (*yogānuśāsanaṁ śāstram adihkṛtaṁ veditavyam*).

Vācaspati Miśra, the ninth-century archcommentator and Classical Scholar of Indian philosophy, is naturally interested in issues of authority and authorship. He is known as an authoritative exponent of each of the classical philosophies (*darśana*).[3] In his commentary on YS 1.1 he elaborates on the issue of Patañjali's originality and type of personal involvement (authorship) in the exposition (*anuśāsana*) of yoga. He ponders how, if the teaching of yoga is known to exist already, Patañjali can have any authority or make any contribution. "Hiraṇyagarbha and no other of ancient days is he who gave utterance (*vākta*) to yoga. How can it be said that Patañjali gives utterance to the authoritative book on yoga?" Vācaspati answers such questions, apparently raised by a virtual opponent (*pūrva-pakṣin*), saying: "In reply the author of the sutra says 'the exposition' (*anuśāsana*); exposition in the sense of expounding something previously expounded."[4]

Since, as suggested above, YS 1.1 is the only meta-sutra in the *Yogasūtra*, it is no accident that the identity of Patañjali—philosopher, compiler, yogin—is most emphatically discussed in ancient as well as in contemporary literature in relation to YS 1.1. Modern commentators concede that the very first sutra is important with respect to Patañjali's intellectual character, authority, and the nature of his work. While in agreement on these as measures of significance, they disagree in their assessment of Patañjali in all three respects. I. K. Taimni thinks that Patañjali was an accomplished yogin:

> From the masterly manner in which he has expounded the subject of *Yoga* in the *Yoga-Sūtras* it is obvious that he was a *Yogi* of a very high order who had personal knowledge of all aspects of *Yoga* including its practical techniques.[5]

Personal knowledge is less evident (and less important) to Hariharananda Aranya, who is more committed to the conventional sense of *anuśāsana:*

> The science of Yoga delineated in these *Sūtras* has been based on the instructions transmitted by the ancient sages. It is not a science newly evolved by the framer of the *Sūtras*.[6]

While Hariharananda Aranya seems indifferent to Patañjali as anything more than a transmitter, Bhagavan Rajneesh sounds much more enthusiastic. Rajneesh glorifies Patañjali as a "rare flower," being someone of experience and poetry as well as a scientist. He elaborates on the tension between being a poet and being a scientist:

> Patañjali is the greatest scientist of the inner. His approach is that of a scientific mind: he is not a poet. And in that way he is very rare, because those who enter into the inner world are almost always poets, those who enter into the outer world are almost always scientists.
>
> To have a scientific attitude and to enter into the inner is almost an impossible possibility. . . . He talks like a mathematician, a logician. He talks like Aristotle and he is a Heraclitus.[7]

In a more scholarly vein, G. Feuerstein reaches a similar conclusion with respect to the combination of seemingly contradictory traits in Patañjali's character. Feuerstein seems undecided with respect to Patañjali's character and the nature of his work. He reflects on the difficulty of integrating Patañjali as a scholar and philosopher with Patañjali the accomplished yogin. These two aspects of the person-in-the-text—a sophisticated, highly verbal scholar and a silent-unto-yogic-death ascetic—are indeed largely incompatible. However, Feuerstein concludes that Patañjali was *both* a scholar and a yogin:

> Reading and re-reading the *Yogasūtra,* one soon begins to piece together a mental image, or profile, quite hypothetical, of its author. It is the picture of a systematic thinker with a traditional bend of mind, a practical metaphysician who is lucid and precise in his formulations, not over-anxious to enter into polemics with other schools and obviously well-established in the *practice* of Yoga. His work is remarkable for its dispassionate temper. This cannot be accounted for by the extreme terseness of his aphoristic style alone. After all, Pascal succeeded in communicating powerful emotive images by the same method. Rather, the conspicuous absence of all emotionality from the *Yoga-Sūtra* must be explained by the author's other-worldly philosophy and his personal character which is that of a genuine renunciant and *yogin.*[8]

Feuerstein's argument is not compelling, as it leads him to ignore in this context the weight of Patañjali's unique expression of his self-understanding (strongly suggested by the word *anuśāsana*). By calling his work an exposition, Patañjali seems to be declaring himself more scholar than ascetic, a self-classification that must be taken into account in any character assessment.

M. Eliade is much closer to Patañjali's spiritual character and the nature of his work. He shares with Patañjali and the classical scholars the definition of the *Yogasūtra* as an "exposition" (*anuśāsana*). He thinks that Patañjali adds nothing to the theory and metaphysics of Sāṅkhya.[9] He makes an astute observation about the nature of Patañjali's work:

> In sum, what can properly be called Patañjali's work was directed principally to the coordination of the philosophical material—borrowed from Sāṅkhya—with the technical prescriptions for concentration, meditation, and ecstasy. Thanks to Patañjali, yoga was advanced from a "mystic" tradition to the level of a "system of philosophy.[10]

However, Eliade does not appreciate the immensity and significance of the intellectual project involved in the "coordination" (integration) of Sāṅkhya metaphysics with the "technical prescriptions for concentration." Indeed, this is the core of the *Yogasūtra*, which is a most daring attempt at a synthesis of practice, attitude, metaphysics, and experience; a closure of the gap between the yogin's life and experience, and the philosophical personality. Indeed, since Eliade so harshly denounces yogic experience (the *siddhis*) as temptations,[11] he cannot respond justly to Patañjali's openness to the paranormal condition of yogic death (*samādhi*) and its domain of experience.

The *Yogasūtra* has been perceived by many as a "compilation." Some scholars, notably E. Frauwallner (1953),[12] J. W. Hauer (1932, 1958)[13] and G. Oberhammer (1965)[14] attempted to identify various "texts" in the *Yogasūtra*, basically on philological grounds. F. Staal (1986) criticizes this "dismemberment" or "dissection" of the *Yogasūtra*, suggesting instead the need for understanding "not texts about Yoga, but Yoga itself."[15] Indeed, Staal's criticism should be extended to the entire tradition of yoga commentaries. The inaccessibility of the yoga universe, and in particular certain aspects of Pātañjala Yoga (such as the yoga experiences, the *siddhis*), makes Staal's assignment extremely difficult for the interpreter of the *Yogasūtra*. A presentation of the *Yogasūtra* as giving expression to the "wholeness," coherence and reality of the *Vivekin*'s life is a small step in the right direction.

"Yoga itself," distinguished from "texts about yoga," is the dying yogin's abysmal quietude. The reality behind the *Yogasūtra* is the silent yogin's presence, and thus, the text about yoga is the transformation of dense, fertile, near-death silence into noisy Sāṅkhya speech. However, if the yogin's being is utter solitude and silence, the philosopher must break it and demolish the yogin's otherness. Explanation is the philosopher's bridge between the yogin's otherness and the philosopher's being. Though speech about yoga destroys or distorts its otherness, it nevertheless points to its existence. Explanation is Patañjali's essential mode of encounter with the yogin's immersion in silence and his rare reports.

There is virtually no statement in the *Yogasūtra* which does not serve the existential need to explain the hard facts contained in the dying yogin's silence and reports. Significantly, the approach toward inaccessible silence produces explanations which often seem incomplete and inadequate. For example, the assertion of the emergence of the ultimate Sāṅkhya insight (*viveka-jaṁ jñānaṁ*) from meditation (*saṁyama*) on the moments (*kṣaṇa*) and their sequence is somewhat ambiguous.[16] It explains the emanation of knowledge as a result of meditation on a certain object. The puzzle, in this case, concerns the relation of "time" with the emergence of *viveka-khyāti*.[17] Other explanations are similarly incomplete.

Meditation (*saṁyama*) on the navel wheel (*nābhi-cakra*) produces knowledge of the arrangement of the body (*kāya-vyūha-jñānaṁ*). Though there is a certain—somewhat tenuous—"thematic relation" between the object of meditation (a point in the body) and the product of meditation (knowledge of anatomy), the dynamic which generates the particular cognition is not made explicit. Why is the navel wheel—and no other bodily point—particularly efficient as an object of meditation the result of which is knowledge of anatomy? In other words, the correspondence between the nature of the object of meditation—a correspondence expressed in the vast majority of the sutras explaining particular experiences—is often underdefined, leaving the explanation incomplete.

YS 3.24 is an example of a closer correspondence of object and outcome of meditation. Meditation on powers (*bala*) produces powers such as those of an elephant (*baleṣu hasti-balādīni*). Vyāsa sees a full correspondence—namely, actual identity—between the object meditated upon and the power (or experience) which results therefrom. Thus he says that *saṁyama* focused on the elephant's strength produces elephant's power (*hasti-bale saṁyamād hasti-balo bhavati*). *Saṁyama* on Vināta's son's (Garuda) strength produces Garuda's power. *Saṁyama* on the power of Vāyu produces the power of Vāyu.[18] Vācaspati generalizes Vyāsa's examples: the yogin attains the powers on which he meditates (*yasya bale saṁyamas tasya balaṁ labhata iti*).[19] Hariharananda Aranya says that "all physical culturists know that by consciously applying the will-power on particular muscles, their strength can be developed. Saṁyama on strength is only the highest form of the same process" (p. 296). Vivekananda translates Patañjali's sutra in accordance with Vyāsa's understanding of the close connection between the object and the outcome of meditation (*saṁyama*): "By making Saṁyama on the strength of the elephant and others, their respective strength comes to the Yogi."[20] He introduces the concept of "energy," thus making an opening for a more abstract interpretation of YS 3.24; "Infinite energy is at the disposal of everyone if he only knows how to get it. The Yogi has discovered the science of getting it."[21]

It is noteworthy that in the vast majority of commentaries on the *Yogasūtra*, there is doubt with respect to the commentator's judgment of the truth-value of Patañjali's statements. Does Vivekananda commit himself to the reality of the potency of *saṁyama*? When he says "The Yogi has discovered the science of getting it," does he intend his statement to be a textual exposition of YS 3.24, or does he corroborate the truth of Patañjali's sutra by addressing extratextual reality (in this case, "infinite energy")?

The narrative of Vivekananda's commentary on YS 3.24 provides an illustration of the difficulty to close the gap between the otherness of the yoga universe and the commentator's own world. Vivekananda starts by accepting Vyāsa's pattern of explanation in his *bhāṣya* on YS 3.24; this pattern—based on the correspondence of object of meditation and the outcome of *saṁyama* on this object—is indeed Patañjali's paradigm for causally explaining the yogin's experiences. Though he seems to feel committed to what he considers the literal meaning of YS 3.24, Vivekananda proceeds to provide also a more abstract wording of the sutra since he also seeks "truth." If he believed in the reality corresponding to the literal conception of YS 3.24, he would not have proceeded to refer to the more abstract interpretation (using the concept of "energy").

While Ultimate Insiders commit themselves to the extratextual reality of the *Yogasūtra*, most of the others seem to feel an urge for abstraction or metaphor in order to avoid devaluation of the *Yogasūtra* as an untrustworthy text. R. Mehta considers literal interpretations such as Vyāsa's, Taimni's,[22] or Aranya's as unlikely. "Patañjali uses the word 'elephant' to denote this spring of limitless energy, for an elephant is regarded as the strongest animal. This does not mean that man comes in possession of animal strength or that the spiritual aspirant gets the strength of the elephant. To interpret the sutra thus is to misunderstand it completely."[23]

Vivekananda's and the other commentators' predicament in interpreting YS 3.24 is significant, since it is largely Patañjali's own, in his listening to the whispers of the yogin—radically subdued, invulnerable, otherworldly, as it were. Patañjali explains the fertile silence which he tries to approach, and thus he conceptualizes the yoga universe, closing the gap between his own world and the dying yogin's. Patañjali's basic speech act is the explanation, the transformation of otherness into the familiar and intelligible.

YS 3.24 is noteworthy, since it sheds light on Patañjali's mode of explanation of the dying yogin's testimony. He posits a measure of correspondence between the object of meditation and the resulting experience. In the case of YS 3.24 it is "complete correspondence" (identity). In other cases, the correspondence is weaker, more partial.

In YS 3.40 Patañjali explains the observation of splendor either emanating from the yogin or experienced by him. From the mastery of the life energy known by the name of *samāna,* there is effulgence (*samāna-jayāj jvalanam*). By using the ablative case in a causal sense, Patañjali explains the phenomenon of light. Vyāsa understands *jvalana* as the light which emanates from the yogin's body, generated by "exciting," (literally) "blowing" (*upadhmānaṁ kṛtvā*). The imagery seems to consist of fire enhanced by blowing, hence Vācaspati's view that "the yogin who has subjugated the *samāna* by causing a pulsation of the flames, becomes radiant."[24]

In this context, Vijñānabhikṣu recalls the famous incident from the life of Satī, Siva's wife, who burnt herself to death because she could not bear her father's insult to her husband. The radiating yogin blows on inner heat much as Satī burnt herself (by means of yoga).[25] Similarly, though lexically different, the literature of neo yoga in our age uses seemingly scientific jargon to create an aura of truth, objectivity, and respectability for Patañjali's explanations. Thus, for example, R. S. Mishra's definition of *samāna*:

> *samāna* is the life force which is responsible for all metabolic forces, all chemical, biochemical, and biological forces. Its residence is the area of the navel in the abdomen and its field of function is all living tissues. Every living cell is a factory in which forces of *samāna* are operating day and night.[26]

Causality based upon the resemblance of object and result of meditation extends thus throughout the exegesis of the *Yogasūtra*. However, sometimes the object/experience relation seems weak. In YS 3.39, the statement preceding YS 3.40, Patañjali connects another type of life energy (*prāṇa*)[27] with certain phenomena observed in the dying yogin's life. By mastery over the *udāna,* the yogin avoids contact with water, mud, thorns,[28] and also maintains "upward motion" (*utkrānti*) (probably at the moment of death).[29] As in the case of YS 3.40, the causal relationship between mastery over the *udāna* and lack of contact with water, is made explicit by the use of the ablative case (*jayāt*). Vyāsa defines life as the action of all the senses, an action characterized by the existence of the fivefold vital breathing (*samastendriya-vṛttiḥ prāṇādi-lakṣaṇā jīvanam / tasya kriyā pañcatayi*).

He further elaborates on the nature of each of the vital breaths:

> *Prāṇa* moves through the mouth and nose and manifests itself up to the region of the heart. *Samāna* manifests itself up to the region of the navel; it is so called because it distributes (food) equally (to all parts of the body). *Apāna* manifests itself up to the region of the soles of the feet; it is so called because it carries away (the waste of the body). *Udāna* manifests itself up to the region of the head; it is so called because it carries upward (the juices of the body). *Vyāna* is so called because it is spread all over the body.[30]

Patañjali's application of the five vital breaths is worth attention since it points to some of the sources of his explanations. We assume that the aura around the yogin's body (or the light he feels inside; YS 3.40) and the absence of the disturbing effects of water, mud, thorns, and the like (YS 3.39) are for Patañjali "hard facts" in need of explanation.[31] Retrieval of the five vital breaths from the ancient traditions of India might be an expression of Patañjali's range of associations and knowledge.

According to A.H. Ewing, references to *prāṇa*, *samāna*, and *apāna* date back to the *Rg-Veda*, and references to the complete series of the five breaths appear in ancient texts such as the Brahmanas, Araṇyakas, and Upanishads.[32] Now, how does Patañjali make use of concepts such as *samāna* (YS 3.40) and *udāna* (YS 3.39)? As seen above, Patañjali connects *samāna* with splendor (*jvalana*) and *udāna* with absence of contact with water and "motion upward" (*utkrānti*). We can speculate and say that Patañjali associates *samāna* with heat and *udāna* with upward motion. Interestingly, this is precisely Śaṅkarācārya's description of *udāna*. According to BSBh 2.4.12, *udāna* is "the breath whose course is upward and which is the cause of departure" (*ūrdhva-vṛttir utkrāntyādi-hetuḥ*).[33]

In YS 3.22 Patañjali explains the fact of the yogin's knowledge of his moment of death. Patañjali introduces the concept of karma which bears fruit faster or more slowly. By meditation on karma the yogin knows the time of his death; and also by omens (*sopakramaṁ nirupakramaṁ ca karma tat-saṁyamād aparānta-jñānam ariṣṭebhyo vā*).[34] There seems to be a "thematic relation" between karma and life span. This relationship is explicated in YS 2.13, according to which karma acts with respect to type of birth (*jāti*), span of life (*āyus*), and experience (*bhoga*).

In YS 3.42 Patañjali causally explains the phenomenon of levitation. By meditation on the relation of space and body, and by identification (*samāpatti*) with light objects such as cotton wool, there is movement in air (*ākāśa-gamana*).[35]

Patañjali's explanations of particular phenomena in the yoga universe are not confined to certain causal relationships expressed in the resemblance, correspondence, and "thematic relationship" between the object of meditation and the yogin's experiences.

The description and prescription of the five *yamas*[36] and five *niyamas*[37] include causal explanations often based upon thematic relationship between the nature of yogic practice and its result. In YS 2.37 Patañjali explains the riches (jewels) reaching the yogin by a reference to the observance (or practice) of yogic nonstealing (*asteya*). Obviously, this is a difficult sutra to interpret. What is precisely nonstealing? How does it provide riches? The classical scholars provide little help towards the understanding of Patañjali's explanation in this case, while an independent seeker such as R. Mehta is particularly helpful in this context: "Why does one steal at all, whether in a crude or in a polished manner? It is only when one feels incomplete within oneself that one steals."[38] Mehta then proceeds to connect nonstealing with "truthfulness" (*satya*) and "noninjury" (*ahiṁsā*):

> We saw while discussing *satya* that one who is rooted in it moves on in life performing complete action from moment to moment. But why is man unable to do this? It is because he is not established in *asteya*. Without non-stealing there can be no establishment in *satya*, and without *satya* there can be no *ahiṁsā*. A person who acts so as to reap a reward is bound to be violent, for he will demand the fruit which another has gained. Thus non-injury depends upon non-falsehood, which in turn depends upon non-stealing. We have said that imitation is an act of stealing, for in imitation one wants to have what the other person has, material goods or beauty or position or so-called spiritual attainments. This trait arises from a feeling that one is incomplete within oneself.[39]

Like most of the explanatory sutras brought forth above, YS 3.35 consists of a complex explanation embedded wholly in the sutra. It defines the nature of experience (*bhoga*), which involves failure to distinguish between *sattva*—which is a "strand" (*guṇa*) of objectivity—and purusha (which is pure, passive, unalloyed subjectivity). The difference between *sattva* and purusha is infinite, since *sattva* cannot possibly exist by itself; it "exists for another."[40] However, everyone is prone to mixing them. By meditation (*saṁyama*) on the nature of the purusha—which exists for its own sake—there emerges knowledge of purusha.[41] The entire Sāṅkhya metaphysics and theory of liberation is implied in this *sutra*. Indeed, the combination of meditation with the ultimate—most abstract—insight is the apex of the *Yogasūtra*. Yogic powers of concentration and absorption bear directly on the prospect of liberation. The role of powerful and transformative meditation—the development of which is the pinnacle and culmination of yogic training—is suggested in this context. YS 3.35 thus provides the core of Patañjali's explanation of liberation (*kaivalya*).

The *Yogasūtra* is a philosophical work of explanation; the basic pattern of explanation is causal. This pattern has a grammatical manifestation, as Patañjali expresses causality through the third (instrumental) and the fifth (ablative) cases. These exegetical sutras show yoga as an efficient means for the emergence of *samādhi*.

For indeed, the *Yogasūtra* introduces one concept—*samādhi*—as the true center of its conceptualization of the multidimensional yoga universe.

Yogic silence, the dying yogin's deathly quiet, is referred to as *samādhi*. In his terse statement—"yoga is *samādhi*" (*yogaḥ samādhiḥ*)[42]—Vyāsa expresses an essential truth. Patañjali uses "yogic death"—*samādhi*—as the ultimate integrative concept in its references to the wholeness of the yoga universe, yogic epistemology, and ontology. The explicit connections of *samādhi* with the domains of experience, practice, and metaphysics constitute the basic paradigm of the *Yogasūtra*. Indeed, it is possible to see *samādhi* simply as the name of the yoga universe.

The richness and paradoxality with which the concept of *samādhi* is infused is the primary intellectual challenge pondered in the *Yogasūtra*. The yogin's life is a movement towards "identification with objects" (*samādhi*) as well as complete dissociation from "objects" (*kaivalya*). The equation of *samādhi* with *kaivalya* is paradoxical and difficult.[43] Any understanding of the *Yogasūtra* as a whole must—in the end—shed some light on this mysterious equation. The integration of Sāṅkhya metaphysics with the yogin's life is plainly the main theme of the *Yogasūtra*.[44] The road to *samādhi* is the most essential undertaking of the yogin towards his initiation as a *Vivekin*.

The yogin starts his journey by moving away from objects and objectivity. By cutting off any trace of externality, he or she creates darkness, rich and real. As the world darkens, the interior looms, abysmally unfamiliar. A host of visions and "altered states of consciousness" become the yogin's lot and reality. Patañjali connected the "death of the senses" with an opening into "total innerness." In the technical speech of the *Yogasūtra*, the yogin on the way to liberation undergoes the condition of complete "sensory deprivation" (*pratyāhāra*). The *Yogasūtra* says that as the senses are dissociated from their respective objects, following the mind, as it were, this is *pratyāhāra*.[45] Vyāsa likens the mind and the senses in the condition of *pratyāhāra* to the queen bee and her bees. While normally the mind follows the senses, the yogin attains an opposite condition, like bees who follow their queen as it flies and as it lands.[46] Thus the mind stops following the senses and stands independent, self-abiding, vulnerable to eruptions from inside. And so it happens for the yogin on the verge of darkness and death. This disconnection of the senses from the "world outside" is the end of life as we know it. It is the ground for the emergence of the *Vivekin*'s organic whole (*samādhi*).

While the *Yogasūtra* is a contemplation of the yoga universe as an organic whole, linearity and fragmentation nevertheless pervade it. The linear and fragmentary presentation and reading of the *Yogasūtra* is reflected structurally in the fourfold division of the *Yogasūtra*, as well as in the fragmentary and often ambiguous import of the individual sutra-statements.

The *Yogasūtra* is a list of 195 short sentences in Sanskrit, divided into four sections called *Pādas*, as follows:

i) The Samādhi-Pāda ("The chapter concerning yogic silence");

ii) The Sādhana-Pāda ("The chapter on yogic discipline and practice");

iii) The Vibhūti-Pāda ("The chapter on unusual attainments");

iv) The Kaivalya-Pāda ("The chapter on liberation").

This division implies a thematic distinction between the various sections. There is a powerful suggestion in the linear arrangement of the *Yogasūtra* in accordance with the thematic titles. Once the linear presentation is given, there arises the need for its justification, hence the commentators of Pātañjala-Yoga have had to interpret the transition from one section to another. I see, for example, Vyāsa's commentary on YS 2.1 as an attempt to justify the boundary between the first section of the *Yogasūtra* (the Samādhi-Pāda) and the second (the Sādhana-Pāda). Vyāsa justifies the "thematic boundary" between the first and second chapters of the *Yogasūtra* by postulating the existence of two distinct "yogic personalities." The first one is the "well-recollected" yogin (*samāhita-citta*); the second is the "outgoing" yogin (*vyutthita-citta*). The first chapter, he says, is intended for the first type of person, the second for one who needs yogic activity in order to get established in yoga. Vyāsa then mentions the three components of *kriyā*-yoga (the yoga of action) which are commensurate with the condition of the *vyutthita-citta* yogin. In particular, he speaks of the need for "austerity" (*tapas*). Yoga cannot succeed for one who is not an ascetic (*nātapasvino yogaḥ sidhyati*).[47]

This structural attention is also seen as the author of the *Vivaraṇa* focuses his attention on the contents of the different sections of the *Yogasūtra*; the first chapter (the Samādhi-Pāda) is thus labeled since it primarily discusses *samādhi*. About the second chapter he says:

> The means to reach liberation (*kaivalya*) is real knowledge (*saṁyag-darśana*). The means to attain this real knowledge are the means of yoga. Since these very means (*sādhana*) are primarily explained in this (second) *pāda*, it is called the "section of means" (*sādhana-pāda*).[48]

Similarly, the author of the *Vivaraṇa* explains the titles of the other two *Pādas* of the *Yogasūtra*; the third section of the *Yogasūtra* is called the Vibhūti-Pāda since the "powers" (*vibhūti*) necessarily follow for one engaged in the practice of yoga; the fourth section (the Kaivalya-Pāda) is so called since this chapter—by way of summing up the entire teaching of yoga—primarily discusses liberation for one who has become indifferent with respect to all attainments (listed in the third chapter).[49]

Thus the classical commentators succumb to the thematic division. They support and explain the need for the boundaries implied by the fourfold division of the *Yogasūtra*, thereby objectifying these boundaries and overlooking their constructed nature.

Objectification also characterizes contemporary commentators who invariably follow the lead of the classical exegetes. I. K. Taimni suggests:

> [The] first section deals with the general nature of *Yoga* and its technique. It is meant really to answer the question "What is *Yoga?*" Since *Samādhi* is the essential technique of *Yoga*, naturally, it occupies the most important position among the various topics dealt with in this Section. This Section is, therefore, called *Samādhi Pāda.*[50]

Conceptualization of the yoga universe as an organic whole is not, however, commensurate with a strictly linear as well as with a thematic division of the text. Indeed, the relation of the titles of the *Pādas* to their contents is not very instructive. It is often the case that certain sutras could be easily embedded in sections other than the one in which they actually appear. We can take each section of the *Yogasūtra* and review its contents; in each instance, the division of the *Yogasūtra* into four thematically distinct sections is problematic.

Let us take, for example, the Samādhi-Pāda. The nature of "yogic unconsciousness" (*samādhi*) is closely related to the yogin's experiences therein as well as to the practices which precede and facilitate it. Indeed, quite a few statements are devoted to the subject of *samādhi* in this chapter. There are references to various types of *samādhi*. According to YS 1.41–45 there are four distinct kinds (or qualities) of *samādhi* (or *samāpatti*). The condition of *samādhi* is described according to its "quality." YS 1.42 depicts the lowest type of meditative identification with the object, where there is mixture of word, object, and cognition.[51] YS 1.43 refers to a more purified and therefore higher condition of meditation, where the object alone shines in consciousness, revealing its (the object's) real nature.[52] YS 1.44 refers to the two stages of absorption (*sa-vicārā* and *nir-vicārā*) defined by the "subtlety" (*sūkṣmatā*) of the respective objects.[53] There are also references to the impact of *samādhi* on karma.[54] However, although the Samādhi-Pāda includes quite a few—and important—references to the condition of *samādhi*, it does not focus exclusively on yogic trance or "yogic death."

There is much material in this section which can be persuasively situated elsewhere in the *Yogasūtra*. Many sutras do not address the nature or meaning of *samādhi* at all. YS 1.3,[55] for example, defines the ultimate condition of liberation (*kaivalya*) according to Sāṅkhya yoga. The sutra states that "then it is a condition of the seer abiding in his own nature." YS 1.3 is thus a definition of the "solitude" (*kaivalya*) of the pure subject (purusha). In this tradition, aloneness (*kaivalya*) means the dissociation of the pure subject from any contact or involvement with objectivity. Now, a statement such as YS 1.3 could be placed in the fourth section of the *Yogasūtra* (the Kaivalya-Pāda) rather than in the first section. Its import indeed is similar to the last sutra of the fourth section (which defines *kaivalya* as the cessation of the *guṇa* activities or the autonomous abiding of the consciousness-capacity).[56]

Likewise, the definition of yoga in YS 1.2 as the "cessation (*nirodha*) of (all) mental activities" is not directly related to the condition of *samādhi*.[57] There is even some tension between the ideal of *nirodha* and the condition of *samādhi*. For in the condition of *sa-bīja-samādhi* there is the presence of an object. It is thus not the state of emptiness associated with *nirodha*. Thus a sutra such as YS 1.2—along with the statements which explicate it[58]—could be placed in the second Pāda, the Sādhana-Pāda.

There are obviously numerous other examples to the same effect. YS 1.12[59] asserts that the erasure or abolition of the activities of the mind is accomplished by "practice" (*abhyāsa*) and "detachment" (*vairāgya*).[60] Such a sutra could be placed in the second *Pāda* (the Sādhana-Pāda) which deals primarily with "practice." On the other hand, the second sutra in the second section[61] refers to *samādhi* as one of the goals of *kriyā-yoga*. Thus—if the thematic division of the *Pādas* were more compelling—could be placed in the first section (Samādhi-Pāda). The references to Īśvara in YS 1.23–29 do not relate to the nature of *samādhi*, and thus need not have necessarily been placed in the Samādhi-Pāda.

Indeed, in great contrast to these thematic divisions, almost all of Patañjali's statements in the *Yogasūtra* are of a connective, integrative character. Consequently, the thematic and taxonomic dismemberment of the text is somewhat misleading, artificial, and difficult.

The relationship of "practice" to Sāṅkhya consciousness is a hallmark of the yoga universe as presented in the *Yogasūtra*. Yogic practice is often seen as *strictly causal* in effecting the ultimate metaphysical insight. A programmatic proposition in this regard is YS 2.28. "From the application of the different practices of yoga, as the contaminations are reduced, there arises the light of knowledge, up to the ultimate discrimination (between subject and object)."[62] This statement defines the *Vivekin* as one who practices yoga up to the point of reaching enlightenment. Now, does such a statement as YS 2.28 belong in the second section, the Sādhana-Pāda, apparently devoted to yogic practice, or does it rather belong in the fourth Pāda, which—according to its title—deals with liberation and enlightenment? Moreover, since the practice of the eight limbs of yoga terminates in the stage of *samādhi*, would it be implausible to include this statement in the Samādhi-Pāda?

The relationship of yogic practice and the yoga experiences (*siddhis*) is also keenly expressed in the *Yogasūtra*. Patañjali devotes a special sutra, the first sutra of the fourth Pāda, to the classification the causes of the *Vivekin*'s unusual experiences;[63] sometimes they occur "naturally."[64] Sometimes they are produced by drugs (*auṣadhi*), by heating practices (*tapas*), by the use of mantras, and also through the most important source of unusual experiences, "meditation" (*samādhi*). Now, this sutra is of a conspicuously integrative nature. It defies any clear-cut classification as a reference to either "practice," "metaphysics," yogic trance, or "experience." It could be housed as naturally in the first, second, third, or fourth sections of the *Yogasūtra*.

Thus, Patañjali explains and connects the dying yogin's testimony with what he already knows and accepts. The strictly causal explanations in the *Yogasūtra* are of the philosopher's making. Yet, the dying yogin's presence provides the holistic principle behind the composition of the *Yogasūtra*. It is, however, a principle at odds with Patañjali's strictly linear exposition.

This friction suggests a sediment of undigested otherness; on the one hand, Patañjali recognizes the significance as well as the abysmal otherness of the yoga universe and the dying yogin's experience. On the other, he tries to appropriate and incorporate the dying yogin's dense innerness. In so doing, causal explanation is Patañjali's instrument. However, such explanations—partially embodied in the linear presentation of the *Yogasūtra*—are visibly incomplete. Such insufficiency is auspicious, since under the cover of the seductive transparence of the cause and effect relationships and verbalization lies—ready to be retrieved—the dark and weakened contours of the dying yogin's existence.

5

Untying the Knot of Existence: Liberation, Deathly Silence, and Their Interpretation in Pātañjala-Yoga

Mankind is confronted by contained, deathly silence in the figure of the emaciated, dying yogin, and is compelled to speak by force of deep concern and anxiety. Black and infinite silence resembles the quiet of postdissolution (*laya*) and is a threat to creation, as the world verges on primordial silence. Experience (*bhoga*) itself fades away and finally ends in deathly silent liberation. Unbearable silence must be broken, interpreted, made sense of, explained, expounded, analyzed, translated into speech. What is alleviation and respite to the yogin is a great burden to other people. It is most urgent for life and creation that humankind act out terrible silence into words. The dying yogin's silence is thus the root of Pātañjala-Yoga; it is the sound of liberation.

Patañjali approaches the dying yogin through an extended paradigmatic image of separation, untying, decomposition, dissolution. This is the primary imagery of Sāṅkhya. Once the fertile, productive, preliminary silence is superseded by ultimate balance (*nir-bīja-samādhi*), the yogin's power of speech weakens and dies. The yogin's deathly silence is postexistence, postdissolution, postdecomposition, a postspeech condition. Thus Patañjali conceives of the dying yogin as the Liberated Human Being.

There are various expressions of the Sāṅkhya imagery of liberation as disintegration; dissolution (*laya*), the untying of the rope of existence by the separation of its constituent threads (*guṇa*),[1] making the distinction between purusha and prakriti, the emergence of the insight of discrimination (*viveka-khyāti*), and—most explicitly in Patañjali's own version of Sāṅkhya—in the dissolution of speech by separating word (*śabda*), object (*artha*) and idea (*pratyaya*). Patañjali thus makes the yogin's silence the true center of his work.

The dying yogin's silence is the end of a process of "loosening," untying, falling apart, disintegration. Sāṅkhya metaphysics focuses on this basic imagery. The *guṇas* are untied; purusha and prakriti are distinguished; mind is purified by the disentanglement of its components—the *guṇas*—and dropped;

separation and dissociation from objects (*vairāgya*) is recommended; and finally, speech itself breaks down into its components: *śabda, artha, pratyaya.*

Responding to the need to interpret and thereby suppress the reality behind the dying yogin's being and testimony, Patañjali makes an attempt at the exposition of silence, distinguishing between creative silence (*sa-bīja-samādhi*) and uncreative silence (*nir-bīja-samādhi*), conceptualizing the yogin's road to silence in the *Yogasūtra.* Explications of silence, basically through the use of Sāṅkhya terminology and metaphysics, are most important in Patañjali's work.

While linear presentation of the *Yogasūtra* is misleading if taken too seriously, the very first and last utterances are justifiably considered more significant. The tradition of Pātañjala-Yoga accords much attention to these most conspicuously programmatic statements in the *Yogasūtra.* Since YS 1.1 is a meta-*sūtra,* YS 1.2—the definition of yoga—is duly considered the first programmatic one. The last statement (YS 4.34) describes the condition of release, liberation (*kaivalya*).

YS 1.2 defines yoga as the cessation of "mind fluctuations."[2] The nature of the activities to be stopped strongly suggests a state of silence at the end of the process of yoga, or as the essence and goal of yoga. In YS 1.6–11 Patañjali describes the five[3] types of activity to be stopped so that the mind is still. Conscious, verbal activities predominate among these: discursive reasoning (*anumāna*),[4] the presence of traditional wisdom (*āgama*), wrong conception (*viparyaya*),[5] empty thinking (*vikalpa*),[6] and memory (*smṛti*) are clearly verbal fluctuations. Thus Patañjali's opening section is evidently a conceptualization of silence,[7] an explication of the dying yogin's abysmal silence. Vyāsa says: *yogaḥ samādhiḥ.*

Contemporary commentators invariably see in YS 1.2 a general statement on the nature of yogic transformation. A common metaphor for this transformation refers to the stilling of the mind which is like a lake. Thus, for example, says Vivekananda in his commentary on YS 1.2:

> The bottom of the lake we cannot see, because its surface is covered with ripples. It is only possible for us to catch a glimpse of the bottom, when the ripples have subsided, and the water is calm. If the water is muddy or is agitated all the time, the bottom will not be seen. If it is clear, and there are no waves, we shall see the bottom. The bottom of the lake is our true Self; the lake is the *Citta* and the waves the *Vṛttis.*[8]

This distinction between the Real Self and the ego, expressed in Vivekananda's passage, is often made the focus by Seekers in their interpretation of YS 1.2. The mind fluctuations, "thought waves," are the mind suffused with ego sense, which is different from the pure subject. Isherwood and Prabhavananda connect this distinction to the problem of suffering and happiness:

> If the thought-wave is pleasant, the ego-sense feels, "I am happy"; if the wave is unpleasant, "I am unhappy." This false identification is the cause of all our misery—for even the ego's temporary sensation of happiness brings anxiety, a desire to cling to the object of pleasure, and this prepares future possibilities of becoming unhappy. The real Self, the Atman, remains forever outside the power of thought waves, it is eternally pure, enlightened and free—the only true, unchanging happiness.[9]

The Seekers' thirst for transformation and transcendence finds full expression in their interpretation of YS 1.2. Rajneesh renders *citta-vṛtti-nirodha* as "cessation of mind" (not only cessation of mind fluctuations), and voraciously proceeds to his central theme, the transition from the known to the unknown. "Cessation of the mind means cessation of the known, cessation of the knowable. It is a jump into the unknown. When there is no mind, you are in the unknown. Yoga is a jump into the unknown."[10] Similarly, R. Mehta also perceives in YS 1.2 an opportunity for relaying his central message, which is not radically different from Rajneesh's. Translating YS 1.2 as "Yoga is the dissolution of all centers of reaction in the mind,"[11] he sums up the meaning of freedom in yoga: "A mind in which there is no centre of reaction or habit is truly a free mind. Yoga is therefore the state of a completely free mind—not a mind free from certain so-called bad habits."[12]

Patañjali's most important—and thought-provoking—assertion in his definition of yoga (YS 1.2) is that the means of right knowledge—*pramāṇa*—are mind fluctuations which should be stopped (or controlled). The means of right knowledge are posited by Patañjali on a par with others such as "mistaken cognition" (*viparyaya*) or "empty cognition" (*vikalpa*).[13] Since Patañjali explicitly counts the mind fluctuations as five in number, there can be no doubt that the *pramāṇas* are lumped together with other activities of seemingly inferior status. Though even the teaching of Sāṅkhya may be included as "*vṛttis*" to be stopped (probably under the category of *āgama*), Vyāsa—a staunch Sāṅkhya philosopher—insists that the five *vṛttis*, with no exceptions, must be stopped (*nirodhavya*).

Whence the need to detail mind fluctuations? Vācaspatii thinks that in order to stop them, one must know them. In this context, he is impressed by the number of mind activities; even a thousand human life spans are insufficient to count these mind modifications (*na ca sahasreṇāpi puruṣāyuṣaīr alam imāḥ kaś-cit parigaṇayitum*). How can such innumerable fluctuations be stopped (*asaṁkhyātāś ca kathaṁ niroddhavyā iti*)?[14] Herein arises the need for the classification of the *vṛttis* into five categories.

Reading primary and secondary expositions of Pātañjala-Yoga, one gets the impression that the strong mystical (antiverbal) note present in Patañjali's interpretation of the yogin's silence is often muted or suppressed. In particular, Universal Philosophers overlook the significance of Y1.5–7, where the treatment of "correct and legitimate verbalization" is the same as wrong or empty cognition.

YS 1.2 is considered the definition (*lakṣaṇa*) of yoga by the Classical Scholars: yoga is the cessation of the mind activities (*yogaś citta-vṛtti-nirodhaḥ*). Since YS 1.2 is a *lakṣana-sūtra*, Vyāsa raises the question of the precise scope of yoga. He concludes that since the sutra does not contain the word "all," Patañjali does not exclude certain types of consciousness of objects from yoga.[15] In the language advanced here, Vyāsa's meaning is that the process of reaching creative silence (*sa-bīja-samādhi*) is also included in yoga.

In YS 1.2 and its unfolding up to YS 1.16, Patañjali does not make use of specifically Sāṅkhya terminology. In his programmatic definition of yoga as the silence consequent upon the stilling of the "turnings of thought." Patañjali's is here a non-Sāṅkhya voice, corresponding (as it were) to a non-Sāṅkhya silence. Although Patañjali speaks of "cessation" (*nirodha*)[16] of mind fluctuations without commitment to the specific Sāṅkhya metaphysics and terminology, Vyāsa focuses his attention on the *guṇa* constitution of the mind, a major aspect of Sāṅkhya thought and its conception of liberation. Vyāsa outlines the procedure of mind purification in terms of the three *guṇas*, which he names *prakhyā* (*sattva*), *pravṛtti* (*rajas*), and *sthiti* (*tamas*).[17]

In the ancient tradition of Sāṅkhya in India, the theory of the *guṇas* is the most explicit conceptualization of creation as the evolution of the primordial, unseen, abstract potential of objectivity into the actual, manifold world in which we live. Prakriti consists of the three threads (*guṇas*).[18] As long as these are found in complete equilibrium, the process of creation does not occur. Creation essentially gets started once the equilibrium between the *guṇas* is disrupted, especially by virtue of the pure subject's presence.

In the *Sāṅkhyakārikā* (SK), Iśvarakṛṣṇa describes the three *guṇas*, the components of objective existence.[19] *Sattva* is associated with pleasure (*prīti*), illumination (*prakāśa*), shining (*prakāśaka*), and "easiness" (*laghutva*). Such qualities predominate in the upper world (*ūrdhvaṁ sattva-viśālaḥ*) (of the gods).[20] *Rajas*, dominant in the human world, is associated with stimulation (*upaṣṭaṁbhaka*) and motion (*cala*), displeasure or pain (*aprīti*), initiative and action (*pravṛtti*). *Tamas* is characterized by inhibition (*niyama*), heaviness (*gurutvā*), and dejection (*viṣāda*).

In his exposition of the definition of yoga as the cessation of modifications of the mind, Vyāsa sees a central and unifying conceptual framework for the description and analysis of the process to liberation in the Sāṅkhya theory of the *guṇas*. Deviating from the relatively Sāṅkhya-free voice of Patañjali, Vyāsa unifies the voice of yoga as emphatically Sāṅkhyan in YSBh 1.2. Vyāsa says that when the *sattva* component is affected by *rajas* and *tamas*, the mind becomes fond of power and objects (*prakhyā-rūpaṁ hi citta-sattvaṁ rajas-tamobhyāṁ saṁsṛṣṭam aiśvarya-viṣaya-priyaṁ bhavati*).[21] When the *sattva* component is overwhelmed by *tamas*, the human tends to be unlawful, ignorant, attached, and weak (*tad eva tamasānuviddham adharmā-jñānāvairāgyānaiśvaryopagaṁ bhavati*).

As the veil of confusion is removed and the (primarily sattvic) mind is influenced exclusively by *rajas*, it is prone to dharma, knowledge (*jñāna*), detachment (*vairāgya*) and power (*aiśvarya*). Vyāsa then proceeds to describe the final stages of mind purification on the road of yoga. When the impact of any trace of *rajas* is removed, the mind abides in its own nature (*sva-rūpa-pratiṣṭhaṁ*). Thus, Vyāsa considers possible the purity of *sattva*, a condition where the incessant contradiction of the three *guṇas* ceases, a pre-*kaivalya* state. When the *sattva* is pure, it conceives and comprehends the infinite difference between itself and the pure subject (purusha). Vyāsa insists that there is a sediment of impurity in the condition of pure *sattva*, a condition in which the ultimate discriminating insight (*viveka-khyāti*) emerges; for the *sattva* is, after all, a *guṇa*. Once the *guṇa*-made mind is totally dropped, and the *guṇas* break down and cease like stones rolling down a mountain slope, final release (*kaivalya*) is effected.

Since Patañjali's conception of yoga in YS 1.2–16 does not refer to the theory of the *guṇas* at all, we may ask about the reason for Vyāsa's emphatic exposition of YS 1.2 in terms of the *guṇa* theory. Why does Vyāsa focus his attention on this aspect of the stilling of the mind activities? Most likely, in this context Vyāsa heeds the import of Patañjali's very last sutra (4.34); in this sutra Patañjali equates liberation (*kaivalya*) with the dissolution of the *guṇas* into their source. It reads thus: "The reabsorption of the *guṇas*, devoid of the object of purusha, is *kaivalya*; or the establishment of the power of consciousness in its own form."[22]

Thus Vyāsa connects YS 1.2 with YS 4.34, a powerful connection which gives coherence and integration to the entire text. Obviously, Vyāsa's connection of YS 1.2 and YS 4.34 lends the *Yogasūtra* an enhanced sense of coherence and unity attractive to its exegetes. And indeed, all the commentators follow this connection. Thus the Classical Scholars (Vācaspati, Vijñanabhikṣu, the author of the *Vivaraṇa*) dwell on the theory of the *guṇas* in their interpretation of YS 1.2.

Vyāsa's interpretation of YS 1.2 is commensurate with some of the more important of Patañjali's sutras. Thus, for example, the movement to liberation as the growing dominance of *sattva* over the other two *guṇas* up to their virtual disappearance is suggested in Patañjali's view of suffering (YS 2.15); *duḥkha* is produced (among other things) by the (incessant) strife of the *guṇas* (*guṇa-virodha*). Hence the description of the diminishing power of *rajas* and *tamas* implies the gradual alleviation of suffering.

The connection between purity of mind and its imminent disappearance is made in the important statement, YS 3.55. YS 3.55 is the last sutra of the Vibhūti-Pāda, the third section of the *Yogasūtra*. Dasgupta considers YS 3.55 the last one in the original composition of the *Yogasūtra*; the fourth Pāda—he thinks—is a late addition. The theme of YS 3.55—the purity of *sattva*—is similar to Vyāsa's interpretation of YS 1.2, although the proposition laid down in YS 3.55 is also different. YS 3.55 defines *kaivalya* as the condition of *sameness* of *sattva* purity and the purity of purusha (*sattva-puruṣayoḥ śuddhi-sāmye kaivalyam iti*). This is a most puzzling statement, since *sattva* is a segment of objective existence (prakriti) and purusha is "infinitely (*atyanta*) different." However, in his *bhāṣya* on this sutra, Vyāsa recapitulates the main imagery of purification within the *guṇa* theory and terminology, which he further connects to the theory of karma and the *kleśas*.

Vyāsa's emphasis in YSBh 3.55 is on the power of correct knowledge. In reality, he says, ignorance is dispelled solely by knowledge (*paramārthatas tu jñānād adarśanaṁ nivarttate*). When misconception disappears, would-be *kleśas* do not emerge (*tasmin nivṛtte na santy uttare kleśāḥ*). Once the *kleśas* do not exist, karma no longer fructifies (*kleśābhavāt karma-vipākābhāvaḥ*). Then, in this condition, having fulfilled their task, they stand no more for purusha to see them. This is the isolation of purusha, stainless, alone, and the light of its own nature.[23]

While untying the knot of existence and thus returning to primordial peace and silence is produced by the loosening of the *guṇas*, the ultimate cognitive attainment is the separation of prakriti and purusha. The relationship between purusha and prakriti is somewhat enigmatic. Although prakriti, objectivity ("nature"), is real, it nevertheless "exists for another," which is the purusha. Prakriti, says Iśvarakṛṣṇa, acts for the release of purusha—which is thus an action for the other's benefit—as if for its own (prakriti's) sake (*prati-puruṣa-vimokṣārthaṁ svārtha iva parārtha āraṁbhaḥ*).[24]

In the Sāṅkhyakārikā, there are several illustrations of this "altruistic" action of the unconscious prakriti towards pure consciousness, the purusha. Milk, which is unconscious (like prakriti), acts for the sake of the calf's growth (*vatsa-vivṛddhi-nimittaṁ kṣīrasya yathā pravṛttir ajñasya*).[25] The world moves in action for the cessation of desire (*autsukya-nivṛtty-arthaṁ yathā kriyāsu pravartate lokaḥ*).[26] Thus, as the purpose of prakriti is fulfilled, it (she) ceases to be active, like a dancer after having been seen by an audience.[27] The definition of the purusha as that which exists for his own sake (*svārtha*) is contrasted with that of the feminine prakriti which wants to be seen. The following *kārikā* of Iśvarakṛṣṇa gives expression to the female's orientation; I think, says the author, that nothing equals the tenderness of prakriti, as she says (at the end of her task): "I was seen," and then shows herself no more to the purusha (*prakṛteḥ sukumārataraṁ na kiṁcid astīti me matir bhavati / yā dṛṣṭāsmīti punar nadarśanam upaiti puruṣasya*).[28] Interestingly, as prakriti recognizes the fact that she has finally been seen, the purusha (simultaneously) sees prakriti, "(peacefully) resting in his own nature, like a spectator."[29] This matter of fact, mutual acknowledgment (or recognition) of the primordial couple (purusha and prakriti) is the climax of the Sāṅkhya story told by Iśvarakṛṣṇa. It is indeed paradoxical, as this mutual recognition is not a beginning of relationship but its very end. It is concomitantly contact and disjunction, a complex, pregnant, crucial moment in the history of existence. The reciprocal, too-delicate-to-occur touch of the eye, contact/nocontact of purusha and prakriti, deserves and demands poetry such as Kalidāsa's. Thus he writes of Śiva's awakening to Pārvati's presence:

> He was a little,
> just a little,
> shaken, like the ocean
> when the moon first rises.[30]

However, this kind of attraction—no more than recognition—at the moment of divorce is—in the case of prakriti and purusha—even more subtle than the touch of moon and ocean.

This peaceful divorce will be the end of creation, and (so) its description in SK 66 is worth full quotation: "I have seen her!" says the Indifferent One (purusha). "I have been seen!" says the other (she, prakriti) and becomes silent. And though they are still in sight of each other, there is no more point for creation."[31]

The separation of purusha and prakriti is the end of creation and the world as we know it. It means the "aloneness" (*kaivalya*) of the purusha, his ultimate fulfillment in self-sufficiency. In YS 3.35[32] Patañjali focuses on "existence for one's own sake" and "existence for another's sake" as the respective characteristics of purusha and prakriti. Meditation applied to the difference between *sattva* and purusha produces "knowledge of purusha" (*puruṣa-jñāna*). YS 3.35 suggests a central theme of the Sāṅkhya theory of liberation, namely, that experience itself (*bhoga*) is a symptom of noisy, samsaric existence. It asserts that experience is (unfortunate) nondistinction between *sattva* and purusha, two apparently slightly similar "entities" but radically, infinitely different, since *sattva* "exists for another" (*parārthatvāt*). Thus analysis of existence disintegrates experience itself. Indeed, this is a most difficult idea to accept for all who desire to live on, whether Seeker, Bodily Practitioner, Philosopher, Ultimate Insider, or Observers' Observer.

Patañjali's conceptualization of liberation includes a major classification of two kinds of silence: *sa-bīja-samādhi* is silence charged with an object; *nir-bīja-samādhi* is silence without an object. When the first—pregnant, fertile—type of silence is hushed, the second one, abysmal silence "without an object," emerges. Patañjali ponders the two kinds of silence in YS 1.51; the condition of silence (*samādhi*) without object emerges as the initial silence, charged with an object (*sa-bīja-samādhi*), is stilled by virtue of the cessation of all mind activities (including the *saṁskāras*) (*tasyāpi nirodhe sarva-nirodhān nir-bīja-samādhiḥ*). Vyāsa considers the more abysmal silence as the condition of liberation: "when the mind ceases to function, purusha gets isolated in Himself, and that is why He is then called pure and liberated."[33] In YS 3.8 Patañjali again explicates the difference between the two kinds of silence. The first kind, charged with an object, consists of the three modes of concentration, or meditation, as these apply to objects. The three types of meditation are *dhāraṇā*, *dhyāna*, and *samādhi*, defined respectively in YS 3.1,[34] YS 3.2[35] and YS 3.3. In YS 3.8 Patañjali classifies this silence as more external than the higher, denser silence (*samādhi*) which is "objectless silence" (*tad api bahir-aṅgaṁ nir-bījasya*).

It is not impossible to imagine the ground for the connection made by Patañjali of the two silences with Sāṅkhya metaphysics. The more obscure silence seems to "structurally" resemble the condition of the motionless, turned-upon-himself purusha in the condition of *kaivalya*. The silence charged with objects corresponds with an image of purusha that is more "involved," connected, not alone. Liberation is silence within silence, enduring and secure. As the silence charged with an object negates noisy existence beyond the boundaries of the yoga universe, so the objectless silence negates the subtle and disembodied noise of the first silence.

Thus the yogin's silence is interpreted by Patañjali as commensurate with negation and disintegration. Imagery of disintegration, discrimination, and separation is central to his character as a Sāṅkhya philosopher. Integration, combination, mixture are symptoms of life in *saṁsāra*. The yogin's postdecomposition silence is the essence of his otherness. This is a particularly difficult otherness to meet, as it is self-contained, whole and hard to approach.

One of the more direct references to "silence" in Patañjali's conceptualization of the yoga universe is the description of discrimination and disintegration in relation to the domain of language. In YS 1.42 and YS 3.17 Patañjali suggests that the three dimensions of speech—word (*śabda*), object (*artha*), and idea (*pratyaya*)—can and should be separated. As in the case of purusha and prakriti, the combination, association, and mixture of these three distinct dimensions in the process of thinking and speech constitutes an inferior state of mind.

Vācaspati elaborates on this point in his exposition of YS (and YSBh) 1.42: "Thus in ordinary life it is evident that, although word and intended object and idea are distinct, in the process of knowing they are not distinguished."[36] Such a condition of impure silence (*samādhi*) accompanied by words (*sa-vitarka*) is evidently the most inferior of the four silences described in YS 1.42–45.[37] Vācaspati says that experts (*parīkṣaka*) can see—by the method of *anvaya-vyatireka*[38]—that the nature of word, object, and idea is radically different; "a word which is nothing but a mutation of sound has such properties as high (pitch)."[39] Objects have other properties, and are in their nature insensate, contoured, and so forth (*jaḍatva-mūrtatvādayaḥ*). Vācaspati refers to the use of nouns without distinguishing word, object, and idea as empty cognition (*vikalpa*), in accordance with the sutra (*gaur ity upāttayoḥ śabdārthayor jñānābheda-vikalpaḥ*).[40] Similarly in YS 3.17, Patañjali refers to "unlawful mixture" (*saṅkara*) of word, object, and idea as due to their mutual superimposition (*adhyāsa*). Meditation (*saṁyama*) on the distinction between the three dimensions of speech produces "knowledge of the sounds of all creatures" (*śabdārtha-prayayānām itaretarādhyāsāt saṅkaras tat-pravibhāga-saṁyamāt sarva-bhūta-ruta-jñānam*). In YS 1.42 and YS 3.17 Patañjali apparently envisions a condition of relative silence, wherein speech disappears. The ensuing silence is of a higher level of existence than the previous, noisy one. The disintegration of speech and the purification of mind, ridding it of its conventional verbalizations, is another aspect of the conceptualization of the yogin's deathly silence according to the *Yogasūtra*.

The yogin's dark silence is a primary datum of the *Yogasūtra*, inducing anxiety and concern, mingled with the desire to live on and on. Patañjali, like others, can hardly bear the burden of the yogin's silence. But equally, he longs for this very silence, the end of creation. Within this tension, Patañjali conceptualizes silence, changing it in the process of exposition, and lives on.

How do the Seekers, Ultimate Insiders, Mere Philologists, Complacent Outsiders, Bodily Practitioners, and Observers' Observers interpret liberation and silence? For the Complacent Outsider, the Mere Philologist, and the Universal Philosopher, this is not a significant question. The Complacent Outsider rejects the foundation of the question, since for him or her—by definition—yoga leads to hallucination. The Mere Philologist as well as the Classical Scholars are deliberately out of touch with the reality of yoga, and exclusively engaged with the text.

For the Seeker, the disappearance of experience is particularly difficult to accept. Is not such disappearance a kind of death? R. Mehta finds a brilliant solution for the integration of life and death: "And what is Yoga but an experience of the fullness of life? Experience of the fullness of life demands an act of dying from moment to moment, for it is in death that life finds its fulfilment. To know how to live, and therefore to know how to die—this is the supreme message of yoga and is the true elixir of life" (p. 452).

The Bodily Practitioner is also embarrassed by the cessation of experience.

Reaching the last sutra, YS 4.34, B. K. S. Iyengar confuses the obvious technical meaning of *puruṣārtha* in YS 4.34, and takes it instead to be the human purpose in life, thus realigning the text with his pursuit.[41]

Vivekananda retains a vague trace of technical, scholarly attitudes when facing the end of Patañjali's *Yogasūtra*. Apparently alarmed by impending isolation, he falls back onto the image of the Mother; thus sweetness and motherhood prevail in Vivekananda's exposition of final dissolution. Indeed, on the verge of death, silence, and dissolution, Vivekananda seems to forget the nature of unconscious objectivity which is prakriti, and he invokes the image of the Mother; an unselfish, untiring woman, who cares for her children:

> Nature's task is done, this unselfish task which our sweet nurse, nature, had imposed upon herself. She gently took the self-forgetting soul by the hand, as it were, and showed him all the experiences in the universe, all manifestations, bringing him higher and higher through various bodies, till his lost glory came back, and he remembered his own nature. Then the kind mother went back the same way she came, for others who also have lost their way in the trackless desert of life. And thus is she working, without beginning and without end. And thus through pleasure and pain, through good and evil, the infinite river of souls is flowing into the ocean of perfection, of self-realization.[42]

Vivekananda's deep, sentimental voice does not suit G. Feuerstein, who wishes to stay calm, striving to neutralize any excessive emotionality at the end. A note of denial can be heard in his concluding remarks. In truth, he seems to say, the most dramatic climax in the narrative is not a real event at all: "Throughout the ups and downs in the life of the *yogin*, no change took place on the level of the Self. What seemed like an unsurpassed achievement from the perspective of the finite consciousness, is an absolute nonevent from the Self's viewpoint" (p. 145).

Stooping over the abyss of final dissolution, irreversible separation of purusha and prakriti, the liberating divorce of the primordial couple, I. K. Taimni, an Ultimate Insider, emits a cry of doubt and revolt:

> Then again, from the literal meaning of *Kaivalya* many people are led to imagine that it is a state of consciousness in which the *Purusha* is completely isolated from all others and lives alone in solitary grandeur like a man sitting on the peak of a mountain. Such a state, if it did exist, would be a horror and not a consummation of bliss.[43]

Indeed, Taimni cannot accept the literal import of YS 4.34. Nowhere else in his entire commentary on the *Yogasūtra* is he so apologetic and confused. He says in the beginning that "we now come to the last sutra which defines and sums up the ultimate state of Enlightenment which is called *Kaivalya*." Subsequently he negates his own literal translation of the sutra: "It should be noted that this is not a description of the content of Consciousness in the state of *Kaivalya*."[44] He then expresses doubt whether anyone can understand *kaivalya* at all: "[No] one living in the world of the unreal can understand or describe the Reality of which the *Yogi* becomes aware on attaining *Kaivalya*."[45] Does the Ultimate Insider concede here, at the end, his self-understanding as located in *saṁsāra*? Full of doubts in the face of Patañjali's clear-cut definition of the state of liberation as deathly silence, when the *guṇas* cease to act and humankind falls apart, the Ultimate Insider converts from Sāṅkhya Yoga to Advaita-Vedānta, as we watch:

> The idea of isolation implied in Kaivalya is to be interpreted in relation to Prakṛti from which the Puruṣa is isolated. This isolation frees him from all the limitations which are inherent in being involved in matter in a state of Avidyā, but leads him, on the other hand, to the closest possible unification with Consciousness in all its manifestations. Complete isolation from Prakriti means complete unification with Consciousness or Reality, because it is matter which divides the different units of consciousness, and in the world of Reality we are all one.[46]

The tensions in this curious confession of conversion from Sāṅkhya to Advaita are obvious. Isolation leads one to the "closest possible unification with Consciousness," and then this same isolation from prakriti (now "complete") means "complete unification with Consciousness." Indeed, Taimni's predicament is immense. He knows well, of course, that Sāṅkhya-Yoga teaches the plurality of purusha*s* (*puruṣa-bahutva*),[47] and that in Sāṅkhya and Yoga there is nothing like a single consciousness beyond this plurality.

The core of Patañjali's encounter with the dying yogin is the philosopher's recognition of silence as the essence of the yogin's otherness. Yet, in the process of explaining, digesting, expounding, and assimilating silence, the yogin's otherness and silence fade away. Nevertheless, silence also remains fresh (as it were), vibrating under cover of Sāṅkhya interpretation, a conceptualization particularly compatible with a view of silence as an implicit default.[48] Many courageous minds falter in contemplating this text, which is but a secondary verbalization of silence. Vivekananda seeks a soothing mother, B. K. S. Iyengar wants fulfilment of all human purposes and only then silence, R. Mehta wishes for life free of projections, for metaphoric dying from moment to moment, in the eternal present, and Taimni wants bliss. Indeed, Taimni's conversion together with the wishes and aspirations of the others sheds light on a central feature of Patañjali's character. As a Sāṅkhya philosopher, he resists the allure of unity and unification, of merging with the One Absolute, and he is not attached to bliss. Patañjali's is an utterly negative conception of life, not in value but cognitively. For indeed, there is nothing beyond disintegration, decomposition, separation, and loosening of all ties and knots. Noises recoil, fall apart and disappear before effective, perspicacious analysis; the rest is silence.

6

The Dying Yogin's Challenge; Homelessness and Truth

Silence and understanding are homeless; they have no precise location. According to Sāṅkhya, true knowledge is extremely paradoxical; it must exist but cannot be situated, since the mind, obviously, cannot contain or sustain it. Silence seems similarly ungrounded. Both knowledge and silence imply cessation, elimination, abnegation. Pātañjala Yoga is preoccupied with this condition, *samādhi*, which "carries truth."

Indeed, the yogin's stark otherness is humanized in the *Yogasūtra* by its preoccupation with truth and knowledge. After all, the naked yogin is divested of almost all human traits. Thus, in the scholarly jargon, he "transcends the human condition." He is not subject to the law of gravitation, he does not need food and drink, he renounces family, friends, and offspring; he does not respond to immediate sensory reality, he knows the moment of his death, seeing, as if with his own eyes, his future and past. Moreover, the yogin resists the most powerful predispositions of thought and emotion allegedly inherent in the human condition. The yogin does not say "I" and "me"; he does not even wish to live on, and is thus, indeed, different from the rest of humankind. Thus Patañjali conceives the yogin and his world in the *Yogasūtra*; thus he makes sense of the yogin's terrible silence.

But Patañjali's main point is not consummated in the explanation of the yoga universe, silence, and wonders, for he is relentless in proposing that there is *truth* in the yogin's silence, or that this silence *is* truth. Such an assertion coming from a sober and sophisticated mind is disturbing. Indeed, by making use of the concept of truth in reference to the yoga universe, Patañjali humanizes the yogin and posits his life as disconcertingly relevant. It is easy (and rational) to dismiss the yogin's pathological silence if it is part of a collection of dumb fakir techniques; it is more difficult if the yogin's silence is associated with "truth."

The connection of enlightenment and silence is one of the central themes in Patañjali's conceptualization of the yoga universe. The road to the silence of *samādhi* is also the road to understanding. Harsh discipline is rewarded, according to YS 2.28: "From the application of the eight practices of yoga, as the contaminations are reduced, there emerges light of knowledge (*jñāna-dīpti*), up to the ultimate discrimination (between subject and object)."[1] *Samādhi*, yogic silence, upholds cosmic truth (*ṛtaṁ-bharā*).[2] By virtue of mastering yogic meditation the light of knowledge dawns (*taj-jayāt prajñālokaḥ*).[3] *Samādhi* is the condition in which things are seen "as they are" (*yathā-bhūta*).[4] *Samādhi* is the condition in which the highest knowledge, *puruṣa-jñāna*, emerges.[5] Indeed, predominant among the unusual experiences and feats described in the *Yogasūtra* are attainments of cognition and knowledge. Knowledge of the universe,[6] of anatomy,[7] astronomy[8] emerges in a silence charged with objects (*sa-bīja-samādhi*).

The description and corroboration of silence as charged with understanding and illumination, coexisting with healthy and productive homelessness, is pivotal to the *Yogasūtra*. All of a sudden, Patañjali penetrates the yogin's thick otherness, mitigating the burden of silence with light. Silence charged with truth and understanding becomes a challenge; an audience emerges, eager to listen. Herein is the meaning of the *Yogasūtra*, providing an occasion for thought and reflection on the dying yogin who, though utterly silent, communicates in accordance with Patañjali's deepest need and interest. Patañjali includes the yogin within the ken of humanity, transforming dumb into enlightened and eloquent silence.

Understanding or enlightenment, however, are neither reasoning nor well-established, traditional knowledge nor even correct perception. As suggested above, Patañjali emphatically rejects normal consciousness and its operation as relevant measures of the yogin's truth.[9] In the technical and conventional terminology, the normal functions of the body and mind are not standards of truth (*pramāṇa*). Thus, people who venture to approach the yoga universe and stay normal and intact are not deemed equal to the task by Patañjali. Universal Philosophers, Complacent Outsiders, Bodily Practitioners, Seekers, Mere Philologists, and even Ultimate Insiders who wish to compromise the yogin's truth with science cannot have access to the truth of yoga. Heavier, deeper, more resonant silence is needed in order to approach the yogin's. Patañjali is obsessed with the hierarchy of silences, a taxonomy of different qualities of silence according to type of object, measure of purity of mind. And yet, Patañjali himself, expounding, explaining, defining, reasoning, and verbalizing, seems to err similarly in approaching the yogin's silence. Patañjali is most definitely normal, balanced, verbal. Is he then a Classical Scholar like Vyāsa and Vācaspati? Is he a Seeker like Yeats and Eliade? In a sense, he is like the others. He is, however, distinctly and intensely pained and disturbed by the prospect of truth which he discerns but which he does not—and cannot—share. This is perhaps the pain behind the composition of the *Yogasūtra*; not historically, of course, but hermeneutically. In a sense, therefore, by virtue of his discerning pain, Patañjali earns access to the yogin's silence.

The dissonance vibrating throughout the *Yogasūtra* consists of two parallel components: acknowledgment of the deficiency of the human mind and constitution (thus the need for its "transcendence") along with the recognition of (inhuman) silence in which there is revelation of truth.

There is perhaps no truth costlier than the yogin's. In Pātañjala Yoga, however, the expense is worth paying; alleviation of illusion and suffering follow upon the realization of truth. While suffering may be alleviated by alternative means, illusion is intractable; hence the deathly attraction of the yogin's claim to live in truth, to discover truth by silence. The yogin's silence is painful to a humanity that wishes growth of consciousness and truth, if it refuses to entertain an inhuman ("divine") condition of truth. Patañjali is thus a representative of sane though threatened humanity, sensing truth potential in the dying yogin's disembodiment and calm. Yet even the perspicacious Patañjali remains as he is: a Sāṅkhya philosopher.

The possibility of homeless understanding troubles the scholar's mind; Is my knowledge, too, he asks himself, void and futile, like that of Vyāsa's impotent husband's promise to his wife? Vyāsa tells of a woman whose sister has children, and the simple-minded woman also wants an offspring; "My dear husband, why don't I have children too?" "I will give you a child when I am dead" (*mṛtas te 'ham apatyam utpādayiṣyāmi*), says the husband, according to Vyāsa's *bhāṣya* on YS 2.24.[10] The obvious meaning is that the impotent husband will be in the future, when he is dead, still more impotent and ineffectual than at present. There is no way, he seems to be saying to his wife, that I will beget a child with you, now or ever.

None of the commentators and scholars refer in detail to the story of the impotent husband. However, the story is not as simple as it may seem. We must ask: Who is the impotent husband in the reality which the story is said to illustrate? I believe it is Vyāsa himself (or, indeed, Patañjali); a scholar who fails to reach *mokṣa*, though he "knows." Is not the story of the impotent husband who pretends to be in charge and control of his simple wife through empty, evasive verbiage—a suggestive allegory of Vyāsa's (and Patañjali's) impotence over the impenetrability of the truth embedded in inaccessible yogic silence?

The virtual opponent (*pūrva-pakṣin*) invoked by Vyāsa in his commentary on YS 2.24 raises a genuine question. If knowledge existing here does not produce the cessation of the mind (*citta-nivṛtti*), how will it deliver once it does not exist (when one is dead)?[11] The opponent's point focuses on the impotence of Sāṅkhya metaphysics—once known—to really change one's mind. Indeed, Vyāsa does not fully meet the challenge leveled at him by the *pūrva-pakṣin*. Vyāsa's answer is that liberation consists precisely in the cessation of the mind (*buddhi-nivṛttir eva mokṣaḥ*), and that this cessation occurs by the disappearance of the cause of misconception (*adarśana-kāraṇābhāvād buddhi-nivṛttiḥ*). Vyāsa adds that correct vision of reality (*darśana*) stops or sublates misconception (*adarśana*) which is the cause of bondage (*tac cādarśanaṁ bandha-kāraṇaṁ darśanān nivarttate*).

But what is the scholar's knowledge? What is its potency? This knowledge and power is, certainly, Sāṅkhya metaphysics, the core of Vyāsa's and Patañjali's identity. But it is apparently insufficient to produce silence and liberation, so Vyāsa's opponent says. In fact, Vyāsa does answer this allegation; he says that correct vision *does* sublate incorrect vision (*adarśanaṁ bandha-kāraṇaṁ darśanān nivarttate*). But most significantly, he does not say that the scholar's knowledge brings about the cessation of mind (*citta-nivṛtti*). And this seems a universal difficulty shared by Patañjali, Vyāsa, other Classical Scholars, Seekers, Mere Philologists, Universal Philosophers, Ultimate Insiders, and all the rest; mind can hardly negate itself. According to Patañjali, silence follows a sustained, relentless negation of noise up to the dissolution of mind.

Doomed to noise, we yet deduce that the rest is silence (*maunaṁ śeṣam*); as noise to silence, so *mokṣa* to *saṁsāra*; thus the rest is *mokṣa* (*śeṣo mokṣaḥ*). Truth abides in an almost unattainable silence; liberation, it seems, is to be sought there as well.

The Essential Yogasūtra*;*
An Exercise in Rereading as Rewriting

The narrative of the composition of the *Yogasūtra* is that of an encounter. This book argues that the act of reading the *Yogasūtra* is, at its fullest, a reenactment of that originary encounter with the myth of the dying yogin. This section attempts to suggest the textual representation of that reenactment, marking some of its sutras as essential and some as secondary in terms of their position relative to the yogic experience. The essential *Yogasūtra* is infused by the flavor of the encounter with the exercising yogins, often immersed in various degrees of silence and absorption. Some of them seem beyond speech; others are more responsive to and productive of verbal output. Some are devoted to Īśvara; some, apparently very calm, seem to concentrate on sense objects. They appear tranquil, content, not unfriendly, compassionate. They are celibates seated in yogic postures, practicing breathing exercises, speaking little. In meditation they appear speechless. Mediating this experience for his readers, Patañjali's basic inspiration is the association of yogic meditation with Sāṅkhya sensibilities, and thus the interpretation of yogic silence in Sāṅkhya vocabulary.

The essential *Yogasūtra* is Patañjali's direct, primary processing of his encounter with the silent yogins. Thus distinguishing between Patañjali (the philosopher) and the silent yogin, I suggest a distinction between an essential and a secondary *Yogasūtra*. The secondary *Yogasūtra* expresses Patañjali's own universe of Sāṅkhya philosophy and religious convictions. It is relatively independent of the silent yogin's presence. While my distinction between essential and secondary *Yogasūtra* is not and cannot be clear-cut, it is—I believe—a useful technique for the explication of the *Yogasūtra*.

This rereading as rewriting posits three levels of the *Yogasūtra*: an immediate verbal response, the subsequent mediated response, and irrelevant considerations, adhering to a logic of encounter and observation and attempting to distinguish between the encounter with the dying yogin and theoretical considerations independent of this encounter. This chapter is an attempt to retrieve and revive Patañjali's original perception, sifting statements related and unrelated to the primary perception.

Almost two-thirds of the *Yogasūtra* is inspired by Patañjali's mythical encounter. The contradictions and tensions between the philosopher's world and the yogin's are audible in the text's four voices: an intellectual; a Sāṅkhya philosopher; one familiar with yogic practice; a witness of yogic experience. Patañjali's unequivocal thrust is the need for disintegration of experience. Within the spectacle of disintegration as silencing, yogic experiences are partial dissolutions and disconnections; the mind is dissociated from the body, thus facilitating entrance into other bodies. This severed identification with the body brings about experiences of levitation, overcoming of hunger and thirst, invisibility. These are conveyed through two primary vehicles, vision and voice. As I have suggested throughout this book in its main thesis, the differences between Patañjali and the silent yogin are central to understanding their encounter. In the poetic condensation of the *Yogasūtra,* its Sāṅkhya interpretation is nourished, stimulated, intrigued, and provoked by silence, leaving a forceful impression of the powerful yet distant yogin.

A book that has attempted to hear and to articulate yogic silence refuses to end, hence this afterword follows my epilogue in yet another attempt to corral the unsaid space in the sutras within textual confines. The very genre of the sutra is poetic in density and condensation, and leads me towards a poetics of the *Yogasūtra,* which could help readers, translators, and interpreters retain some of the vital complexity of the original text. My strategy aims at a translation that is not definitive but allows the different voices of the text to echo and engage.

To that end I offer here a sample rewriting of the sutras, in a new order. My division into essential sutras (those closest to the experience of the dying yogin) and secondary ones (those closer to the experience of the philosopher engaged with the dying yogin) is meant to suggest a reading strategy, not a taxonomy. The translations I propose are relatively free and sometimes state the implications of the sutras, as I see them, rather than restating their words and phrases mechanically. Their intertextual resonances may help make yogic silence somewhat more audible.

The Essential Yogasūtra

Samādhi-Pāda

1.1 *atha yogānuśāsanam*

1.1.1 Now the explanation of yoga.

1.1.2 Now the explanation of the yogin's world (in terms of Sāṅkhya).

1.1.3 Now the explanation of the inexplicable silence of the yogin immersed in innerness, in terms of disintegration of subject (purusha) and object (prakriti).
1.1.4 Now the explanation of silence.

1.2 *yogaś citta-vṛtti-nirodhaḥ*
1.2.1 Yoga is the cessation of mind activities.
1.2.2 Yoga is the end of any mind activity.
1.2.3 Due to separation of subject and object, every combination stops.
1.2.4 Yoga is the icy silence of postdisintegration.

1.3 *tadā draṣṭuḥ sva-rūpe 'vasthānam*
1.3.1 Then the seer abides in his own form.
1.3.2 At this moment (of liberation), the seer exists in his own nature.
1.3.3 In the condition of liberation, there is no more contact between the light of the consciousness and any objective otherness.
1.3.4 Liberated, the seer is alone, and the seen as well.
1.3.5 At the moment of release and icy silence, the light of consciousness turns upon itself.
1.3.5 Absolutely silent and motionless, the most adept yogins reach the condition of *kaivalya*.

1.4 *vṛtti-sārupyam itaratra*
1.4.1 Otherwise, the form of the mind activities.
1.4.2 In conditions other than that, the seer is (as it were) identical with his mind activities.
1.4.3 In the prerelease state, the seer is not separated from the seen.
1.4.4 In formal life, the subject pours out its light outside of itself.
1.4.5 Ordinary life is the ongoing process of the subject in contact with objects.
1.4.6 Suffering is grounded in the ongoing contact of subject and object.
1.4.7 Ordinary people identify themselves with objects they contact.

1.5 *vṛttayaḥ pañcatayyaḥ kliṣṭākliṣṭāḥ*
1.5.1 The mind fluctuations are fivefold, painful and nonpainful.
1.5.2 Mind activities are painful or unpainful.
1.5.3 The motions of the mind—whether painful or unpainful—are to be abolished.

1.6 *pramāṇa-viparyaya-vikalpa-nidrā-smṛtayaḥ*
1.6.1 The motions of the mind are the following: correct mode of normal cognition, wrong mode of normal cognition, merely verbal fluctuation, mind activities during sleep, memory.

1.6.2 Correct modes of normal cognition are lumped together with other—less respectable—modes as mind activities to be abolished.

1.6.3 Mind activities of many kinds are considered noises of mind, and are to be silenced.

1.7 *pratyakṣānumānāgamāḥ pramāṇāni*

1.7.1 The means of knowledge are perception, reasoning, and trustworthy, traditional knowledge.

1.7.2 The correct sources of cognition are perception, reasoning, and reliable tradition.

1.7.3 The action of senses, thinking, and tradition are the correct normal mind activities (sources of right knowledge).

1.7.4 Normal functions of the mind—however venerated as valid, right means of knowledge—are to be silenced along with other, less venerated ones.

1.8 *viparyayo mithyā-jñānam a-tad-rūpa-pratiṣṭham*

1.8.1 False conception is incorrect knowledge based on an unreal form (of the object).

1.8.2 Wrong cognition is representation of a thing not as it is in reality.

1.8.3 Mind activities associated with wrong knowledge involve distorted representation of things.

1.8.4 Mind activities leading to wrong cognition are to be abolished (silenced), as are mind activities leading to correct cognition.

1.9 *śabda-jñānānupātī vastu-śūnyo vikalpaḥ*

1.9.1 *Vikalpa* is a cognition devoid of a real object, cognition which follows mere words.

1.9.2 Mind activities engaged in mere words, which do not correspond to things, are "empty cognition" (*vikalpa*).

1.10 *abhāva-pratyayālambanā vṛtti-nidrā*

1.10.1 Mind activities during sleep have nonexistence as their basis.

1.11 *anubhūta-viṣayāsaṁpramoṣaḥ smṛtiḥ*

1.11.1 Memory is the preservation of an object experienced in the past.

1.12 *abhyāsa-vairāgyābhyāṁ tan-nirodhaḥ*

1.12.1 The extinction of all the mind activities is carried out by exercise and detachment.

1.13 *tatra sthitau yatno 'bhyāsaḥ*
1.13.1 In this context, practice is an effort at stabilization.
1.13.2 Yogic effort aims at the maintenance of silence (the extinction of mind activities).
1.13.3 Yogic practice minimizes the fluctuations of mind and body.

1.14 *sa tu dīrgha-kāla-nairantarya-satkārāsevito dṛḍha-bhūmiḥ*
1.14.1 Yogic practice exercised for a long time, ceaselessly, and in earnest, becomes firmly grounded (well-established).

1.15 *dṛṣṭānuśrāvika-viṣaya-vitṛṣṇasya vaśī-kāra-saṁjñā vairāgyam*
1.15.1 Detachment is awareness of mastery of one free of attachment to things heard about and seen.
1.15.2 Observing dissociation from objects, the yogin feels powerful and free.
1.15.3 Detachment is independence and freedom.

1.16 *tat-paraṁ puruṣa-khyāter guṇa-vaitṛṣṇyam*
1.16.1 Ultimate detachment emerges from awareness of the pure subject. And (this detachment) signifies absence of thirst for the very action of the *guṇas*.
1.16.2 True vision of the pure subject (purusha) is a powerful cognition. It overcomes the lethal attraction for natural combinations and confusions.

1.17 *vitarka-vicārānandāsmitā-rūpānugamāt saṁprajñātaḥ*
1.17.1 By virtue of association with gross reasoning, abstract (subtle) thinking, feeling of joy, and sense of ego, there is yogic discipline and *samādhi* called "cognitive" (*saṁprajñāta*).
1.17.2 There are yogins absolutely empty and silent, and there are others seen to undergo processes of cognition, feeling.

1.18 *virāma-pratyayābhyāsa-pūrvaḥ saṁskāra-śeṣo 'nyaḥ*
1.18.1 The other (type of yoga *samādhi*) is preceded by exercises towards the cessation of verbalized mind activities, and is grounded in the remaining *saṁskāras*.

1.19 *bhāva-pratyayo videha-prakṛtilayānām*
1.19.1 For those bodiless yogins absorbed in prakriti there is existence in thought only.

1.20 *śraddhā-vīrya-smṛti-samādhi-prajñā-pūrvaka itareṣām*
1.20.1 Others reach that condition (of *asaṁprajñāta samādhi*) preceded by faith, power, memory, *samādhi*, and understanding.

1.21 *tīvra-saṁvegānām āsannaḥ*
1.21.1 For those relentless and determinate—ultimate (*asaṁprajñāta*) *samādhi* comes soon.

1.22 *mṛdu-madhyādhimātratvāt tato 'pi viśeṣaḥ*
1.22.1 Another relevant distinction among yogins concerns degrees of intensity; yogic efforts are mild, medium, or intense.

1.23 *Īśvara-praṇidhānād vā*
1.23.1 Or, by surrendering to *Īśvara.*
1.23.2 By contact with a "perfect being," deep silence comes into being.

1.29 *tataḥ pratyak-cetanādhigamo 'py antarāyābhāvaś ca*
1.29.1 Then there is direct perception of the inner self and absence of obstacles.
1.29.2 Surrender to the perfected being—Īśvara—brings about vision of true self and the yogin overcomes obstacles.
1.29.3 Meditative repetition of the syllable *oṁ* generates the yogin's self-understanding.

1.30 *vyādhi-styāna-saṁśaya-pramādālasyāvirati-bhrānti—darśanālabdha-bhūmikatvānavasthitatvāni citta-vikṣepās te 'ntarāyāḥ*
1.30.1 The obstacles are mind distractions (caused by) disease, idleness, doubt, intoxication, sloth, lack of detachment, incorrect vision, failure to attain the appropriate level of expertise, instability.

1.31 *duḥkha-daurmanasyāṅgam-ejayatvā-śvāsa-praśvāsā vikṣepa-sahabhuvaḥ*
1.31.1 Sorrow, dejection, trembling limbs, inhalation, and exhalation are associated with the distractions of the mind.

1.32 *tat-pratiṣedhārtham eka-tattvābhyāsaḥ*
1.32.1 For the restriction of these (distractions and obstacles) exercise (of concentration) over one entity (is recommended).

1.33 *maitrī-karuṇā-muditopekṣāṇāṁ sukha-duḥkha-puṇyāpuṇya-viṣayāṇāṁ bhavanātāś citta-prasādanam*
1.33.1 Well-being of mind emerges from exercising friendship toward (people who experience) pleasure, compassion toward (those who undergo) pain, joy over the pure, and equanimity toward vice.
1.33.2 Yogins are often seen to be friendly, compassionate, happy, and indifferent.

1.33.3 Ordinary people have natural feelings (such as envy) towards happy people, avoidance or pity (towards unhappy ones), wonder (or doubt) towards saintly persons, and rejection or criticism of evil ones. Yogins are different from ordinary people on account of their different attitudes to many kinds of people.

1.34 *pracchardana-vidhāraṇābhyāṁ vā prāṇasya*

1.34.1 Or by (controlled) exhalation and retention of breath (the yogin obtains well-being of mind).

1.35 *viṣayavatī vā pravṛttir utpannā manasaḥ sthiti-nibandhanī*

1.35.1 Or, there arises stability of mind accompanied by intense action on an object.

1.36 *viṣokā vā jyotiṣmatī*

1.36.1 Or, (an intense sense activity focused on an object) is effulgent and painless (bringing about well-being, stabilization of mind).

1.37 *vīta-rāga-viṣayaṁ vā cittam*

1.37.1 Or, the mind (is stabilized) and devoid of attachment to (any) object.

1.38 *svapna-nidrā-jñānālambanaṁ vā*

1.38.1 Or (the mind becomes stabilized) having support in knowledge obtained in sleep and dream.

1.39 *yathābhimata-dhyānād vā*

1.39.1 Or by meditation on any object according to one's desire.

1.40 *paramāṇu-paramamahattvānto 'sya vaśī-kāraḥ*

1.40.1 The yogin obtains mastery over the smallest particle and the greatest expansion.

1.41 *kṣīṇa-vṛtter abhijātasyeva maṇer grahītṛ-grahaṇa-grāhyeṣu tat-stha-tad-añjanatā samāpattiḥ*

1.41.1 For the mind whose activities (fluctuations) have been reduced, which is like a transparent jewel, there is a reflection of the object of identification, whether this is the subject, the means of contacting the object, or the object itself.

1.42 *tatra śabdārtha-jñāna-vikalpaiḥ saṁkīrṇāṁ savitarkā samāpattiḥ*

1.42.1 *samāpatti* with thought (is attained) where word, object, cognition, and empty cognition are mingled together.

1.42.2 In this state, as the mind is mixed up (and beclouded) by empty verbalization (consisting in mutual superimposition) of word, object, and idea, there is the condition of verbalized meditation (identification) (with the object of meditation).

1.42.3 Inner speech—like any other speech—implies combination of word, its reference, and the idea thereof. Such a combination results in noisy verbalization.

1.42.4 A silent mind, free of verbalization, emerges by analysis of speech followed by its disintegration.

1.42.4 Yogic meditative states accompanied with verbalization are inferior (noisy) in comparison with others.

1.43 *smṛti-pariśuddhau svarūpa-śūnyevārtha-mātra-nirbhāsā nirvitarkā*

1.43.1 (*samāpatti*) without thought (is attained) where memory is purified, the mind is, as it were, devoid of its own form, and the object alone shines forth.

1.43.2 In the purification of consciousness (of its verbalized, conventional associations), as the mind becomes void as it were of its own nature, the object (of meditation) alone shines forth. This condition is called *nirvitarka* (*samāpatti*).

1.43.3 Removal of the veil of verbalization is purification of mind. In this purified condition, the contact of the mind with its object carries the truth of the object.

1.43.4 Analysis of speech removes distorted perception.

1.43.5 Yogic analysis of speech creates silence.

1.44 *etayaiva savicārā nirvicārā ca sūkṣma-viṣayā vyākhyātā*

1.44.1 Thereby, (*samāpatti*) with reflection and without reflection, having subtle objects, are explained.

1.44.2 By this (paradigm of explanation brought forth in the two forgoing sutras, 1.42–43), the two conditions of the mind focused on subtle objects—*savicāra* and *nirvicāra samāpatti*—have also been explained.

1.44.3 Verbalization interferes with the meditative contact of the mind with its subtle objects. The analysis of speech according to its three functions (word, object, idea) purifies the mind of the noisy combination underlying any speech act.

1.45 *sūkṣma-viṣayatvaṁ cāliṅga-paryavasānam*

1.45.1 The subtle objects of meditation reach the subtlety of the object without signs (prakriti).

1.46 *tā eva sa-bījaḥ samādhiḥ*
1.46.1 These are states of *samādhi* focused on objects.
1.46.2 These (four conditions of identification with objects—*sa-vitarka, nir-vitarka, sa-vicāra, nir-vicāra*) are accompanied with consciousness of objects.
1.46.3 There are degrees of yogic silence. Four types of silence are silence rooted in objects.
1.46.4 Degree of verbalization and measure of grossness of objects (of meditation) determine the quality of yogic silence.

1.47 *nir-vicāra-vaiśāradye 'dhyātma-prasādaḥ*
1.47.1 In the lucidity of the *nir-vicāra* condition, graceful light flows from the inner self.
1.47.2 In the silence classified as *nir-vicāra*, the graceful sound of the inner self is heard.
1.47.3 Veils of visual and auditorial defects (darkness and noise, respectively) are removed in the state of meditation on supersubtle objects and beyond verbalization.

1.48 *ṛtaṁ-bharā tatra prajñā*
1.48.1 There, cognition is truth bearing.
1.48.2 In this condition consciousness carries truth.

1.49 *śrutānumāna-prajñābhyām anya-viṣayā viśeṣārthatvāt*
1.49.1 The cognition arising from the *nir-vicāra* meditative state (which "carries truth") is different from knowledge brought about by scripture and reasoning. This is due to the particular nature of the objects known in yogic meditation.

1.50 *taj-jaḥ saṁskāro 'nya-saṁskāra-pratibandhī*
1.50.1 The potent impressions produced by this (advanced state of *samādhi*) counteract other (past) impressions.
1.50.2 Yogic meditation is a powerful means of deconditioning (undoing the past).

1.51 *tasyāpi nirodhe sarva-nirodhān nir-bījaḥ samādhiḥ*
1.51.2 In the disappearance of the condition of *sa-bīja-samādhi* (along with the impressions created in this condition), by virtue of the extinction of all the impressions, there comes into being the condition of *samādhi*—without object.
1.51.3 There is a condition of "silence within silence."
1.51.4 Ultimate silence defies further classification of silence types.

Sādhana-Pāda

2.1 *tapaḥ-svādhyāyeśvara-praṇidhānāni kriyā-yogaḥ*

2.1.1 The "yoga of action" consists of heating practices (*tapas*), study of scripture, and surrender to Īśvara.

2.2 *samādhi-bhavanārthaḥ kleśa-tanū-karaṇārthaś ca*

2.2.1 The objects (of *kriyā* yoga) are bringing about *samādhi* and attenuating the roots of misery.

2.2.2 The goal (of *kriyā yoga*) is the production of *samādhi* and decrease of the power of inner tormenting predispositions (*kleśa*).

2.2.3 *Kriyā* yoga is a means for bringing about peace and silence.

2.10 *te pratiprasava-heyāḥ sūkṣmāḥ*

2.10.1 They (subtle, tormenting predispositions) are avoided by counteraction.

2.11 *dhyāna-heyās tad-vṛttayaḥ*

2.11.1 The mind activities resulting from these (predispositions) are avoided by meditation.

2.28 *yogāṅgānuṣṭhānād aśuddhi-kṣaye jñāna-dīptir āviveka-khyāteḥ*

2.28.1 Through the application of the eight practices of yoga, as the contaminations are reduced, the light of knowledge (intensifies) into the ultimate discrimination (between subject and object.

2.28.2 By the observance and practice of the means of yoga, in the reduction of impurities, the light of knowledge arises, up to the separation of subject and object.

2.29 *yama-niyamāsana-prāṇāyāma-pratyāhāra-dhāraṇā-dhyāna-samādhayo 'ṣṭāv aṅgāni*

2.29.1 Restrictions, observances, postures, breathing exercises and control, dissociation of the senses, concentration on one point, meditation, and meditative absorption are the eight limbs of yoga.

2.30 *ahiṁsā-satyāsteya-brahmacaryāparigrahā yamāḥ*

2.30.1 Nonviolence, truthfulness, abstention from theft, continence, and nonpossessiveness are the restrictions (*yama*).

2.31 *jāti-deśa-kāla-samayānavacchinnāḥ sarva-bhaumā mahā-vratam*

2.31.1 The commitment to (these restrictions) without differentiation concerning social group, place, time, and occasion is the great vow.

2.32 *śauca-saṅtoṣa-tapaḥ-svādhyāyeśvara-praṇidhānāni niyamāḥ*
2.32.1 Cleanliness, contentment, heating practices, study of scripture, and surrender to Īśvara are the observances (*niyama*).

2.33 *vitarka-bādhane pratipakṣa-bhāvanam*
2.33.1 For the restriction of improper thoughts, opposite-cultivation (is recommended).
2.33.2 For the restriction of mental noise, cultivation of silence (should be exercised).

2.34 *vitarkā hiṁsādayaḥ kṛta-kāritānumoditā lobha-krodha-moha-pūrvakā mṛdu-madhyādhimātrā duḥkhājñānānanta-phalā iti pratipakṣa-bhāvanam*
2.34.1 Cultivation of opposite is the following: "thoughts such as of injuring living creatures either done (by oneself), or being compelled (by another), or being recommended (by another) follow delusion, anger, and greed." Such thoughts have unending fruits such as ignorance and suffering of different degrees—mild, medium, and great.

2.35 *ahiṁsā-pratiṣṭhāyāṁ tat-saṁnidhau vaira-tyāgaḥ*
2.35.1 In the vicinity of the yogin well-established in *ahiṁsā*, violence ceases.

2.36 *satya-pratiṣṭhāyāṁ kriyā-phalāśrayatvam*
2.36.1 For the yogin well-grounded in truthfulness, the fruit resides in the action.
2.36.2 For the yogin established in truth, action bears its expected results.
2.36.3 The truthful yogin obtains (in his actions) anything he wishes for.
2.36.4 Yogic practice and observance produces experiences of power and achievement.

2.37 *asteya-pratiṣṭhāyāṁ sarva-ratnopasthānam*
2.37.1 For the yogin grounded in nonstealing, there is an abundance of jewels all around him.
2.37.2 Whatever the yogin renounces, he may receive in abundance.
2.37.3 Renunciation brings about experiences of power and control.

2.38 *brahmacarya-pratiṣṭhāyaṁ vīrya-lābhaḥ*
2.38.1 when firmly established in continence, vigor (is attained).
2.38.1 The yogin controlling his sexual drive is powerful.
2.38.2 Yogic control of sexual desire is associated with independence and power.

2.39 *aparigraha-sthairye janma-kathaṁtā-saṁbodhaḥ*
2.39 Stable in the condition of nonpossessiveness, the yogin becomes conscious of details concerning (previous) births.

2.40 *śaucāt svāṅga-jugupsā parair asaṁsargaḥ*
2.40.1 By (invasive) practices of yogic cleanliness, there arises aversion towards one's body and abstention of contact with others.

2.41 *sattva-śuddhi-saumanasyaikagryeṇḍriya-jayātma-darśana-yogyatvāni*
2.41.2 There emerge dispositions for purity of *sattva*, mental well-being, concentration, control of the senses, and perception of the self.

2.42 *saṁtoṣād anuttamaḥ sukha-lābhaḥ*
2.42.1 Through contentment, the attainment of supreme happiness.
2.42.2 From self-sufficiency (contentment) arises unsurpassed pleasure.

2.43 *kayeṇdriya-siddhir aśuddhi-kṣayāt tapasaḥ*
2.43.1 By virtue of the reduction of impurities due to heating practices of austerity, there comes into being perfection of senses and body.

2.44 *svādhyāyād iṣṭa-devatā-saṁprayogaḥ*
2.44.1 Study of scripture brings about communion with beloved deities.

2.45 *samādhi-siddhir Īśvara-praṇidhānāt*
2.45.1 From surrender to Īśvara there arises success in *samādhi.*
2.45.2 Total devotion to God is also a means of reaching absorption and silence.

2.46 *sthira-sukham āsanam*
2.46.1 Yogic posture is stable and comfortable.

2.47 *prayatna-śaithilyānanta-samāpattibhyām*
2.47.1 By relaxation of effort and meditation on the infinite (yogic posture is perfected).

2.48 *tato dvandvānabhighātaḥ*
From that (mastery of yogic posture) the yogin is not overwhelmed by the opposites.

2.49 *tasmin sati śvāsa-praśvāsayor gati-vicchedaḥ prāṇāyāmaḥ*
2.49.1 This being so, *prāṇāyāma*, which is the stoppage of inhalation and exhalation (is explained).

2.50 *bāhyābhyantara-stambha-vṛttir deśa-kāla-saṅkhyābhiḥ paridṛṣṭo dīrgha-sūkṣmaḥ*

2.50.1 (This *prāṇāyāma*) is an external, internal, and blocking action, distinguished by place, time, and number, and is subtle and long.

2.51 *bāhyābhyantara-viṣayākṣepī caturthaḥ*

2.51.1 The fourth *prāṇāyāma* goes beyond the range of external and internal.

2.52 *tataḥ kṣīyate prakāśāvaraṇam*

2.52.1 Then the veil on the (mind's) effulgence diminishes.

2.53 *dhāraṇāsu ca yogyatā manasaḥ*

2.53.1 And also there is readiness of the mind for concentration.

2.54 *sva-viṣayāsaṁprayoge citta-sva-rūpānukāra ivendriyāṇāṁ pratyāhāraḥ*

2.54.1 *pratyāhāra* is the state where the senses follow as it were the mind's own nature, as they are disconnected from their respective objects.

2.54.2 *pratyāhāra* is as though the senses were imitating the mind's essential form, in dissociating themselves from their objects.

2.54.3 In the condition of *pratyāhāra* the yogin cuts off his relationship with the world of the senses and enters into his own interior.

2.55 *tataḥ paramā vaśyateindriyāṇām*

2.55.1 Then there is ultimate control (mastery) over the senses.

Vibhūti-Pāda

3.1 *deśa-bandhaś cittasya dhāraṇā*

3.1.1 The fixation of the mind on one spot is *dhāraṇā.*

3.1.2 Concentration (*dhāraṇā*) is keeping the mind in (one) point.

3.2 *tatra pratyayaika-tanatā dhyānam*

3.2.1 In the condition of *dhāraṇā*, when the mind flows uniformly onto the object, this is *dhyāna.*

3.2.2 Meditation (*dhyāna*) is the uniform streaming of attention on that (object of concentration).

3.3 *tad evārtha-mātra-nirbhāsaṁ sva-rūpa-śūnyam iva samādhiḥ*

3.3.1 That (meditation, *dhyāna*) shining forth with the object only, as if empty of its own nature, is absorption (*samādhi*).

3.3.2 *samādhi* is a condition when the meditative consciousness becomes empty of its own form, as it were, and the object (of meditation) alone shines forth.

3.3.3 Consciousness is noisy by nature. Deep meditation is noiseless.

3.3.4 Silence is renunciation of noise.

3.4 *trayam ekatra saṁyamaḥ*

3.4.1 Yogic meditation called *saṁyama* is the process of applying the three (degrees of absorption) to one object.

3.5 *taj-jayāt prajñālokaḥ*

3.5.1 By mastery of that, lucidity of knowledge (is attained).

3.5.2 In the mastery of this (meditation, *saṁyama*) there arises the effulgence of knowledge.

3.6 *tasya bhūmiṣu viniyogaḥ*

3.6.1 Its application is done in stages.

3.7 *trayam antar-aṅgaṁ pūrvebhyaḥ*

3.7.1 These three (levels of meditation) are more internal than the (five) preceding ones.

3.8 *tad api bahir-aṅgaṁ nir-bījasya*

3.8.1 This (meditation, *saṁyama*) is an external limb of *nir-bīja-samādhi.*

3.8.2 Being necessarily charged with objects, *saṁyama* constitutes silence less deep and total than consciousness free of all object-relationship.

3.8.3 *saṁyama* is a predisintegration condition.

3.16 *pariṇāma-traya-saṁyamād atītānāgata-jñānam*

3.16.1 By meditation (*saṁyama*) on the three transformations knowledge of the past and future (is obtained).

3.17 *śabdārtha-pratyayānām itaretarādhyāsāt saṅkaras. tat-pravibhāga-saṁyamāt sarva-bhūta-ruta-jñānam*

3.17.1 The mutual superimposition of word, object, and idea is an (undesired) confusion. By virtue of meditation on their difference, knowledge of the sounds of all creatures is obtained.

3.17.2 As referential speech disintegrates, there arises silence which makes possible penetration of other creatures' sounds.

3.17.3 The yogin who separates (the apparently inseparable) dimensions of ordinary speech obtains a sense of comprehending sounds normally unintelligible.

3.18 *saṁskāra-sākṣāt-karaṇāt pūrva-jāti-jñānam*

3.18.1 Through (meditative) direct contact with the subliminal impressions (*saṁskāra*) knowledge of previous births is obtained.

3.19 *pratyayasya para-citta-jñānam*

3.19.1 There arises knowledge of other people's mind (due to perception of) the ideas.

3.20 *na ca tat-sālambanaṁ tasyāviṣayī-bhūtatvāt*

3.20.1 But not (knowledge of) the others' mind's objects, since these objects are not available (for meditation).

3.21 *kāya-rūpa-saṁyamāt tad-grāhya-śakti-stambhe cakṣuḥ-prakāśāsamprayoge 'ntardhānam*

3.21.1 By the performance of *saṁyama* on the shape of the body, as the power of the body to be seen is blocked, and as there is thus no contact of light (emanating from the body) with the eye, there is (the yogin's) invisibility.

3.21.2 By meditation on the shape—or nature—of the body, as light (emanating from the body) is blocked and contact of the eye with this light is stopped, there is disappearance (of the body).

3.22 *sopakramaṁ nir-upakramaṁ ca karma. tat-saṁyamād aparānta-jñānam ariṣṭebhyo vā*

3.22.1 Karma is fast to produce its results and slow to do it. Meditation (*saṁyama*) on that brings about knowledge of death. Or, this knowledge arises from omens.

3.22.2 Karma is either ripe or unripe; by meditation (*saṁyama*) on it, or by omens, knowledge of death (is attained).

3.23 *maitryādiṣu balāni*

3.23.1 (By meditation) on friendliness and so on, strengths (are attained).

3.23.2 (Meditation on feelings such as) friendship produces powers.

3.24 *baleṣu hasti-balādīni*

3.24.1 Meditation on powers produces strengths such as of an elephant.

3.25 *pravṛtty-āloka-nyāsāt sūkṣma-vyavāhita-viprakṛṣta-jñānam*

3.25.1 By focusing the light of mental activity, knowledge of the subtle, the obstructed and the remote (is attained).

3.25.2 From placing the light of (mental) activity (on the respective objects) there is knowledge of subtle, hidden, and distant objects.

3.26 *bhuva-jñānaṁ sūrye saṁyamāt*

3.26.1 By meditation (*saṁyama*) on the sun, knowledge of the world is attained.

3.27 *candre tārā-vyūha-jñānam*

3.27.1 (Meditation on) the moon produces knowledge of the arrangement of the stars.

3.28 *dhruve tad-gati-jñānam*

3.28.1 Meditation on the pole-star produces knowledge of its motion.

3.29 *nābhi-cakre kāya-vyūha-jñānam*

3.29.1 Meditation on the navel wheel results in knowledge of the arrangement of the body.

3.30 *kaṇṭha-kūpe kṣut-pipāsā-nivṛttiḥ*

3.30.1 (By meditation) on the hollow of the throat (gullet), cessation of hunger and thirst (is attained).

3.30.2 *saṁyama* focused on the pit of the throat produces cessation of hunger and thirst.

3.31 *kūrma-nāḍyāṁ stharyam*

3.31.1 Meditation on the tortoise-channel brings about stability.

3.32 *mūrdha-jyotiṣi siddha-darśanam*

3.32.1 *saṁyama* on the light of the head produces visions of the *siddhas* (perfected beings).

3.33 *prātibhād vā sarvam*

3.33.1 Or by intuition—everything (is known).

3.34 *hṛdaye citta-saṁvit*

3.34.1 Meditation on the heart brings about awareness of the mind.

3.35 *sattva-puruṣayor atyantāsaṁkīrṇayoḥ pratyayāviśeṣo bhogaḥ parārthatvāt svārtha-saṁyamāt puruṣa-jñānam*

3.35.1 Experience is grounded in the failure of discrimination between the radically distinct (qualities of) *sattva* and purusha; by meditation (*saṁyama*) on (purusha's) independence of another's purpose, knowledge of purusha (is attained).

3.35.2 Experience (*bhoga*) is grounded in the nondistinction of the *sattva* component and the pure subject, however infinitely different are those two (*sattva* and purusha) by virtue of their radical otherness. Meditation on what exists for itself produces knowledge of the pure subject (self).

3.36 *tataḥ pratibhā-śrāvaṇa-vedanādarśāsvāda-vārtā jāyante*

3.36.1 From that arises intuition, (celestial) hearing, (unusual powers of) touch, supranormal power of vision, taste, and smell.

3.37 *te samādhāv upasargā vyutthāne siddhayaḥ*

3.37.1 They are obstacles in *samādhi*, and attainments in a state of wakefulness.

3.37.2 These (experiences) are obstacles in the condition of *samādhi*, but achievements in the condition of active (outgoing) orientation.

3.37.3 The yogin's unusual experiences in the condition of *sa-bīja-samādhi* obstruct transformation into *nir-bīja-samādhi*.

3.37.4 Unusual experiences are noise in comparison with postintegration silence.

3.38 *bandha-karaṇa-śaithilyāt pracāra-saṁvedanāc ca cittasya para-śarīrāveśaḥ*

3.38.1 By loosening the causes of bondage and awareness of the mind's motions, consciousness can enter another's body.

3.38.2 By virtue of the weakening of the causes of bondage, and also due to the knowledge of the motions of the mind, there is entrance into others' bodies.

3.39 *udāna-jayāj jala-paṅka-kantakādiṣv asaṅga utkrāntiś ca*

3.39.1 From mastery of the *udāna* (up-breathing) there is no contact (of the yogin's body) with water, mud, and thorns, and also upward motion (in the time of death).

3.40 *samāna-jayāj jvalanam*

3.40.1 From mastery of the *samāna* breathing there arises effulgence.

3.41 *śrotrākāśayoḥ saṁbandha-saṁyamād divyaṁ śrotram*

3.41.1 By meditation (*saṁyama*) on the connection between the ear and space, divine hearing (is attained).

3.42 *kāyākaśayoḥ saṁbandha-saṁyamāl laghu-tūla-samāpatteś cākāśa-gamanam*

3.42.1 By meditation (*saṁyama*) on the relation of body and space, and also by identification with light cotton, movement in space can be perceived.

3.42.2 from *saṁyama* on the relation of the body with space and also from the meditative identification with light-weight objects such as cotton there is motion in space.

3.43 *bahir-akalpitā vṛttir mahā-videha tataḥ prakāśāvaraṇa-kṣayaḥ*

3.43.1 The action of thinking outside the body is the great bodilessness. From this there is decrease in the veil over (the mind's) illumination.

3.44 *sthūla-sva-rūpa-sūkṣmānvayārthavattva-saṁyamād bhūta-jāyaḥ*

3.44.1 By *saṁyama* focused on the gross, the essence, the subtle, and purposefulness, there arises mastery over the elements.

3.45 *tato 'ṇimādhi-pradurbhavaḥ kāya-saṁpat taddharmāṇabhigātaś ca*

3.45.1 Then there arise becoming infinitely minute and the like; and also perfection of the body, and its immunity to the qualities (of things).

3.46 *rūpa-lāvaṇya-bala-vajra-saṁhananatvāni kāya-saṁpat*

3.46.1 The perfection of the body is (good) shape, radiance, strength, and thunderbolt-solidity.

3.47 *grahaṇa-sva-rūpāsmitānvayārthavattva-saṁyamād indriya-jayaḥ*

3.47.1 *saṁyama* on the cognitive process, on the essence, on the sense of ego, on inherence, and on the purposefulness (of experience), produces mastery over the senses.

3.48 *tato mano-javitvaṁ vikaraṇa-bhāvaḥ pradhāna-jayaś ca*

3.48.1 Then there is speed of the mind, knowledge obtained independently of the ordinary means, and mastery over the primary cause (prakṛiti).

3.49 *sattva-puruṣānyatā-khyāti-mātrasya sarva-bhāvādhiṣṭhātṛtvaṁ sarva-jñātṛtvaṁ ca*

3.49.1 For the yogin immersed solely in the awareness of the difference of the pure subject and the *sattva* component (of objectivity), there is mastery over all existence, and omniscience as well.

3.50 *tad-vairāgyād api doṣa-bīja-kṣaye kaivalyam*

3.50.1 As even this awareness is renounced, in the destruction of the seed of (every) fault, there is liberation (independence, aloneness, *kaivalya*).

3.50.2 Even the most advanced of the contents of consciousness—the difference of *sattva* and purusha—is renounced in favor of ultimate, postintegration silence.

3.51 *sthāny-upanimantraṇe saṅga-smayā-karaṇaṁ punar aniṣṭa-prasaṅgāt*

3.51.1 Being invited by divine authorities, the yogin should avoid (resist) smiles inviting attachment, for undesired consequences follow.

3.52 *kṣaṇa-tat-kramayoḥ saṁyamād viveka-jaṁ jñānam*

3.52.1 By meditation (*saṁyama*) on the moment and the sequence, knowledge born of discernment (is attained).

3.52.2 By the application of *saṁyama* to the moments and their sequence there is attainment of knowledge born of the distinction (between subject and object).

3.53 *jāti-lakṣaṇa-deśair anyatānavacchedāt tulyayos tataḥ pratipattiḥ*

3.53.1 Then (due to the awareness of the distinction between subject and object) there is ability to distinguish between two things absolutely similar regarding type, characteristic qualities, and place.

3.53.2 The yogin's ability to realize the most subtle distinction (between subject and object) results in his power to distinguish between other (extremely similar) entities.

3.54 *tārakaṁ sarva-viṣayaṁ sarvathā-viṣayam akramaṁ ceti viveka-jaṁ-jñānam*

3.54.1 Knowledge born of discernment is without sequence, comprising everything and all objects, and is a means of deliverance (*tāraka*).

3.55 *sattva-puruṣayoḥ śuddhi-sāmye kaivalyam*

3.55.1 When *sattva* and purusha are of equal purity, *kaivalya* (is attained).

3.55.2 Though infinitely different (*sattva* being a force in objectivity, the purusha a subject) Patañjali associates *sattva* with purusha by their common feature—purity.

3.55.3 Reduction of noise in objectivity is mysteriously connected by Patañjali with postdisintegration silence.

Kaivalya-Pāda

4.1 *janmauṣadhi-mantra-tapaḥ-samādhi-jāḥ siddhayaḥ*

4.1.1 The *siddhis* are produced by birth, herbs, mantras, heating practices, and *samādhi*.

4.1.2 The unusual experiences (*siddhi*) come about from birth, use of herbs (drugs), use of meditative recitations (mantra), heating practices (*tapas*), and absorption (*samādhi*).

4.1.3 There are various sources of yogic experiences.

The Secondary Yogasūtra

Sāmādhi-Pāda

1.24 *kleśa-karma-vipākāśayair aparāmṛṣṭaḥ puruṣa-viśeṣa Īśvaraḥ*
1.24.1 Untouched by the roots of misery, action, its fruits, and mental imprints, Īśvara is a special purusha.
1.24.2 Īśvara is a particular purusha unaffected by natural predispositions and by conditioning due to past impressions and actions.

1.25 *tatra niratiśayaṁ sarvajña-bījam*
1.25.1 There the seed of omniscience is unsurpassed.

1.26 *sā pūrveṣām api guruḥ kālenānavacchedāt*
1.26.1 Since time is undivided (in the yogin's eyes) he (Īśvara) is also the teacher (*guru*) of all those (*yogins*) who lived in the past.

1.27 *tasya vācakaḥ praṇavaḥ*
1.27.1 He is denoted by the syllable *oṁ*.

1.28 *taj-japas tad-artha-bhāvanam*
1.28.1 The meditative repetition of that syllable brings about its meaning.

Sādhana-Pāda

2.3 *avidyāsmitā-rāga-dveṣābhiniveśāḥ kleśāḥ*
2.3.1 The inner tormenting predispositions are: ignorance, sense of ego, attraction (attachment), aversion, and persistent will to live on.
2.3.2 The most elemental ("natural") human inclinations are tormenting predispositions.
2.3.3 Yoga opposes and undermines the most fundamental characteristics of human identity and behavior.

2.4 *avidyā kṣetram uttareṣāṁ prasupta-tanu-vicchinnodārāṇām*
2.4.1 Ignorance (*avidyā*) is the source of the other four tormenting predispositions; each of these (four) may be in a condition of dormancy, weakness, interruption, and stimulation.

2.5 *anityāśuci-duḥkhānātmasu nitya-śuci-sukhātma-khyātir avidyā*
2.5.1 Ignorance (*avidyā*) is the imposition of the permanent on what is impermanent, of the pure on the impure, of pleasure on what is

essentially pain, of essence and selfhood (*ātman*) on what is devoid of essence and selfhood (*anātman*).

2.5.2 Worldly phenomena are essentially impermanent, impure, painful to live in, and without self or permanent essence. *Avidyā* creates the nonyogin's universe by projection.

2.5.3 The vision of *avidyā* unfolded in YS 2.5 is essentially Buddhist, deviating from Patañjali's other conceptualization of *avidyā* as "combination" of purusha and prakriti.

2.6 *dṛg-darśana-śaktyor ekātmatevāsmitā*

2.6.1 Sense of ego (*asmitā*) is the identification of the power of the seer with the power of perception.

2.7 *sukhānuśayī rāgaḥ*

2.7.1 Attraction follows pleasure.

2.8 *duḥkhānuśayī dveṣaḥ*

2.8.1 Aversion follows pain.

2.9 *svarasavāhī viduṣo 'pi tathā rūḍho 'bhiniveśaḥ*

2.9.1 The will to live, flowing by its own force, is thus ingrained even in the wise.

2.9.2 The wish to live conditions every creature; it goes on by itself in the wise as well as in the unlearned.

2.12 *kleśa-mūlaḥ karmāśayo dṛṣṭādṛṣṭa-janma-vedanīyaḥ*

2.12.1 Accumulation of past actions is the source of the tormenting inner dispositions, and this accumulation may be known by types of birth present as well as unseen.

2.13 *sati mūle tad-vipāko jāty-āyur-bhogāḥ*

2.13.1 As the root (of the *kleśa*) exists, its fruition is manifest in type of birth, span of life, and nature of experiences.

2.14 *te hlāda-paritāpa-phalāḥ puṇyāpuṇya-hetutvāt*

2.14.1 These (manifestations of karma—birth, span of life, experience) are accompanied by joy and pain due to pure and impure actions (in the past).

2.15 *pariṇāma-tāpa-saṁskāra-duḥkhair guṇa-vṛtti-virodhāc ca duḥkham eva sarvaṁ vivekinaḥ*

2.15.1 Owing to the suffering inherent in mutability, in anxiety, and in the *saṁskāras*, as well as in the strife of fluctuating *guṇas*, all is suffering to the discerning.
2.15.2 On account of sufferings associated with change, tormenting practices, binding effects of previous deeds, and also by virtue of the ongoing mutual contradiction between the three dispositions in nature (*guṇa*), everything is sheer suffering in the eyes of the one who discerns (*Vivekin*).
2.15.3 The spiritual hero is sensitive and perceptive.

2.16 *heyaṁ duḥkham anāgatam*
2.16.1 Suffering which is not yet come is to be avoided.

2.17 *draṣṭṛ-dṛśyayoḥ saṁyogo heya-hetuḥ*
2.17.1 The combination of the seer with the seen is the cause of what should be abandoned.
2.17.2 The cause of suffering is the contact of the seer and the objects.
2.17.3 Integration of subject and object is the cause of "life" and misery.

2.18 *prakāśa-kriyā-sthiti-śīlaṁ bhūtendriyātmakaṁ bhogāpavargārthaṁ dṛśyam*
2.18.1 The object (that which may be seen) consists of the three dispositions—illumination, action, and inertia. It is the nature of the senses, and it (the object) exists for the sake of experience and liberation.

2.19 *viśeṣāviśeṣa-liṅga-mātrāliṅgāni guṇa-parvāṇi*
2.19.1 Objects may be specific or unspecified, have characteristic signs, or lack such signs.

2.20 *draṣṭā dṛśi-mātraḥ śuddho 'pi pratyayānupaśyaḥ*
2.20.1 The seer consists of pure seeing; although pure, he observes ideas.

2.21 *tad-artha eva dṛśyasyātmā*
2.21.1 The purpose of this (seen) is its essence.
2.21.2 Objective existence exists for the subject.

2.22 *kṛtārthaṁ prati naṣṭam apy anaṣṭaṁ tad-anya-sādhāraṇatvāt*
2.22.1 Although (for the yogin who reached understanding and thus liberation) the world has accomplished its purpose and thus has come to an end, it is still existent (in a sense) by virtue of its common reality for others.

2.23 *sva-svāmi-śaktyoḥ sva-rūpopalabdhi-hetuḥ saṁyogaḥ*

2.23.1 The combination (contact) (of the subject and object) is the reason for the (wrong) identification between the master and his power.

2.24 *tasya hetur avidyā*

2.24.1 Ignorance is its source.

2.24.2 The connection between the subject (observer) and the object is the root of ignorance.

2.25 *tad-abhāvāt saṁyogābhāvo hānaṁ tad-dṛśeḥ kaivalyam*

2.25.1 In the nonexistence of that (ignorance), the connection (of subject and object) also does not exist, and "aloneness" (liberation) is the cessation of seeing this (the object).

2.25.2 Real understanding of the infinite difference between the seer and the potentially seen transforms the human into two completely independent, inactive essences (subject and object).

2.25.3 Liberation is disintegration.

2.26 *viveka-khyātir aviplavā hānopāyaḥ*

2.26.1 The remedy for ignorance, the means of undoing the knot between purusha and prakriti is well-established, constant realization of the difference between subject and object.

2.27 *tasya saptadhā prānta-bhūmiḥ prajñā*

2.27.1 Realization of that (ultimate truth) is of seven degrees.

Vibhūti-Pāda

3.9 *vyutthāna-nirodha-saṁskārayor abhibhava-prādurbhāvau nirodha-kṣaṇa-cittānvayo nirodha-pariṇāmaḥ*

3.9.1 The transformation of *nirodha* accompanies the mind in a moment of cessation, which appears and disappears in accordance with the emergence of karmic impressions (*saṁskāra*) producing outgoing motion or cessation.

3.10 *tasya praśānta-vāhitā saṁskārāt*

3.10.1 From (appropriate) impressions its flow is calm.

3.11 *sarvārthataikāgratayoḥ kṣayodayau cittasya samādhi-pariṇāmaḥ*

3.11.1 The transformation into *samādhi* is (conditioned by) the reduction and growth of dispersion of attention and of concentration.

3.12 *tataḥ punaḥ śāntoditau tulya-pratyayau cittasyaikāgratā-pariṇāmaḥ*
3.12.1 Then again the transformation of one-pointedness of mind is when the ideas (awareness) of tranquility and arousal are the same.

3.13 *etena bhūtendriyeṣu dharma-lakṣanāvasthā-pariṇāmā vyākhyātāḥ*
3.13.1 By this the transformations of nature (essence), characteristic signs, and condition in relation to the sense organs and their objects have been explained.

3.14 *śāntoditāvyapadeśya-dharmānupāti dharmī*
3.14.1 The substance follows the qualities dormant, aroused, or inherent in it.

3.15 *kramānyatvaṁ pariṇāmānyatve hetuḥ*
3.15.1 The cause for the difference in transformation is the difference in sequence.

Kaivalya-Pāda

4.2 *jāty-antara-pariṇāmaḥ prakṛty-āpūrāt*
4.2.1 The transformation into another type of birth comes about from the fullness of objective potentiality.

4.3 *nimittam aprayojakaṁ prakṛtīnāṁ varaṇa-bhedas tu tataḥ kṣetrikavat*
4.3.1 There is no direct causality of the primary potencies of nature, but rather the removal of obstacles, as in the case of the farmer (who manipulates the flow of water by the removal of walls of mud or clay).

4.4 *nirmāṇa-cittāny asmitā-mātrāt*
4.4.1 Created mind originates from mere sense of ego.

4.5 *pravṛtti-bhede prayojakaṁ cittam ekam anekeṣām*
4.5.1 By virtue of the difference in initiation of action (creating other minds), one mind becomes the cause of many.

4.6 *tatra dhyāna-jam anāśayam*
4.6.1 In this case, (the mind) born of meditation does not have accumulated karma (transferred on from previous lives).

4.7 *karmāśuklākṛṣṇaṁ yoginas tri-vidham itareṣām*
4.7.1 The yogi's karma is neither white nor black; the karma of others is of three kinds.

4.8 *tatas tad-vipākānuguṇānām evābhivyaktir vāsanānām*

4.8.1 Then there is manifestation of only those karmic impressions following the quality (color) of the respective fruition of this.

4.9 *jāti-deśa-kāla-vyavāhitānām apy ānantaryaṁ smṛti-saṁskārayor eka-rūpatvāt*

4.9.1 From the uniformity of nature of memory and karmic impressions, though hidden by birth, place, and time (the manifestation of karma) is uninterrupted.

4.10 *tāsām anāditvaṁ cāśiṣo nityatvāt*

4.10.1 Karmic impressions are beginningless by virtue of the eternity of the will to live which sustains them.

4.11 *hetu-phalāśrayālambanaiḥ saṁgṛhītatvād eṣām abhāve tad-abhāvaḥ*

4.11.1 Due to the connectedness of the karmic impressions with the basic network consisting of cause and effect, in the cessation of these (causes and effects) there is cessation of these (karmic impressions).

4.12 *atītānāgataṁ sva-rūpato 'sty adhva-bhedād dharmāṇām*

4.12.1 Past and future do exist in their essential nature, by virtue of the difference in the qualities of their course.

4.13 *te vyakta-sūkṣmā guṇātmānaḥ*

4.13.1 These, both tangible and subtle, are grounded in the forces of nature.

4.14 *pariṇāmaikatvād vastu-tattvam*

4.14.1 The essence of an entity is determined by its uniformity through the various changes (of the thing).

4.15 *vastu-sāmye citta-bhedāt tayor vibhaktaḥ panthāḥ*

4.15.1 Though a thing is the same, it may look different (from itself) due to the difference of the (spectator's) mind.

4.16 *na caika-citta-tantraṁ vastu tad-apramāṇakaṁ tadā kiṁ syāt*

4.16.1 If an object depended on one mind, how would it be real in accordance with considerations of valid knowledge?

4.17 *tad-uparāgāpekṣitvāc cittasya vastu jñātājñātam*

4.17.1 A thing is known or unknown according to its color in the mind.

4.18 *sadā jñātāś citta-vṛttayas tat-prabhoḥ puruṣasyāpariṇāmitvāt*
4.18.1 The mind activities are always known to their master, due to the unchangeability of the pure subject (purusha).

4.19 *na tat-svābhāsaṁ dṛśyatvāt*
4.19.1 The mind activities, since they are perceived (by another), cannot illuminate themselves.

4.20 *eka-samaye cobhayānavadhāraṇam*
4.20.1 Both mind activity and the pure subject cannot be fully known on one and the same occasion.

4.21 *cittāntara-dṛśye buddhi-buddher ati-prasaṅgaḥ smṛti-saṁkaraś ca*
4.21.1 If one mind perceives another, there is the logical fault (of infinite regression) of one intelligence illuminating another. There follows also confusion of memory.

4.22 *citter apratisaṁkramāyās tad-ākārāpattau sva-buddhi-saṁvedanam*
4.22.1 The mind knows itself when pure consciousness takes on the contents of the mind without any residue of its own.

4.23 *draṣṭṛ-dṛśyoparaktaṁ cittaṁ sarvārtham*
4.23.1 The mind is colored by the seer (pure subject) and the seen (object), and can take on (the form of) any object.

4.24 *tad-asaṁkhyeya-vāsanābhiś citram api parārthaṁ saṁhatya-kāritvāt*
4.24.1 The mind is made to act as a combination for the sake of another through its countless impressions.

4.25 *viśeṣa-darśina ātma-bhāva-bhāvanā-vinivṛttiḥ*
4.25.1 For the one who makes the distinction (between *sattva* and purusha) there is cessation of the cultivation of personal being.

4.26 *tadā hi viveka-nimnaṁ kaivalya-prāg-bhāraṁ cittam*
4.26.1 Then, the mind immersed in the consciousness of the distinction (between subject and object) tends towards complete liberation.

4.27 *tac-chidreṣu pratyayāntarāṇi saṁskārebhyaḥ*
4.27.1 In the intermissions of this (discriminating consciousness) there arise other contents of the mind, due to (remaining) karmic impressions.

4.28 *hānam eṣāṁ kleśavad uktam*

4.28.1 The abolition of these (disturbing impressions) is accomplished as explained with respect to the tormenting dispositions (*kleśa*).

4.29 *prasaṁkhyāne 'py akusīdasya sarvathā viveka-khyāter dharma-meghaḥ samādhiḥ*

4.29.1 For the one indifferent even with regard to the meditation of *prasaṁkhyāna*, there arises constant immersion in the meditative silence known as the "cloud of essence," due to the discriminative consciousness.

4.30 *tataḥ kleśa-karma-nivṛttiḥ*

4.30.1 Then there is cessation of the tormenting predispositions and karma.

4.31 *tadā sarvāvaraṇa-malāpetasya jñānasyānantyāj jñeyam alpam*

4.31.1 Then, due to the infinity of understanding purified of all the veiling stains, there is but little to be understood.

4.32 *tataḥ kṛtārthānāṁ pariṇāma-krama-samāptir guṇānām*

4.32.1 Then there is an end to the series of changes due to the forces of nature, as these forces have accomplished their goal.

4.33 *kṣaṇa-pratiyogī pariṇāmāparānta-nirgrāhyaḥ kramaḥ*

4.33.1 Sequence is a series of moments perceived at the end of change.

4.34 *puruṣārtha-śūnyānāṁ guṇānāṁ pratiprasavaḥ kaivalyaṁ sva-rūpa-pratiṣṭhā vā citi-śakter iti*

4.34.1 The reabsorption of the *guṇas*, devoid of the object of purusha, is *kaivalya*; or the establishment of the power of consciousness in its own form.

4.34.2 Liberation (*kaivalya*) is the involution of the forces of nature, as these forces have fulfilled their goal and become void; or it is the power of consciousness abiding in its self (turning upon itself).

Notes

Introduction

1. This is the import of YS 2.15.

2. Considering the imagery of separation and falling apart underlying yoga, the name of *viyoga* would be more appropriate.

3. *The Science of Yoga*, p. 445.

4. See, for example, *Yoga, Immortality and Freedom*, p. xx.

5. Ibid., p. 97.

6. *Yoga; Discipline of Freedom*, p. 2.

7. Ibid., p. 1.

8. Ibid., p. 3.

9. See *The Vedānta-sūtras*, with the commentary of Śaṅkarācārya, pp. 55–56.

10. *Yoga-Sūtras of Patañjali with the Exposition of Vyāsa,* p. xii.

11. See W. Halbfass, "The Therapeutic Paradigm and the Search for Identity in Indian Philosophy," in *Tradition and Reflection*, pp. 243–64.

12. See my "Yogic Revolution and Tokens of Conservatism in Vyāsa-Yoga," *Journal of Indian Philosophy* 25, 129–38, 1997.

13. YS 1.48.

14. In accordance with the famous YS 1.2: "Yoga is the cessation of the mind-fluctuations" (*yogaś citta-vṛtti-nirodhaḥ*).

15. References to "empty words" (*vikalpa*) and ordinary, valid, verbal source of knowledge (*āgama*) as mind-fluctuations to be eradicated indicate the overall perception of verbalization in opposition to an accomplished, yogic condition.

16. See YS 3.50.

17. R. Thapar, *A History of India*, p. 15.

18. See YS 3.16; YS 2.39; YS 3.18.

19. YS 4.5.

20. YS 2.15.

21. YS 3.21.

22. YS 2.39.

23. YS 2.40.

24. YS 2.49–51.

25. YS 3.30.

26. *Encyclopedic Dictionary of Yoga*, p. 258.

27. S. Dasgupta, *Yoga as Philosophy and Religion*, p. ix.

Chapter 1. Eight Characters in Search of the Yogasūtra

1. Yeats quotes as his source "a man from Malabar," who said: "Buddha tried to put down both Brahman and soldier, failed against the Brahman, was too successful against the soldier, for he destroyed our power of self-protection. We have been conquered by race after race, Syrian, Persian, French, English" (see his introduction to *Yoga Aphorisms of Patañjali*, p. 14).

2. See his *Yoga: the Art of Integration*, 1986.

3. YS 2.9: *sva-rasa-vāhī viduṣo 'pi tathā rūḍho 'bhiniveśaḥ* ("The will to live, flowing by its own force, is thus ingrained even in the wise").

4. The roots of misery (*kleśa*) are five: *avidyā* (wrong mode of knowledge), *asmitā* (ego sense), *rāga* (attachment), *dveṣa* (aversion), and *abhiniveśa*. (See YS 2.3.)

5. *Rāja-Yoga*, p. 111.

6. See YS 2.40.

7. See, for example, Eliade's view of the various types of yogic meditation as "Techniques for Autonomy," in *Yoga: Immortality and Freedom*, pp. 47–100.

8. Among the topics discussed by Rawcliffe in *Occult and Supernatural Phenomena*: stigmata, poltergeists, seances, ESP, telepathy, hypnotism, firewalking, mystical experience, lycanthropy, peyotl visions, auras, levitation, automatic writing, and more.

9. *Occult and Supernatural Phenomena*, p. 280.

10. M. Eliade strongly opposes such a view of yogic bliss and superconsciousness (*samādhi*); he says: "[From] time immemorial India has known the many and various trances and ecstasies obtained from intoxicants, narcotics, and all other means of

emptying consciousness; but any degree of methodological conscience will show us that we have no right to put *samādhi* among these countless varieties of spiritual escape. Liberation is not assimilable with the 'deep sleep' of prenatal existence, even if the recovery of totality through undifferentiated enstasis seems to resemble the bliss of the human being's fetal preconsciousness. . . . [The yogin] enters into 'deep sleep' and into the 'fourth state' (*turīya*, the cataleptic state) with the utmost lucidity; he does not sink into self-hypnosis." See *Yoga: Immortality and freedom*, p. 99.

11. Pp. 280–81.

12. P. 297. Rawcliffe sums up his consideration of the Indian rope trick as follows: "It is safe to say that the traditional rope-trick has never been performed in actual fact. It has never been anything other than one of the stock hallucinations suggested by the itinerant oriental magus or fakir to the credulous and highly suggestible audiences of the East" (p. 301).

13. Rawcliffe acquired his knowledge of yoga from K. Behanan's book, *Yoga: a Scientific Evaluation* (1937).

14. G. Feuerstein—a Spiritual Seeker—sums up his opinion of ideas such as Rawcliffe's: "There is no shortage of criticism and outright denunciations. For the most part, these show a conspicuous lack of objectivity and sound information. At the root of such biased attitudes lies the critics' unwillingness to find the way to authentic experimentation with Yoga, based on their complacent belief in a false 'scientific objectivity' which only permits of an 'outside' point of view. Today, at a time when Yoga has become an undeniable sociological reality in the West, petty pseudo-criticism of such kind is no longer justifiable" (*The Essence of Yoga*, p. 12).

15. *Aphorisms of Yoga*, p. 65

16. The account of the twentieth-century Indian mystic Gopi Krishna is significantly similar to Purohit's. (See *Kundalini: Evolutionary Energy in Man*, 1971, pp. 12–13.)

17. Ibid, p. 58. Purohit continues: "During that period, I could not sit in any posture, I could not stand, I used to lie down on my bed and repeat the name of Lord Dattatreya. I know of cases where the fire was not brought under control for six or eight months; one mahatma told me that he used to sit under a cold water tap for eight hours every day. There is no danger to life, unless the rules and discipline are disregarded; it is only an act of purification, through which every one must go if he wants to attain" (ibid.).

18. See, for example, his commentary on YS 3.21, in which he corroborates Patañjali's assertion by reference to his experiences of invisibility (pp. 66–67).

19. See his commentary on YS 1.2 (p. 25).

20. *Autobiography of a Yogi*, pp. 14–15.

21. Ibid., p. 317.

22. "As I closed my eyes in meditation, my consciousness was suddenly transferred to the body of a captain in command of a battleship. The thunder of guns split the air as the shots were exchanged between shore batteries and the ship's cannons. A huge shell hit the powder magazine and tore my ship asunder. I jumped into the water, together with the few sailors who had survived the explosion.

Heart pounding, I reached the shore safely. But alas! A stray bullet ended its swift flight in my chest. I fell groaning to the ground. My whole body was paralyzed, yet I was aware of possessing it as one is conscious of a leg gone to sleep.

At last the mysterious footstep of death has caught up with me, I thought. With a final sigh, I was about to sink into unconsciousness when lo! I found myself seated in the lotus posture in my Garpar Road room.

Hysterical tears poured forth as I joyously stroked and pinched my regained possession: a body free from a bullet hole in the breast. I rocked to and fro, inhaling and exhaling to assure myself that I was alive. Amidst these self-gratulations, again I found my consciousness transferred to the captain's dead body by the gory shore. Utter confusion of mind came upon me" (p. 318).

23. P. 314.

24. However, Taimni concedes that "the facts of higher Yoga can neither be proved nor demonstrated. Their appeal is to the intuition and not to the intellect" (p. vii).

25. Ibid., p. vi.

26. In his assessment of Radhakrishnan's intellectual profile, W. Halbfass refers to Radhakrishnan's emphasis on experience as the "soul of religion." According to Halbfass, Radhakrishnan considers Hinduism as "the religion of experience par excellence." However, Halbfass says that Radhakrishnan "does not ever refer to his own experiences" (*India and Europe*, p. 383).

27. See *Indian Philosophy*, v. 2, fn 4, p. 358.

28. P. 364.

29. P. 368.

30. Ibid.

31. Ibid.

32. P. 368.

33. *Yoga as Philosophy and Religion*, p. viii.

34. See below, Ch. 3.

35. *Philosophies of India*, p. 284.

36. "Man's problem is, simply, that his permanent, ever-present actual freedom is not realized because of the turbulent, ignorant, distracted condition of his mind" (p. 286).

37. *Yoga: Immortality and Freedom*, pp. xvii–xviii, 11.

38. Eliade starts with Haridas's case, moves on to Buddha's denouncement of "powers," and then gets to the main point: yoga and freedom. He is enchanted by the connection of yoga and freedom. He mentions "absolute freedom," "indescribable freedom."

39. "The ideal of Yoga, the state of *jivan-mukti*, is to live in an 'eternal present,' outside of time" (*Yoga: Immortality and Freedom*, p. 363).

40. Ibid., p. 364.

41. Ibid.

42. Ibid.

43. *Aphorisms of Yoga*, translated by Shree Purohit Swami, p. 11.

44. YS 2.45: *samādhi-siddhir Īśvara-praṇidhānāt* ("From surrender unto Īśvara there arises success in *samādhi*").

45. *Yoga; The Science of the Soul*, p. 7.

46. *How to Know God*, pp. viii–ix.

47. Ibid., p. 57.

48. Ibid., p. ix.

49. Thus for example says W. B. Yeats: "Some years ago I bought *The Yoga-System of Patañjali*, translated and edited by James Haughton Woods and published by the Harvard Press. It is the standard edition, final, impeccable in scholastic eyes, even in the eyes of a famous poet and student of Samskrit, who used it as a dictionary" (*Aphorisms of Yoga*, p. 11).

50. P. ix.

51. Ibid., p. x.

52. *The Tree of Yoga*, p. 68.

53. Iyengar even ventures to describe the mystical end of the road: "So in the culminating moment, the self too is forgotten, but you forget it by going deep into it" (p. 69).

54. R. Mehta considers the move from body to mind and soul implausible. "To seek to control the mind with physical processes is to reverse the course of nature" (*Yoga: the Art of Integration*, p. 186).

55. *The Tree of Yoga*, p. 8.

56. See, for example, the definition of *samādhi* in YS 3.3: *tad-evārtha-mātra-nirbhāsaṁ sva-rūpa-śūnyam iva samādhiḥ* ["*samādhi* is a condition when the meditative consciousness becomes empty of its own form, as it were, and the object (of meditation) alone shines forth"].

57. See my articles "Experience and Observation in Traditional and Modern Pātañjala Yoga" (*Beyond Orientalism*, pp. 557–66) and "Yogic Revolution and Tokens of Conservatism in Vyāsa Yoga," *Journal of Indian Philosophy* 25, 129–38, 1997.

58. The ability to experience objects without any trace of pleasure or displeasure is the essence of "dispassion," or *vairāgya*, and a central feature of the yogin's lifestyle. R. Mehta nicely describes the nature of pleasure (in contrast with joy) in his commentary on YS 2.38. See *Yoga: the Art of Integration*, 1990, pp. 167–70.

59. See YS 1.4: *vṛtti-sārūpyam itaratra* ("Otherwise, the form of the mind-activities").

60. See YS 1.3: *tadā draṣṭuḥ svarūpe 'vasthānam* ("Then the seer abides in his own form").

61. See YS 1.24: *kleśa-karma-vipākāśayair aparāmṛṣṭaḥ puruṣa-viśeṣa Īśvaraḥ* ("Untouched by the roots of misery, action, its fruits and mental imprints, Īśvara is a special purusha.")

62. See YS 2.42: *saṁtoṣād anuttamaḥ-sukha-lābhaḥ* ("Through contentment, the attainment of supreme happiness").

63. See YS 3.42: *kāyākāśayoḥ saṁbandha-saṁyamāl laghu-tūla-samāpatteś cākāśa-gamanam* ["By meditation (*saṁyama*) on the relation of body and space and also by identification with light cotton, movement in space can be perceived"].

64. See YS 3.30: *kaṇṭha-kūpe kṣut-pipāsā-nivṛttiḥ* ["(By meditation) on the hollow of the throat (gullet), cessation of hunger and thirst (is attained)"].

65. See YS 3.21: *kāya-rūpa-saṁyamāt tad-grāhya-śakti-stambhe cakṣuḥ-prakāśāsaṁprayoge 'ntardhānam* ["By meditation on the shape—or nature—of the body, as light (emanating from the body) is blocked and contact of the eye with this light is stopped, there is disappearance (of the body)"].

66. See YS 3.22: *sopakramaṁ nirupakramaṁ ca karma tat-saṁyamād aparānta-jñānam ariṣṭebhyo vā* ["Karma is either ripe or unripe; by meditation (*saṁyama*) on it, or by omens, knowledge of death (is attained)"].

67. See YS 3.38: *bandha-kāraṇa-śaithilyāt pracāra-saṁvedanāc ca cittasya para-śarīrāveśaḥ* ("By loosening the causes of bondage and perceiving passages, consciousness can enter another's body").

68. See YS 3.41: *śrotrākaśayoḥ saṁbandha-saṁyamād divyaṁ śrotram* ["By meditation (*saṁyama*) on the connection between the ear and space, divine hearing (is attained)"].

69. See his introduction to YS 3.16, which is the first one in the particular *siddhi* sutras of the Vibhūti-Pāda.

70. See YSBh 2.1.

71. See YSBh 2.35.

72. TV 2.35: *saṁpraty apratyūhaṁ yama-niyamābhyāsāt tat-siddhi-parijñāna-sūcakāni cihnānyupanyasyati yat parijñānād yogī tatra tatra kṛta-kṛtyaḥ kartavyeṣu pravartate* ["Now, in the absence of obstacles due to the practice of *yamas* and *niyamas*, (the author) will point to the indicatory signs which are the *siddhi*-experiences; upon their discernment, the yogi who has accomplished his task proceeds to what is (yet) to be accomplished"].

73. See YV 3.16.

74. Language, of course, profoundly influences thinking. In the case of the "paranormal facts of yoga" the relevance of the choice of language is immediately perceptible. The language of experience applied to the *siddhis* predisposes one to questions such as: Is it true? Is it compatible with what we already know? What is the thematic relationship of yoga experience with Sāṅkhya metaphysics? The language of the (improper) desire associated with the *siddhis*, their being ("worldly") powers and attainments (and therefore temptations), and their consequent rejection, are somewhat less productive of questioning. Indeed, the only issue which comes to mind here is: Why does Patañjali bother so much about the explanation and interpretation of these numerous obstacles on the way to liberation?

75. *The Six Systems of Indian Philosophy*, 1919, p. 351.

76. Ibid., p. 352.

77. Ibid., p. 356.

78. See Ramakrishna, *Sayings of Sri Ramakrishna*, 1920, p. 201.

79. See the translation of his *Yogasūtra* into Arabic, translated into English by S. Pines and T. Gelblum, *Bulletin of the School of Oriental and African Studies*, 46, 1983, p. 264.

80. See A. Osborn, *Ramana Maharshi and the Path of Self-Knowledge*, p. 153.

81. P. V. Kane is obviously wrong in counting the *siddhis* as 35 in number. The theories of transformation directly focused on the structure of power experience are broached in YS 2.35, with the theory of the transformative potency of *ahiṁsā*. Each of the *yamas* and *niyamas* has attached to it a theory of transformation (a *siddhi-sūtra*). In the tradition of Pātañjala-Yoga the powers consequent upon the *yamas* have been explicitly considered *siddhis*. See, for example, Vyāsa on YS 2.39 (*etā yama-sthairye siddhayaḥ*: "these are the *siddhis* pertaining to the steadfast practice of *yamas*").

82. *History of Dharmaśāstra*, 1962, pp. 1451–52.

83. *Indian Philosophy*, 1993, p. 366.

84. Ibid., p. 367.

85. See S. Dasgupta, p. 156.

86. *Yoga: Immortality and Freedom*, 1973, p. 177.

87. *Structural Depths of Indian Thought*, 1985, p. 350.

88. See *Yoga: the Method of Re-Integration*, 1949, p. 137.

89. *Yoga and the Hindu Tradition*, 1976, p. 133.

90. *A Survey of Hinduism*, 1990, p. 366.

91. See J. Ghosh, *A Study of Yoga*, 1977, p. 35.

92. *An Introduction to Indian Philosophy*, 1960, p. 306.

93. *Religion, Philosophy, Yoga*, trans. Maurice Shukla, p. 370.

94. The dominant attitude of Patañjali, the compiler of the *Yogasūtra*, is that the unusual yoga experiences are real; they are the "hard facts" of existence in yoga. As suggested below, it is likely that Patañjali makes the *siddhi* phenomena the root of his philosophical enquiry; the *siddhis* could serve as a necessary link between Sāṅkhya philosophy and yogic practice. Seen in this light, Patañjali's project in the *Yogasūtra*—connecting practice and Sāṅkhya-consciousness—is made more intelligible as we see that "experience" mediates between blind practice and metaphysics. Essentially, yogic practice is described in the *Yogasūtra* as the (causal) explanation of yoga experience, while Sāṅkhya metaphysics is its interpretation. Thus explained by yogic practice and interpreted by Sāṅkhya categories, the *siddhis* are the major "data" of the *Yogasūtra*.

Chapter 2. Daily Life in Samādhi

1. YS 4.7: *karmāśuklākṛṣṇaṁ yoginas tri-vidham itareṣām* ("The yogi's karma is neither white nor black; the karma of others is of three kinds.")

2. Śaṅkarācārya gracefully describes the condition of *Īśvara* as being without desire and any motive for action. In BSBh 2.1.33 he compares God to princes and other dignitaries who play in amusement parks. Such people do not miss anything; all their desires are satisfied (they are *āpta-kāma*). Thus, they do not seem to have any motive for their activities except mere playfulness. God's actions are also similar to breathing: "Just as inhalation and exhalation proceed from their own being, without aiming at any external purpose, so God's activity, too, proceeds from his own being in the form of play, without aiming at any other purpose." (See D. Handelman and D. Shulman, *God Inside Out,* p. 48.)

3. Purusha is the unchanging pure subject or seer. According to Sāṅkhya metaphysics—of which our knowledge owes much to Patañjali—there is a plurality of passive "pure seers" who must be distinguished and dissociated from any trace of objectivity. However, objectivity is also real. It is referred to as prakriti or *pradhāna*. In its primordial condition, objectivity is potential, balanced, unseen. The realization

of the distinction between purusha and prakriti is called *viveka-khyāti*, and it embodies the condition of liberation (*kaivalya*).

4. See YS 3.42: *kāyākāśayoḥ saṁbandha-saṁyamāl laghu-tūla-samāpatteś cākāśa-gamanam* ["By meditation (*saṁyama*) on the relation of body and space and also by identification with light cotton, movement in space can be perceived"].

5. See YS 3.21: *kāya-rūpa-saṁyamāt tad-grāhya-śakti-stambhe cakṣuḥ-prakāśāsaṁprayoge 'ntardhānam* ["By meditation on the shape—or nature—of the body, as light (emanating from the body) is blocked and contact of the eye with this light is stopped, there is disappearance (of the body)"].

6. There are many kinds of knowledge-expansions explained in the *Yogasūtra* as part of the adept's experiences and attainments. Even the ultimate cognition—concerning the difference between purusha and prakriti—is obtained by meditation (See YS 3.35). Other unusual expansions of cognition are, for example, the knowledge of "anatomy" ("the arrangement of the body," YS 3.29), knowledge of the (entire) universe (YS 3.26), knowledge of other creatures' sounds (YS 3.17), and so forth.

7. See *The Haṭhayogapradīpika* 2.26 (trans. P. Sinh), p. 17.

8. Ibid., 2.25; *Gheranda-Saṁhitā* 1.36–41.

9. Vyāsa is supposed to have lived in the 6th century A.D.

10. *kiñ ca parair asaṁsargaḥ kāya-svabhāvālokī svam api kāyaṁ jihāsur mṛj-jalādibhir ākṣālayann api kāya-śuddhim apaśyan kathaṁ para-kāyair atyantam evāprayataiḥ saṁsṛjyeta* ["(The yogi) does not come into contact with others. He perceives the true nature of the body. He is even desirous of giving up his own body, seeing its impurity even when cleansed with water and other purifying substances. How should he come into contact with other bodies, which are all the more impure?"].

11. YS 3.38: *bandha-kāraṇa-śaithilyāt pracāra-saṁvedanāc ca cittasya para-śarīrāveśaḥ* ("By loosening the causes of bondage and perceiving passages, consciousness can enter another's body").

12. See, for example, YS 1.50–51.

13. TV 2.39.

14. See W. Halbfass, "The Therapeutic Paradigm and the Search for Identity in Indian Philosophy," in *Tradition and Reflection*, pp. 234–64.

15. See YSBhV 2.39.

16. *Rāja-Yoga*, p. 210.

17. *The Science of Yoga*, p. 244.

18. *Yoga: the Art of Integration*, p. 170.

19. Ibid., p. 171.

20. YS 3.26: *bhuvana-jñānaṁ sūrye saṁyamāt* ["By meditation (*saṁyama*) on the sun, knowledge of the world is attained"].

21. The commentators interpret the "sun" (*sūrya*) in different ways. Vyāsa understands it as the "sun-opening" (*sūrya-dvāra*), Vācaspati as the central energy-channel (*suṣumnā-nāḍī*) and King Bhoja as the physical sun.

22. *The Yoga-Sūtra of Patañjali*, p. 105.

23. Ibid., p. 106.

24. *The Science of Yoga*, p. 315.

25. See *Tradition and Reflection*, p. 291.

26. At the end of his long *bhāṣya* on YS 2.13, Vyāsa notes that the "course of karma is complex and hard to know" (*karma-gatir vicitrā dur-vijñānā*).

27. See for example, YS 1.50–51; YS 2.12–14; YS 4.7–11.

28. YS 3.22: *sopakramaṁ nirupakramaṁ ca karma tat-saṁyamād aparānta-jñānam ariṣṭebhyo vā* ["*Karma* is either ripe or unripe; by meditation (*saṁyama*) on it, or by omens, knowledge of death (is attained)]".

29. *Rāja-Yoga,* pp. 228–29.

30. TV 3.22: *tataś ca yogī sopakramam ātmanaḥ karma vijñāya bahūn kāyān nirmāya sahasā phalaṁ bhuktvā svecchayā mriyate* ["Thus the yogi, discovering his ripe karma, creating many bodies and tasting the fruits (of karma) at once, dies at his own will"].

31. YS 2.15: *pariṇāma-tāpa–saṁskāra-duḥkhair guṇa-vṛtti-virodhāc ca duḥkham eva sarvaṁ vivekinaḥ* ["Owing to the suffering inherent in mutability, in anxiety and in the *saṁskāras*, as well as in the strife of fluctuating *guṇas*, all is suffering to the discerning"].

32. See W. Halbfass, "The Therapeutic Paradigm and the Search for Identity in Indian Philosophy," in *Tradition and Exploration*, pp. 243–63.

33. See W. Halbfass, *Tradition and Reflection*, p. 291.

34. YSBh 2.34.

35. BS 4. 4.22: *anāvṛttiḥ śabdād anāvṛttiḥ śabdāt.*

36. P. 311.

37. *Selfless Persons,* p. 191.

38. BV 3.18.

39. Actually, Vyāsa considers the meditation on the *saṁskāras* as capable also of producing knowledge of the other's previous lives. See YSBh 3.18.

40. The practice or observance of *santoṣa* ("contentment") results in "supreme happiness" (YS 2.42: *santoṣād anuttamaḥ sukha-lābhaḥ*).

41. YS 2.16: *heyaṁ duḥkham anāgatam* ("Suffering which is not yet come is to be avoided").

42. See below, ch. 5.

43. *Yoga and the Hindu Tradition*, p. 11.

44. Ibid.

45. Ibid., p. 133.

46. Ibid., p. 181.

47. *Yoga: Immortality and Freedom*, p. 177.

48. See below, ch. 3.

49. The definition of *samādhi* in YS 3.3 is most relevant in this context. YS 3.3 asserts that *samādhi* is a condition where only the object is in sight. "*Samādhi* is (a state of awareness) devoid as it were of its own nature, in which only the object of meditation shines forth" (*tad evārthamātra-nirbhāsaṁ svarūpa-śūnyam iva samādhiḥ).* The condition of *dhyāna* becomes void of its own "form" or "identity" (*svarūpa*).

50. See YS 2.54, which defines *pratyāhāra* as the condition of total sensory deprivation.

51. See YS 3.42.

52. YS 3.45.

53. Ibid.

54. YS 3.30.

55. See YS 3.29; YS 3.30.

56. See YS 3.19; YS 3.38.

57. See YS 3.26.

58. YS 3.27.

59. See YS 3.17.

60. YS 3.35.

61. See YS 3.29.

62. See YS 3.25.

63. See above, YS 3.18.

64. YS 3.22.

65. See YS 2.35. "In the immediate enviornment of the yogin well established in *ahiṁsā* violence ceases" (*ahiṁsā-pratiṣṭhāyāṁ tat-saṁnidhau vaira-tyāgaḥ*).

66. See above, YS 2.40.

67. See YS 2.38 [*brahmacarya-pratiṣṭhāyāṁ vīrya-lābhaḥ;* "when firmly established in continence, vigor (is attained)]."

68. See YS 2.33–34; YS 3.53.

69. See YS 2.39, above.

70. See YS 2.37.

71. See YS 2.42: [*saṅtoṣād anuttamaḥ-sukha-lābhaḥ* ("Through contentment, supreme happiness (is attained)"].

72. See YS 2.36.

73. See YS 3.32.

74. See YS 3.1.

75. See YS 3.2.

76. See YS 2.34 and YS 3.53.

77. YS 3.42.

78. YS 2.42.

79. YS 2.8.

80. YS 2.7.

81. This could be the meaning of invisibility (YS 3.21).

82. See YS 3.22.

83. W. Doniger and B. Smith, *The Laws of Manu* 6.45.

84. Technically, this balance can be represented as that among the three *guṇas* (*sattva*, *rajas*, *tamas*); according to Sāṅkhya, a complete balance of these constituents of prakriti is the primordial state, preceding the process of creation.

Chapter 3. The Yogasūtra and the Dying Yogin's "Lively Interior"

1. Being in a "predeath" condition does not mean that the yogin is about to die soon. A predeath condition is a state of being rather than a point in time. It is similar to the "near-death condition and experience"; see below.

2. Handelman and Shulman refer to the difference between "unconsciousness" and "nonconsciousness." They say that unconsciousness "may allow for states of dreaming, and is thus already a movement toward consciousness." On the other hand,

the state of nonconsciousness does not allow dreaming, and is thus "more distant from a state of awareness" (*God Inside Out*, n 10, p. 190).

3. See, for example, YS 3.18, which refers to the retrieval of previous lives.

4. See YS 3.38.

5. YS 3.21.

6. See YS 3.25: *pravṛtty-āloka-nyāsāt sūkṣma-vyavāhita-viprakṛṣṭa-jñānam* ["By focusing the light of mental activity, knowledge of the subtle, the obstructed and the remote (is attained)"].

7. The superior beings are *siddhas*. See YS 3.32.

8. *God Inside Out*, p. 190. The citation directly refers to the condition of the primordial being before creation, according to the famous creation hymn, *Rg-Veda* 10.129.

9. Patañjali is not necessarily an individual. I consider the reference "Patañjali" to be an archetype of a philosophically minded personality, whether an individual, a group of people.

10. The essentials of the encounter between the yogin and the philosopher can be viewed as an internal dialogue. Unconscious experiences are retrieved as the contents of a dream.

11. Bhagavan Rajneesh emphasizes the paradoxical character of Patañjali, who is both a poet and a mathematician. See *Yoga: The Science of the Soul*, p. 10. However, his account seems to me to exaggerate the expressive quality of the *Yogasūtra*.

12. Patañjali, as a Sāṅkhya philosopher, embodies in his outlook the "composite nature of Sāṅkhya." About the various components of this school of thought, G. J. Larson remarks: "Influences were traced from the old Upaniṣadic notions of *ātman* and *brahman*; from ancient creation myths; from analysis of the breaths and speculations concerning the states of waking, dreaming and dreamless sleep; from ancient and later yogic theories and techniques; and even from some doctrines of Jainism and Buddhism" (*Classical Sāṅkhya*, p. 154).

13. See below the discussion of YS 1.7; YS 3.37; YS 1.43; YS 3.55; YS 3.35.

14. The *Sāṅkhyakārikā* is the most authoritative systematic exposition of Sāṅkhya metaphysics and theory of liberation. Although the text is late (its date of composition is most often said to be the fifth century A.D.), it is the earliest systematic composition on Sāṅkhya. The final redaction of the *Yogasūtra* is usually considered to be of the same period. G. J. Larson considers the date of the *Yogasūtra* to be between 300 and 400 A.D. (see *Classical Sāṅkhya*, p. 252).

15. See YS 1.3–4; YS 2.28; YS 3.35; etc.

16. See in particular YS 2.15.

17. See the definition of *avidyā* in YS 2.5. "Ignorance (*avidyā*) is the perception of what is impermanent as permanent, what is impure as pure, what is suffering as pleasure, what is devoid of selfhood as of selfhood" (*anityāśuci-duḥkhānātmasu nitya-śuci-sukhātma-khyātir avidyā*).

18. Humankind, according to YS 2.15, is in a condition of permanent inner war.

19. See W. Halbfass, "The Therapeutic Paradigm and the Search for Identity in Indian Philosophy," in *Tradition and Reflection*, pp. 243–64.

20. *Bhagavadgītā* 2.54: *sthita-prajñasya kā bhāṣā samādhi-sthasya keśava / sthita-dhīḥ kiṁ prabhāṣeta kim āsīta vrajeta kim.*

21. YS 2.28 connects phenomena which are observable in principle—*ahiṁsā, brahmacārya, śauca, aparigraha*, with liberating insight—*viveka-khyāti*. Van Buitenen's suggestion of the blunt superimposition of "Sāṅkhya-rationalization" on the yogin's "trance-states," though containing an opening for further thoughts on the relationship of Sāṅkhya metaphysics with yoga experience, is biased against the value of yoga experience. It overlooks the positive, stimulating presence of the yogin, and the nature of Pātañjala-Yoga as reflection on yoga experience.

22. See below, ch. 5.

23. See the reference to the yogin "immersed in *samādhi*" (*samādhi-stha*) in *Bhagavadgītā* 2.54.

24. YS 3.52: *kṣaṇa-tat-kramayoḥ saṁyamād viveka-jaṁ jñānam* ["By meditation (*saṁyama*) on the moment and the sequence, knowledge born of discernment (is attained)"].

25. YS 3.55: *sattva-puruṣayoḥ śuddhi-samye kaivalyam* ["When *sattva* and purusha are of equal purity, *kaivalya* (is attained)"].

26. "The yogi ought to die when he realizes *samādhi* . . ." (J. Varenne, *Yoga and the Hindu Tradition*, p. 137.)

27. *Bhagavadgitā* 2.69: *yā niśā sarva-bhūtānāṁ tasyāṁ jāgarti saṁyamī / yasyāṁ jāgrati bhūtāni sā niśā paśyato muneḥ* ("In that which is night to all beings, the yogi awakes; that in which all beings awake, is night to the sage who sees").

28. Indra proceeds in his journey by a process of elimination. He finds fault with each of the teachings presented to him by Prajāpati. Significantly, Indra rejects Prajāpati's suggested notions of the self by the recurring argument that these teachings are "useless," rather than false. He says time and again: "I do not see any benefit in this" (*nāham atra bhogyaṁ paśyāmi*).

29. The Upanishad emphasizes that the body is mortal, covered by death (*martyaṁ vā idaṁ śarīram āttaṁ mṛtyunā*). Embodiment is the great obstacle to transcendence of life conditioned by pleasure and displeasure. However, pleasure and displeasure do not touch the disembodied one (*aśarīraṁ vāva santaṁ na priyāpriye spṛśataḥ*). As the tranquil one rises from his body and reaches the supreme light, he abides in his own

nature (*evam evaiṣa samprasādo 'smāc-charīrāt samutthāya paraṁ jyotir upasampadya svena rūpeṇābhiniṣpadyate*). The climax of Prajāpati's teaching of innerness is the concise description of "life in creative disembodiment."

30. *sa tatra paryeti jakṣat krīḍan ramamānaḥ strībhir vā yānair vā jñātibhir vā.*

31. David Shulman tells me that this story is exceptional in the Upanishadic tradition.

32. *nopajanaṁ smarann idaṁ śarīraṁ.*

33. *sa yathā prayogya ācarane yukta evam evāyam asmiñ charīre prāṇo yuktaḥ.*

34. See below, Ch. 4.

35. There is an irreducible sediment of "experience" in the teaching of the *siddhis* in the *Yogasūtra* as well as in the *Chāndogya* story. In the stunningly new condition of total intentionality or creative disembodiment, there is no cessation of experience of the kind implied by the descriptions of nirvāṇa, *kaivalya*, or *mokṣa*.

36. See YS 1.6–1.11.

37. See, for example, the four types of *samāpatti* in YS 1.42–45.

38. See YS 1.24–28.

39. See YS 1.23.

40. YS 3.29: *nābhi-cakre kāya-vyūha-jñānam* ("Meditation on the navel wheel results in knowledge of the arrangement of the body").

41. YS 3.42.

42. See Ch. 4.

43. See, for example, BG 3.3; 5.4–5; 13.24.

44. Van Buitenen considers the philosopher's attitude to the yogin's "trance states" as a kind of Sāṅkhya-inspired rationalization. See his "*Dharma* and *Mokṣa*," in *Philosophy East and West*, 1975, p. 38.

45. R. A. Moody, *Life After Life*, p. 102.

46. See C. G. Jung, "Visions: Life After Death," from *The Near-Death Experience: A Reader*, p. 108.

47. R. A. Moody, *Life After Life*, pp. 102–3.

48. The recognition of yogic meditation as a privileged means of knowledge (*pramāṇa*) is expressed most succinctly by Vyāsa in YSBh 1.43. He refers to meditation as "superior perception" (*paraṁ pratyakṣaṁ*).

49. *The Six Systems of Indian Philosophy*, p. 356.

50. See S. Radhakrishnan, *Indian Philosophy* (1992), p. 367.

51. See S. Dasgupta, p. 156.

52. See "Dharma and Mokṣa," in *Philosophy East and West*, 1975, p. 38. Van Buitenen's idea is reminiscent of the myth of the dying yogin. However, he does not consider the yogin/philosopher relationship to be of any importance and worth exploring. He says that the philosopher's attitude to the "trance states" of yoga is that of "Sāṅkhya-inspired rationalization," and that "Sāṅkhya cosmogony was superimposed on the practices." He, however, considers the "trance states" as "primitive" and philosophically inferior. He notes, that "yoga itself has never got rid of it." (ibid.)

53. *Yoga: Immortality and Freedom*, p. 177.

54. *Yoga and Indian Philosophy*, p. 133.

55. *Yoga: the Art of Integration*, p. 137.

56. *Structural Depth of Indian Philosophy*, p. 350.

57. *Study of Yoga*, p. 35.

58. *The Oceanic Feeling*, pp. 125–41.

59. See *Beyond Orientalism*, p. 591. W. Halbfass seems to suggest that there is something worthwhile exploring concerning this "embarassment" and recognizes that the *siddhis* might serve as a potent "suggestion," but he does not go as far as to say that they constitute yoga experience.

60. This avoidance, by the way, can never fully succeed. There are always questions which remain unanswered. For suppose there are two Patañjalis, why and how did the purely philosophical one introduce the inferior magician's teaching into his composition? Was there a compromising third? Or, if the *siddhis* are alluring temptations, what makes them so dangerous for the adept yogin who has already mastered yoga?

61. J. Varenne, *Yoga and the Hindu Tradition*, p. 133.

62. See Kloistermaier, *A Survey of Hinduism*, pp. 366–67.

63. See YS 3.37. This sutra seems to deny the connection between *samādhi* and the *siddhis*. It says that in the condition of *samādhi* the *siddhis* are "obstacles" (*upasargā*), while in the condition of "arousal" (outward orientation) the *siddhis* are "attainments" [*te samādhāv upasargā vyutthāne siddhayaḥ* ("They are obstacles in *samādhi*, and attainments in a state of wakefulness")]. Since *samādhi* is the primary source or cause of the *siddhis*, YS 3.37 contradicts the rest of the *Yogasūtra*.

64. This receptivity to the yoga experience is the most salient difference between Pātañjala-Yoga and the nonyogic classical Sāṅkhya.

65. See YSBh 1.2.

66. *ṛtambharā tatra prajñā* ("There, cognition is truth-bearing").

67. YS 3.5: *taj-jayāt prajñāloka:* ["By mastery of that, lucidity of knowledge (is attained)"].

68. Eliade, M. *Yoga: Immortality and Freedom*, p. 76.

69. YS 1.41–145.

70. *Samādhi* is instrumental in changing the karmic sediment accumulated in previous life cycles. See in particular YS 1.50–51.

71. YS 2.2: *samādhi-bhāvanārthaḥ kleśa-tanū-karaṇārthaś ca* ["The objects (of *kriyā* yoga) are bringing about *samādhi* and attenuating the roots of misery"].

72. See YS 2.29.

73. *Samādhi* being the final stage of *aṣṭāṅga* yoga.

74. See YS 4.4.

75. I refer here to *sa-bīja-samādhi,* which—by definition—applies to a seed, or support (the object).

76. The pronoun *tat* refers to the previous condition of meditation, *dhyāna*, which is the subject of the statement.

77. The descriptions of *siddhis* follow this definition in YS 3.3.

78. *janmauṣadhi-mantra-tapaḥ-samādhi-jāḥ sīddhayaḥ.*

79. Vyāsa follows Patañjali in featuring *samādhi* as a condition grounded in temperament rather than an experience; there are *samāhita-citta* yogins and others.

80. See YS 1.51 and YS 3.8. See also discussion below, Ch. 5.

81. On Sāṅkhya metaphysics and yogic silence, see discussion below, Ch. 5.

Chapter 4. Causality, False Linearity, and the Silent Yogin's Presence in the Yogasūtra

1. TV 1.1.

2. *Yogasūtras of Patañjali with the Exposition of Vyāsa*, p. 63.

3. Thus Vācaspati wrote the *Bhamatī* on Śaṅkara's *Brahmasūtrabhāṣya*, the *Nyāya-vārttika-tatpārya-tīka* on the *Nyāya* system, the *Tattva-kaumudi* on Sāṅkhya philosophy, the *Tattva-vaiśāradi* on Yoga, the *Nyāya-kanika* and the *Tattva-bindu* on *Pūrva-Mīmāṁsā*.

4. J. H. Woods's translation, p. 5.

5. *The Science of Yoga*, p. 3.

6. *Yoga Philosophy of Patañjali*, p. 2.

7. *Yoga: the Science of the Soul*, v. 2, pp. 2–4.

8. *The Yogasūtra of Patañjali*, p. 5. Feuerstein proceeds to reflect on the meaning of Patañjali's character within the larger context of the history and nature of

mysticism. He says that "Patañjali is visible proof for the fact that mysticism *can* be approached rationally and that, equally importantly, contemplative interests and intellectual pursuits *can* be fruitfully combined in one person. This lesson is not new, for it has long been taught within the context of Christianity by such outstanding theologians and mystics as St. Augustine and Meister Eckhart. They, together with Patañjali, demonstrate a further truth, namely that the cultivation of mystical inwardness is not, in principle, incompatible with the Establishment—a particularly relevant observation at a time when mysticism tends to be mingled with social protest and even militancy." (ibid).

9. "Patañjali's personal contribution with respect to the theoretical framework and the metaphysical foundation that he gave to these practices was minimal" (*Patañjali and Yoga*, p. 16).

10. Ibid.

11. See above, Ch. 1.

12. See *History of Indian Philosophy*, 1953.

13. See Hauer, J. W., *Der Yoga: Ein indischer Weg zum Selbst*, 1958.

14. See Oberhammer, G., "Meditation und Mystik im Yoga des Patañjali," 1965.

15. Staal, F., *Exploring Mysticism*, 1986, p. 89.

16. See YS 3.52: *kṣaṇa-tat-kramayoḥ saṁyamād viveka-jaṁ jñānam* ["By meditation (*saṁyama*) on the moment and the sequence, knowledge born of discernment (is attained)"].

17. In this case, even the correspondence of object of meditation with the result—a correspondence which is the foundation of Patañjali's conceptualization of the power of meditation—is not made clear.

18. YSBh 3.24.

19. TV 3.24.

20. *Rāja-Yoga*, p. 229.

21. Ibid.

22. In his commentary on YS 3.23 [*maitryādiṣu balāni*; "(By meditation) on friendliness and so on, strengths (are attained)"], Taimni notes: "It is a well-known law of psychology that if we think of any quality persistently, that quality tends to become more and more a part of our character. This effect is heightened by meditation in which the concentration of mind is far more intense than in ordinary thinking. The effect is increased tremendously in *Samādhi*" (*The Science of Yoga*, p. 322).

23. *Yoga: the Art of Integration*, p. 328.

24. J.H. Woods's translation, p. 268.

25. YV 3.40: *uttejanaṁ kṛtvā jvalati satīvat sva-sarīraṁ dahati.*

26. *The Textbook of Yoga Psychology*, p. 272. In a similar vein, I. K. Taimni equates *samāna* with "gastric fire." "The relation of *Samāna Vāyu* with the gastric fire and the digestion of food is well known. Control over *Samāna* will naturally enable the *Yogi* to increase the intensity of the gastric fire to any extent and to digest any amount of food" (*The Science of Yoga*, p. 346).

27. The root *an* ("to breathe") occurs in the names of all five vital breaths (*prāṇa, samāna, apāna, udāna, vyāna*).

28. Shree Purohit Swami takes *udāna* to be "living fire." He translates YS 3.39: "By concentration on *udāna*, living fire, the yogi remains unaffected in water, in swamps, or amid thorns; leaves his body at will" (p. 70). Purohit further illustrates YS 3.39: "Recently the case of a yogi sitting with crossed legs floating on water for three days was reported in Indian papers, cases of walking on fire happen every year. I know the case of a yogi who always walked with bare feet, thorns did not prick them, snow did not chill them. The yogi can enter into or take any form he likes, and when his karma is exhausted, he can disintegrate his body at his pleasure" (pp. 70–71).

29. According to Woods, Vācaspati identifies the motion upward at the time of death with entrance onto the way of the gods (*devayāna*) expounded in the *Bṛhadāraṇyakopaniṣad* 6.1.3 and the *Chāndogyopaniṣad* 5.10. Literally, Vācaspati says that at the moment of death (*prāyaṇa-kāle*) there is upward movement into the fire on the "first (*primary*) way (*ādi-mārga*)" (*utkrāntiś cārcir ādi-mārgeṇa bhavati prāyaṇa-kāle*). See *The Yoga-System of Patañjali*, p. 268.

30. In T. S. Rukmani, *Yogavārttika of Vijñānabhikṣu*, v. 3, pp. 146–47.

31. In other words, they are the dying yogin's testimony.

32. See *The Hindu Conception of the Functions of Breath*, JAOS 1902, pp. 249–308.

33. See A. H. Ewing, p. 305.

34. In this sutra (YS 3.22) Patañjali refers to the two causal agents of knowing the time of one's death by the use of the ablative case.

35. Shree Purohit Swami says: "I saw a Mahatma sitting in the *Siddhāsana* posture with crossed legs, hanging in the air. The same Mahatma went to Benares from Nagpur with the speed of thought through air and dissolved his body in the Ganges." A fuller account is given in *An Indian Monk,* p. 37 (*Aphorisms of Yoga,* p. 70).

36. The *yamas* are: *ahiṁsā* (nonviolence), *satya* (truth), *asteya* (nonstealing), *brahmacarya* (celibacy), and *aparigraha* (nonpossessiveness). See YS 2.30.

37. The *niyamas* are: *śauca* (cleanliness), *saṅtoṣa* (contentment), *tapas* (austerity), *svādhyāya* (study), and *Īśvara-praṇidhāna* (surrender to Īśvara). See YS 2.32.

38. *Yoga: the Art of Integration*, p. 164.

39. Ibid., p.165

40. See Ch. 5 for a discussion of the mutual relationship of purusha and prakriti.

41. *sattva-puruṣayor atyantāsaṅkīrṇayoḥ pratyayāviśeṣo bhogaḥ parārthāt svārtha-saṁyamāt puruṣa-jñānam* ["Experience is grounded in the failure of discrimination between the radically distinct (qualities of) *sattva* and purusha; by meditation (*saṁyama*) on (purusha's) independence of another's purpose, knowledge of purusha (is attained)"].

42. YSBh 1.1.

43. See discussion below, Ch. 5.

44. See below, Ch. 5.

45. YS 2.54: *sva-viṣayāsaṁprayoge citta-sva-rūpānukāra ivendriyāṇāṁ pratyāhāra* ("*Pratyāhāra* is as though the senses were imitating the mind's essential form, in dissociating themselves from their objects").

46. YSBh 2.54: *yathā madhukara-rājānaṁ makṣikā utpatantam anutpatanti niviśamānam anuniviśante, tathendriyāṇi citta-nirodhe niruddhāni* ("Just as the bees follow their queen in her flight, and come to rest when she rests, so the senses are curbed with the curbing of the mind").

47. Vācaspati notes that the practice of *tapas* has to be limited: "Self-castigation should be performed only as long as it does not bring on a disorder of the humours." (Woods's translation, p. 104.)

48. See YSBhV 2.1.

49. YSBhV 2.1: *tathā sakala-yogaiśvarya-vibhūtibhyo viraktasya sarvopasaṁhāra-dvāreṇa kaivalyasya prādhānyena pradarśanāt kaivalya-pāda ity ucyate caturthaḥ* ["Since it treats primarily of one who is liberated by means of total involution of the senses, who is dispassionate with respect to the powers and mastery of the parts of yoga, the fourth (chapter) is called Kaivalya-Pāda"].

50. *The Science of Yoga*, p. viii.

51. YS 1.42: *śabdārtha-jñāna-vikalpaiḥ saṅkīrṇā savitarka-samāpattiḥ* ["*Samāpatti* with thought (is attained) where word, object, cognition and empty cognition are mingled together"].

52. YS 1.43: *smṛti-pariśuddhau sva-rūpa-śūnyevārtha-mātra-nirbhāsā nir-vitarkā* ["(*Samāpatti*) without thought (is attained) where memory is purified, the mind is, as it were, devoid of its own form, and the object alone shines forth"].

53. YS 1.44: *etayaiva savicārā nirvicārā ca sūkṣma-viṣayā vyākhyātā* ["Thereby, (*samāpatti*) with reflection and without reflection, having subtle objects, are explained"].

54. See YS 1.50–51.

55. YS 1.3: *tadā draṣṭuḥ svarūpe 'vasthānam* ("Then the seer abides in his own form").

56. YS 4.34: *puruṣārthaśūnyānāṁ guṇānāṁ pratiprasavaḥ kaivalyaṁ sva-rūpa-*pratiṣṭhā *vā citi-śaktir iti* ["The reabsorption of the *guṇas*, devoid of the object of purusha, is *kaivalya*; or the establishment of the power of consciousness in its own form"].

57. See discussion of YS 1.2 in Ch. 5.

58. YS 1.6–11 list the various mind activities the abolition of which constitute the "cessation" mentioned in YS 1.2 as the essence of yoga.

59. YS 1.12: *abhyāsa-vairāgyābhyāṁ tan-nirodhaḥ.*

60. Patañjali describes the five *vṛttis* in YS 1.6–11, and asserts the way to still the mind in YS 1.12, as follows: "The cessation of these is accomplished by practice and detachment."

61. YS 2.2: *samādhi-bhāvanārthaḥ kleśa-tanū-karaṇārthaś ca* ["The objects (of *kriyā* yoga) are bringing about *samādhi* and attenuating the roots of misery"].

62. YS 2.28: *yogāṅgānuṣṭhānād aśuddhi-kṣaye jñāna-dīptir āviveka-khyāteḥ* ["Through the application of the eight practices of yoga, as the contaminations are reduced, the light of knowledge (intensifies) into the ultimate discrimination (between subject and object)"].

63. YS 4.1: *janmauṣadhi-mantra-tapaḥ-samādhi-jāḥ siddhayaḥ* ("The *siddhis* are produced by birth, herbs, mantras, heating practices and *samādhi*.").

64. Literally, "by birth" *(janma)*.

Chapter 5. Untying the Knot of Existence

1. See discussion below, and in particular YSBh 1.2. Vyāsa describes here the road to liberation in terms of the theory of the *guṇas*. Ultimately, the constitution of the *guṇas* changes to the point where *sattva* dominates, detaching itself entirely from *rajas* and *tamas*.

2. Scholars call the mind activities—*citta-vṛtti*—mentioned in YS 1.2 by different names. Some refer to *citta-vṛtti* as "modifications of the mind"; see, for example, T. S. Rukmani, in *Yogavārttika of Vijñānabhikṣu*, v. 1., p. 31; Hariharananda Aranya, in *Yoga Philosophy of Patañjali*, p. 6; I. K. Taimni in *The Science of Yoga*, p. 6; and more. B. S. Miller, in *Yoga: Discipline of Freedom*, p. 29 translates *citta-vṛtti* as "turnings of thought"; J. H. Woods as "fluctuations of mind-stuff" (p. 8); Rama Prasada takes *citta-vṛtti* as "mental modifications."

3. In YS 1.5 Patañjali counts five mind-fluctuations that should be stopped, sometimes painful and sometimes not (*vṛttayaḥ pañcatayyaḥ kliṣṭākliṣṭāḥ*; "the mind-fluctuations are fivefold, painful and nonpainful").

4. See YS 1.7: *pratyakṣānumānāgamāḥ pramāṇāni* ("The means of knowledge are perception, reasoning and trustworthy, traditional knowledge").

5. See YS 1.8: *viparyayo mithyā-jñānam atad-rūpa-pratiṣṭham* ["False conception is incorrect knowledge based on an unreal form (of the object)"].

6. YS 1.9: *śabda-jñānānupātī vastu-śūnyo vikalpaḥ* ("*Vikalpa* is a cognition devoid of a real object, cognition which follows mere words").

7. Other functions of the mind such as perception (*pratyakṣa*) and dreaming involve disruption of silence in another sense.

8. *Rāja-Yoga*, p. 118.

9. *How to Know God: The Yoga Aphorisms of Patañjali*, p. 13.

10. Bhagavan Rajneesh, *Yoga: the Science of the Soul*, p. 22.

11. *Yoga: the Art of Integration*, p. 8.

12. Ibid., p. 10.

13. B. S. Miller says that "even the most subtle and benign workings of thought are obstructions to freedom of the spirit" (*Yoga: Discipline of Freedom*, p. 31).

14. TV 1.5. In his YSBh 1.5 Vyāsa suggests that the great number of modifications is the reason for their classification into five kinds, painful and nonpainful (*tāḥ punar niroddhavyā bahutve sati cittasya vrittayaḥ pañcatayyaḥ kliṣṭākliṣṭāḥ*; "these then, the mind modifications to be curbed, in their multiplicity, are fivefold, painful and nonpainful").

15. See Vyāsa's YSBh. 1.2.

16. Commentators differ in their rendering of the concept of *nirodha*; some choose "control," some "inhibition," some "suppression," some "annihilation," and so forth. G. Feuerstein counts four types of *nirodha* ("restriction"): *vṛtti-nirodha* ("restriction of the 'fluctuations'"); *pratyaya-nirodha* ("restriction of the presented-ideas"); *saṁskāra-nirodha* ("restriction of the 'subliminal activators'"); *sarva-nirodha* ("complete restriction, coinciding with self-realization.") See *Yogasūtra of Patañjali*, p. 28.

17. See his YSBh. 1.2.

18. T. S. Rukmani: "Yoga considers the *guṇas* '*sattva*,' *rajas*,' and '*tamas*' as substances, directly responsible for the entire creation; they are, in that sense, called constituents which are found in all the created things. The example of threads makes the idea clear; threads are themselves constituents in the making of the rope, and not qualities" (*Yogavārttika of Vijñānabhikṣu*, v. 1, p. 34).

19. See, in particular, SK 12–14. For more details and complexities involved in the descriptions of the *guṇas* in the SK, see G. J. Larson's *Classical Sāṅkhya*, pp. 162–67.

20. SK 54: *ūrdhvaṁ sattva-viśālas tamo-viśālaś ca mūlataḥ sargaḥ / madhye rajo-viśālo / brahmādi-stamba-paryantaḥ* ("In the upper regions, predominance of *sattva*; predominance of *tamas* in the lower creation; in the middle, predominance of *rajas*; extending from Brahma and the rest to a tuft of grass").

21. YSBh 1.2.

22. *puruṣārtha-śūnyānāṁ guṇānāṁ pratiprasavaḥ kaivalyaṁ sva-rūpa-pratiṣṭhā vā citi-saktir iti.*

23. See Vyāsa's YSBh 2.27 on the transcendence of the *guṇa* condition: *pratiprasave cittasya muktaḥ kuśala ity eva bhavati guṇātītatvād iti* ("As the mind is dissolved, the human is called released, by transcendence of the *guṇa* condition").

24. SK 56.

25. SK 57.

26. SK 58.

27. SK 59.

28. SK 61.

29. SK 65: *prakṛtiṁ paśyati puruṣaḥ prekṣakavad avasthitaḥ sva-sthaḥ* ("Purusha, like a spectator, abiding in his essential state, sees prakriti, her activity ceased through the fulfillment of her purpose, withdrawn from the seven forms").

30. *God Inside Out*, p. 169.

31. SK 66: *dṛṣṭā mayety upekṣaka ekā dṛṣṭāham ity uparamaty anyā / sati saṁyoge 'pi tayoḥ prayojanaṁ nāsti sargasya* [" 'She is seen by me,' says the indifferent one. 'I am seen,' says the other, and ceases. Though the two remain in relation, there is no (further) motive for creation"].

32. YS 3.35: *sattva-puruṣayor atyantāsaṅkīrṇayoḥ pratyayāviśeṣo bhogaḥ parārthatvāt svārtha-saṁyamāt puruṣa-jñānam* ["Experience is grounded in the failure of discrimination between the radically distinct (qualities of) *sattva* and purusha; by meditation (*saṁyama*) on (purusha's) independence of another's purpose, knowledge of purusha (is attained)"].

33. Hariharananda Aranya, *Yoga Philosophy of Patañjali*, p. 110.

34. YS 3.1: *deśa-bandhaś cittasya dhāraṇā* ("The fixation of the mind on one spot is *dhāraṇā*").

35. YS 3.2: *tatra pratyayaikatānatā dhyānam* ("In the condition of *dhāraṇā*, when the mind flows uniformly onto the object, this is *dhyāna*").

36. Woods's translation, *The Yoga-System of Patañjali*, p. 81.

37. Vācaspati says: "When it is said that a yogin has come into a state of balance with one of these intended objects, such as a cow, then the lower perception of the yogin has been described." (*tad anena yoginoparaṁ pratyakṣam uktam*) (p. 81).

38. W. Halfbass defines *anvaya-vyatireka* as the method of "positive and negative concomitance," "continuity and discontinuity," "coordinate presence and absence" (*Tradition and Reflection*, p. 162).

39. Ibid.

40. See the definition of *vikalpa*, in YS 1.9, one of the *vṛttis* that should be stopped.

41. See *Light on the Yogasūtra*, p. 265.

42. *Rāja-Yoga*, p. 267.

43. *The Science of Yoga*, p. 445.

44. Ibid., p. 443

45. Ibid., pp. 443–44.

46. Ibid., p. 445.

47. See, for example, SK 18. In this context, see also G. J. Larson, *Classical Sāṅkhya*, p. 170. Larson emphasizes that "the purusha is individual but not personal" (p. 170).

48. As suggested above, there are several types of silence; Sāṅkhya silence is subsequent to the purification of *sattva* and the mind, the untying of the *guṇa* knot (or *guṇa* rope). Sāṅkhya silence of a possibly different quality also follows from the distinction between purusha and prakriti. Yoga silence is also of two kinds: *sa-bīja-samādhi* and *nir-bīja-samādhi*. The silence of *sa-bīja-samādhi* produces the *siddhi* experiences. *Nir-bīja-samādhi* is different.

Chapter 6. The Dying Yogin's Challenge

1. YS 2.28: *yogāṅgāuṣṭhānād aśuddhi-kṣaye jñāna-dīptir āviveka-khyāteḥ.*

2. YS 1.48: *ṛtaṁ-bharā tatra prajñā.*

3. YS 3.5.

4. YSBh 1.20.

5. YS 3.35.

6. YS 3.26.

7. YS 3.29.

8. YS 3.27–28.

9. See Ch. 5.

10. Patanjali's YS 2.24 identifies misconception, *avidyā*, as the source of the connection of purusha and prakriti *(tasya hetur avidyā)*.

11. *tathedaṁ vidyamānaṁ jñānaṁ citta-nivṛttiṁ na karoti vinaṣṭaṁ kariṣyatīti kā pratyāśā.*

Bibliography

Primary sources

Bādarāyaṇa

Brahmasūtra, Varanasi: Chowkhamba Vidyabhawan, 1969

Īśvarakṛṣṇa

Sāṁkhyakārikā

Patañjali

Yogasūtra

- with the commentaries by Bhogarāja, Bhāvāgaṇeṣa, Nāgojī Bhaṭṭa, Rāmānanda Yati, Anantadeva Pandit, Sadāṣivendra Sarasvati, Varanasi: Chowkhamba, 1930
- with the commentaries *Tattva-vaiśāradi* of Vācaspati Miśra, Bombay: Government Central Press, 1917

Rukmani T. S.

Yogavārttika of Vijñānabhikṣu, Munshiram Manoharlal Publishers, 1984

Śaṅkarācārya

Brahmasūtrabhāṣya

Vācaspati Miśra

Tattva-Vaiśāradī

Vyāsa

Yogasūtrabhāṣya

King Bhoja

Bhoja Vṛttī

Bhagavadgītā

Gheranda-Saṁhitā

Yogasūtrabhāṣyavivaraṇa

Secondary sources

Arya Usharbudh
Yogasūtras of Patañjali with the Exposition of Vyāsa, Pennsylvania: The Himalayan International Institute of Yoga Science and Philosophy of the U.S.A., 1986

Āraṇya Swami Hariharānanda
Yoga Philosophy of Patañjali, Calcutta: University of Calcutta, 1977

Behanan, K.
Yoga: a Scientific Evaluation, NY: Dover, 1937

Chatterjee S. and Datta D.
An Introduction to Indian Philosophy, University of Calcutta, 1960

Collins S.
Selfless Persons, Cambridge: Cambridge University Press, 1987

Danielou A.
Yoga: the Method of Re-Integration, New York: University Books, 1955

Dasgupta S.N.
Yoga as Philosophy and Religion, India, Delhi: Motilal Banarsidass, 1998

Doniger W. and Smith B.
The Laws of Manu, London: Penguin Classics, 1991

Eliade M.
Yoga: Immortality and Freedom, New Jersey: Princeton/Bollingen, 1973

Ewing A. H.
The Hindu Conception of the Functions of Breath, JAOS, 1902

Buitenen Van
"Dharma and Mokṣa," in *Philosophy East and West*, Bombay: Blackie, 1975

Feuerstein G.
Encyclopedic Dictionary of Yoga, London: Unwin. 1990

Feuerstein G.
The Essence of Yoga, NY: Grove Press, 1976

Feuerstein G.
The Yoga-Sūtra of Patañjali, England: Wm Dawson & Sons Ltd, 1979

Filliozat J.
Religion, Philosophy, Yoga, Delhi: Motilal Banarsidass, 1991

Frauwallner E.
History of Indian Philosophy, Delhi: Motilal Banarsida, 1993

Grinshpon Y.
"Yogic Revolution and Tokens of Conservatism in Vyāsa–Yoga," *Journal of Indian Philosophy*, 1997

Ghosh J.
A Study of Yoga, Dehli: Motilal Banarsidass, 1977

Krishna Gopi
Kundalini: Evolutionary Energy in Man, Berkeley: Shambala, 1970

Halbfass W.
"The Therapeutic Paradigm and the Search for Identity in Indian Philosophy," *Tradition and Reflection,* State University of New York Press, 1991

Halbfass W.
Beyond Orientalism: Experience and Observation in Traditional and Modern Pātañjala-Yoga, State University of New York Press, 1996

Handelman D. and Shulman D.
God Inside Out, NY: Oxford University Press, 1997

Hariharananda Aranya
Yoga Philosophy of Patañjali, University of Calcutta, 1981

Hauer J. W.
Der Yoga: Ein indischer Weg zum Selbst, W. Kohlhammer Verlag, 1958

Iyengar B. K. S.
Light On the Yoga Sutras of Patañjali, London: Aquarian Press, 1993

Iyengar B. K. S.
The Tree of Yoga, CO: Shambala Publications, 1989

Jung C. G.
"Visions: Life After Death," in Bailey, Lee W., *The Near-Death experience; A Reader,* Routledge, 1996

Kane P. V.
History of Dharmaśāstra, Poona: Bhandarkar Oriental Research Istitute, 1972

Kloistermaier K.
A Survey of Hinduism, India: Munshiram Manoharlal, 1990

Larson G. J.
Classical Sāṅkhya: An Interpretation of its History and Meaning Motilal Banarsidass, 1969

Leggett T.
Śaṅkara on the Yogasūtra-s: The Vivaraṇa sub-commentary to Vyāsa-bhāṣya on the Yogasūtra-s of *Patañjali*, London: Routledge and Kegan Paul, 1983

Masson J.
The Oceanic Feeling. The Origins of Religious Sentiment in Ancient India, Boston, 1980

Mehta R.
Yoga: the Art of Integration, Theosophical Publishing House, 1975

Miller B. S.
Yoga; Discipline of Freedom, University of California Press, 1996

Mishra R. S.
The Textbook of Yoga Psychology, NY: Julian Press, 1971

Moody R. A.
Life After Life, NY: Bantam Books, 1988

Müller M.
The Six Systems of Indian Philosophy, London: Longmans Green, 1899

Osborn A.
Ramana Maharshi and the Path of Self-Knowledge, London: Century,1970

Paramahansa Yogananda
Autobiography of a Yogi, Self-Realization Fellowship, Los Angeles, 1983

Pines S. and Gelblum T.
"Al-Bīrūnī's Arabic Version of Patañjali's *Yogasūtra*," *Bulletin of the School of Oriental and African Studies,* 29, 1966

Radhakrishnan S.
Indian Philosophy, Princeton University Press, 1973

Rajneesh Bhagavan
Yoga: The Science Of the Soul, Rajneesh Foundation, 1984

Raju P. T.
Structural Depths of Indian Thought, New Delhi: South Asian Publishers, 1985

Rāma Prasāda
The Yogasūtras of Patañjali with the Commentary of Vyāsa And the Gloss of Vācaspati Miśra, NY: AMS Press, 1974

Ramakrishna Shri
Sayings of Śri Ramakrishna, Madras, India: Śri Ramakrishna Math, 1971

Rawcliffe D. H.
Occult and Supernatural Phenomena, NY: Dover Publications, 1959

Sinh P.
The Hathayogapradīpika, Munshiram Manoharlal, India, 1997

Prabhavananda Swami
How to Know God: The Yoga Aphorisms of Patañjali, London: George Allen & Unwin, 1960

Purohit, Shree Swami
An Indian Monk: His Life and Adventures, Macmillan, 1932

Taimni I. K.
Science of Yoga; a Commentary on the Yogasūtras of Patañjali in the Light on Modern Thought, Theosophical pub. House, 1968

Thapar R.
A History of India, London: Penguin, 1974

Varenne J.
Yoga and the Hindu Tradition, Chicago: University of Chicago Press, 1976

Vivekananda Swami
Raja Yoga, NY: Brentano's, 1920

Woods J. H.
The Yoga-System of Patañjali, Delhi: Motilal Banarsidass, 1998

Zimmer H.
Philosophies of India, Bollingen/Princeton University Press, 1974

Index

abhiniveśa, 14
abhyāsa, 77
Absolute, 5, 14, 58, 90
adhyāsa, 7, 87
ahiṁsā, 10, 50, 58, 73, 105, n129, n134, n136
Al-Bīrūnī, 32
anuśāsana, 66, 67
aparigraha, 39, 40, 58, n136
Āraṇya, Swami Harwharānanda, 66, 69, 70, n143, n145
Arya, Ushrabudh, 5, 65
āsana, 27–29
aṣṭāṅga yoga, 27, 63, n139
Ātman, 26, 40, 57, 115, n135
avidyā, 55, 89, 114, 115, n124, n136, n146

Bādarāyaṇa, 11, 45, 50
Behanan, Kovoor, n125
Bhagavadgītā, 56, 57, 59, n136
Bhoja (the king), 6, 19, 29, 40, 46, n132
bhūmi, 30
brahmacarya, 58, n134, n136
Brahman, 26, n124, n135, n144
Brahmasūtra. *See* Bādarāyaṇa
Bṛhadāraṇyakopaniṣad, n141
Buddha, 14, 23, 44, 45, n124, n127
Buddhism, 6, 10, 13, 26, 46, 54, 59, 115, n135
Buitenen, Van, 60, n136–8

Chāndogya Upaniṣad, 57, 58, n137, n141
  See also Upanishads
Chatterjee, Satischandra, 34
Collins, Steven, 46
commentators, 2, 3, 6–10, 13, 15, 18, 20, 27, 31–33, 35, 42, 65, 68, 75, 76, 93, n135, n143, n144
  Classical Scholar, 3, 4, 6, 13, 19, 24, 29, 30, 41, 66, 67, 72, 82, 83, 87, 92, 94
  Insider, 3, 13–20, 27, 29, 30, 35, 70, 86–9, 92, 94
  Observer's Observer, 3, 5, 13, 21, 28–30, 86, 87
  Outsider, 3, 13–6, 24, 27, 29, 30, 35, 87, 92
  Philologist, 3, 13, 14, 20, 26, 27, 29, 31, 35, 87, 92, 94
  Philosopher, 3, 13–5, 19, 20, 27, 29–31, 35, 82, 86, 87, 92, 94
  Practitioner, 3, 13, 27–31, 35, 86–88, 92
  Seeker, 3, 15, 20, 25–7, 29–31, 35, 80, 81, 86, 87, 92, 94
    Existential, 14, 25, 27
    Romantic, 3, 13, 20–4, 27
    Spiritual, 13, n125
    Stimulated, 24

Danielou, Alain, 33, 60
Dasgupta, Surendranath, 20, 33, 60, 84, n124, n129, n138

Datta, Dhirendramohan, 34
death, 1, 2, 10, 11, 14, 17–24, 28, 29, 31, 34, 35, 37, 43–57, 59, 60, 62, 64, 68, 74, 76, 88, 91, 109, 111, n126, n132, n134, n136, n141
dharma, 21, 43, 83, n137
disintegration, 1–5, 9, 14, 27, 79, 86, 87, 90, 96, 97, 102, 108, 113
Doniger, Wendy, n134
duḥkha, 9, 10, 44, 46, 84
dying yogin, 6–8, 11, 13, 15, 21, 30, 34, 35, 37, 47, 53–9, 62, 63, 69, 78–80, 93, 95, 96, n138, n141

Eliade, Mircea, 4, 13, 21–3, 33, 49, 60, 67, 68, 92, n124, n127, n139
Ewing, Arthur, 72, n141

Feuerstein, Georg, 10, 13, 42, 67, 88, n125, n139, n144
Filliozat, Jean, 34
Frauwallner, Erich, 68
Freud, Sigmund, 1

Ghosh, Jajneswar, 34, 60, n129
guṇa, 4, 29, 47, 55, 61, 73, 79, 82–4, 89, 99, 116, n132, n134, n143–6
See also sattva

Halbfass, Wilhelm, 5, 43, n123, n126, n131, n132, n136, n138, n145
Handelman, Don, n130, n134
Haridas, 22, 23, n127
Haṭha Yoga, 27
Hauer, Jakob Wilhelm, 68, n140
Hinduism, 18, n126, n130

Indra, 57, n136
innerness, 4, 5, 11, 20, 21, 28, 29, 49, 53, 64, 74, 78, 97
integration, 2–7, 11, 38, 39, 86, n130
Isherwood, Christopher, 25, 26, 81
Īśvara, 31, 37, 40, 58, 77, 95, 100, 104–6, 114, n128, n130
Īśvarakṛṣṇa, 55, 82, 84, 85
Iyengar, B. K. S., 13, 27–9, 88, 90, n127

Jainism, n135
Jung, Carl Gustav, 59, n137

kaivalya, 4, 7, 49, 56, 58, 64, 73–5, 77, 80, 83, 84, 86, 89, 97, 112, 113, 117, 120, 121, n131, n136, n137, n142, n143
Kalidāsa, 85
Kane, P. V., 32, n129
karma, 8, 31, 37–9, 43, 50, 51, 55, 72, 76, 84, 109, 115, 118–21, n128, n130, n132, n139, n141
kleśa, 14, 31, 51, 55, 84, 104, 114, 115, 121, n124
Kloistermaier, Klaus, 33, n138
Krishna, Gopi, n125
Krishnamurti, 14
kriyāyoga, 63, 77, 104, n143
kundalini, 16, 17

Larson, Gerald James, n135, n144, n146

Masson, Jeffry, 60
meditation, 2, 6, 7, 15, 24, 29, 31, 38, 41–3, 47, 51, 54, 58, 62–4, 68–73, 78, 85–7, 92, 95, 101–4, 106–13, 118, 121, n124, n126, n137, n140
dhāraṇā, 51, 86, 107, n145
dhyāna, 51, 63, 86, 107, n133, n139, n145
saṁyama, 2, 8, 32, 41, 43, 56, 63, 69, 70, 73, 86, 87, 108–113, n128, n131, n132, n136, n140, n142, n145
Mehta, Rohit, 3, 14, 24, 25, 41, 70, 72, 73, 81, 87, 90, n127, n128
Miller, Barbara Stoler, 4, 10, n143, n144

Mishra, Ramamurti, 71
mokṣa, 11, 44, 46, 93, 94, n137
Moody, Raymond, n137
Müller, Max, 10, 14, 32, 60

Naciketas, 57
nirodha, 77, 82, n144
niyama, 58, 72, 73, 105, n129, n141
Nyāya and Vaiśeṣika, 26, n139

Oberhammer, Gerhard, 68, n140
oṁ, 65, 100, 114
otherness, 1–11, 13, 15, 22, 24, 26, 27, 29–31, 34, 35, 40, 42, 49, 50, 60, 64, 68, 70, 78, 86, 90–2, 97, 111

Paramahansa, Yogananda, 14, 17–9, 45
Patañjali
as a Sāṅkhya philosopher, 13, 30, 31, 34, 35, 79–83, 95, 96, n130, n135
meeting the dying yogin, 2, 21, 53–56, 58–64, 70–74, 77, 78, 90–6
as seen by commentators, 17, 23, 26, 40, 65–69, n138, n139
as the composer of the Yogasūtra, 6–10, 37–48, 84–90, n129, n135, n140, n141, n143
Prabhavananda, Swami, 25, 26, 81
Prajāpati, 57, n136, n137
prakriti, 2, 3, 6, 9, 26, 32, 38, 39, 44, 55, 61, 79, 82, 84, 85, 87, 88, 97, 99, 102, 115, n130, n134, n142, n145, n146
pramāṇa, 60, 81, 92, n137
prāṇa. *See* vital breaths
prāṇāyāma, 58, 106, 107, n133, n142
prasaṅkhyāna, 26
pratyāhāra, 74, 107, n133, n142
Purohit, Shree Swami, 16–8, n125, n127, n141
purusha, 2, 3, 6, 9, 21, 32, 38, 44, 55, 56, 61, 73, 77, 79, 83–8, 97, 99, 110, 112, 113, 115, 121, n128, n130, n136, n142, n143, n145, n146

Radhakrishnan, Sarvepalli, 14, 19, 20, 33, 60, n126, n137
Rajneesh, Bhagavan, 20, 24, 25, 66, 81, n135, n144
Raju, P. T., 33, 60
Rama, Prasada, n143
Ramakrishna, Shri, 32, n129
Ramana, Maharshi, 32, n129
Rawcliffe, Donovan,15, 16, n124, n125
Rukmani, Trichur Subramaniam, n141, n143, n144

samādhi
according to Patañjali, 73, 76, 77, 86, 99, 100, 103, 104, 106–108, 111, 113, 117, n133
as means of knowledge, 60, 75
as meditation, 63, 78, n127, n139, n143
as silence, 47, 51, 54, 64, 74, 76, 82, 86, 87, 91, 92, n125, n136, n146
as source of the siddhis, 34, 61–64, n138
as yogic death, 29, 39, 43, 56–8, 64, 68, 74
inaccessible, 6, 14, 15, 19, 20, 22, 24, 27, 28, 33
samāna. *See* vital breaths
saṁsāra, 3, 5, 21, 39, 44–7, 50, 86, 89, 94
saṁskāra, 6, 40, 46, 47, 55, 99, 109, 116, 117, n132, n144
Śaṅkarācārya, 4, 11, 40, 72, n123, n130, n139
Sāṅkhya, 2, 4, 9, 10, 31, 39, 54–7, 59, 62, 64, 68, 69, 73, 74, 77, 79, 81–3, 86, 89–91, 93, 95, 96, n129, n135–9

saṅtoṣa, n133
sattva, 2, 56, 73, 82–86, 106, 110–3, 120, n136, n142, n145, n146
See also guṇa
śauca, 38, 39, 58, 106, n136
Shulman, David Dean, n130, n134, n137
siddhi, 6, 10, 11, 19, 29–34, 48–50, 53, 54, 57–64, 68, 78, 96, 109–111, 113, n125, n128–32, n134, n137–9, n143
cessation of hunger and thirst, 58
effulgence, 70
knowing the time of one's death, 72
knowledge of the sounds of all creatures, 42, 87
knowledge of the Universe, 41
levitation and moving in air, 58, 72
power of elephant, 69
reaching of jewels, 72
revealing of anatomical arrangement of the body, 58, 69
seeing of previous lives, 46, 47
silence, 2–8, 11, 29–31, 34, 54–7, 64, 69, 70, 74, 79–106, 108, 111–3, 121, n139
Smith, Brian, n134
śraddhā, 63
Staal, Fritz, 68

Taimni, I. K., 3, 18, 19, 40–2, 66, 70, 76, 88–90, n126, n140, n141, n143
tapas, 24, 35, 64, 75, 78, 104, 113, n142
Thapar, Romila, n123
trance, 15, 16, 19, 24, 49, 55, 60, 76, 78, n137, n138
turīya, 24, n125

Upanishads, 11, 21, 22, 27, 57–9, n135–7

Vācaspati, Miśra, 19, 24, 29, 32, 40, 43, 65, 66, 69, 71, 81, 87, 92, n132, n139, n141, n142, n145
vairāgya, 77, 80, n128
Varenne, Jean, 10, 33, 48, 60, n136, n138
Veda, 32, n135
Vedānta, 5, 6, 25, 89
verbalization, 2, 7–10, 53, 54, 58, 59, 78, 82, 87, 90, 92, 99, 102, 103
Vijñānabhkṣu, 6, 29, 32, 40, 71, 83
Virocana, 57
vital breaths, 70–2, n141
viveka, 4, 56, 79, n131, n136
Vivekananda, Swami, 14, 40, 43, 69, 70, 80, 88, 90
vivekin, 8, 37, 38, 41, 43, 44, 46, 47, 50, 51, 68, 74, 77, 78, 116
vṛtti, 8, 80, 81, n143, n144, n146
Vyāsa, 6, 8, 14, 19, 24, 29, 32, 39, 40, 41, 43–6, 62, 66, 69–71, 74, 75, 80–4, 86, 92–4, n128, n131, n132, n137, n139, n143–5

Woods, James Hauton, 14, 26, n127, n139–43, n145

Yājñavālkya, 24
Yama (the god), 57
yama, 28, 58, 72, 73, 104, n129, n141
Yeats, William Butler, 5, 13, 16, 23, 24, 92, n127
yogic death. *See* samādhi
yogin. *See* dying yogin

Zimmer, Heinrich, 21